LUTHER ON CONVERSION

LUTHER
on Conversion

✝

The Early Years

Marilyn J. Harran

Cornell University Press

Ithaca and London

Cornell University Press gratefully acknowledges a grant from
the Andrew W. Mellon Foundation that aided
in bringing this book to publication.

First published 1983 by Cornell University Press.
Published in the United Kingdom by Cornell University Press, London.

International Standard Book Number 0-8014-1566-7
Library of Congress Catalog Card Number 83-7194
Printed in the United States of America
*Librarians: Library of Congress cataloging information
appears on the last page of the book.*

*The paper in this book is acid-free and meets the guidelines
for permanence and durability of the Committee on Production
Guidelines for Book Longevity of the Council on Library Resources.*

TO MY PARENTS

Contents

Preface

In his biography of Martin Luther the English historian John Todd wrote that when one visits any major library, one soon discovers that more books have been written about Luther than about any other person in history with the exception of Jesus Christ. This tremendous literature is swelled by many new volumes on Luther's life, thought, and influence offered in 1983, the five hundredth anniversary of his birth. This book explores Luther's views on conversion during his early years as a professor of theology, when he was on his way to becoming the reformer of world renown. It is intended to be a building block in the imposing structure of Luther scholarship. It deals with the development of a key concept in his theology. Luther's union of conceptual understanding and his own personal experience not only changed the course of his own life, but had profound consequences for history.

I owe much to others, not only to the learned scholars who have explored other facets of Luther's theology and his progress in it, but to mentors, colleagues, students, and friends. I recall with gratitude the encouragement toward religious studies and Reformation scholarship of John Geerken, of Scripps College; Robert G. Hamerton-Kelly, Dean of the Chapel at Stanford University; William Clebsch, Stanford University; and the eminent late Luther scholar Wilhelm Pauck. William J. Courtenay, of the University of Wisconsin, Madison, drew my attention to medieval documents and sources related to the concept of conversion. I am particularly indebted to Leif Grane, University of Copenhagen, for his careful reading of the manuscript and his perceptive suggestions for a number of changes. Lewis Spitz, of Stanford University, deserves my special thanks and appreciation for his scholarly counsel and direction.

I am indebted to Lawrence J. Malley and Barbara H. Salazar of Cornell University Press for their help in bringing this volume to publication. Thanks are also due to Thomas Boslooper for preparation of the index.

My research for this volume was aided by a summer Mellon Foundation grant from Barnard College. I thank Charles S. Olton, Dean of the Faculty and Vice President for Academic Affairs of Barnard College, in particular for that assistance. A grant from the Deutscher Akademischer Austauschdienst made possible my initial studies at the Institut für Spätmittelalter und Reformation at the University of Tübingen, Germany, under the directorship of Heiko A. Oberman. A full year's fellowship from the National Endowment for the Humanities provided the sustained time necessary for the revision of this manuscript.

Among colleagues at Barnard College who provided constant encouragement, friendship, and an ideal situation for both research and teaching, I owe particular gratitude to Elaine Pagels, now at Princeton University; David Sperling, now at Hebrew Union College; Joel Brereton, now at the University of Missouri; and Alan Segal, chairperson, Religion Department, Barnard College. Seth Kasten and Betty Bolden of the Union Theological Seminary Library were most generous and helpful in making available to me the resources of that distinguished institution. I am grateful to Concordia Publishing House, St. Louis, and to Fortress Press, Philadelphia, for their kind permission to quote from *Luther's Works*. Unless I have indicated otherwise, additional translations are my own. Biblical quotations are from *The Oxford Annotated Bible, Revised Standard Version*.

MARILYN J. HARRAN

Barnard College, Columbia University

Abbreviations

ARG   *Archiv für Reformationsgeschichte.* Berlin, 1904–

HTR   *Harvard Theological Review.* Cambridge, Mass., 1908–

LW   *Luther's Works.* 55 vols. General Editors: Jaroslav Pelikan, vols. 1–30; Helmut T. Lehmann, vols. 31–55. St. Louis: Concordia Publishing House, and Philadelphia: Fortress Press, 1955–1976.

PL   *Patrologia Latina.* Edited by J.-P. Migne. 221 vols. Paris: Garnier Fratres, 1844–1890.

WA   *D. Martin Luthers Werke: Kritische Gesamtausgabe.* 58 vols. Weimar: Hermann Böhlau and Hermann Böhlaus Nachfolger, 1883–

WA Br   *D. Martin Luthers Werke: Kritische Gesamtausgabe. Briefwechsel.* 15 vols. Weimar: Hermann Böhlaus Nachfolger, 1930–1978.

WA TR   *D. Martin Luthers Werke: Kritische Gesamtausgabe. Tischreden.* 6 vols. Weimar: Hermann Böhlaus Nachfolger, 1912–1921.

LUTHER ON CONVERSION

[1]

Introduction

For a full century Luther's theology has been the subject of intense research and detailed analysis. The renaissance of Luther study that followed upon the four hundredth anniversary of his birth continued unabated throughout the twentieth century and intensified with the approach of the five hundredth anniversary in 1983. Through his challenging essays the great Berlin church historian Karl Holl led the way to the careful study not only of Luther's person and place in history but of his developing theology.[1] The roster of eminent Luther scholars includes such names as Heinrich Boehmer, Heinrich Bornkamm, Emanuel Hirsch, Otto Ritschl, and Erich Vogelsang.[2]

[1] Karl Holl, *Gesammelte Aufsätze zur Kirchengeschichte*, vol. 1: *Luther*, 2d and 3d eds. (Tübingen: J. C. B. Mohr [Paul Siebeck], 1923; first published 1921).

[2] Heinrich Boehmer, *Der junge Luther*, 6th rev. ed. (Stuttgart: K. F. Koehler, 1971; first published 1925); Heinrich Bornkamm, *Eckhart und Luther* (Stuttgart: W. Kohlhammer, 1936), and "Luthers Bericht über seine Entdeckung der iustitia dei," *ARG* 37 (1940), 117–128; Emanuel Hirsch, "Initium theologiae Lutheri," in *Lutherstudien*, vol. 2 (Gütersloh: C. Bertelsmann, 1954), pp. 9–35; Otto Ritschl, *Dogmengeschichte des Protestantismus*, vol. 2: *Orthodoxie und Synkretismus in der altprotestantischen Theologie*, pt. 1: *Die Theologie der deutschen Reformation und die Entwicklung der lutherischen Orthodoxie in der philippistischen Streitigkeiten* (Leipzig: J. C. Hinrichs, 1912); Erich Vogelsang, *Die Anfänge von Luthers Christologie nach der ersten Psalmenvorlesung* (Berlin and Leipzig: Walter de Gruyter, 1929). Many other names could be added—for example, Paul Althaus, Adolf Hamel, Rudolf Hermann, Hans Iwand, Wilhelm Link, Walther von Loewenich, Otto Scheel, Erich Seeberg, and Ernst Wolf.

It is a fascinating fact of Luther scholarship that to this date only Otto Ritschl has considered Luther's concept of conversion.[3] This fact becomes all the more surprising when one realizes the extraordinary amount of attention that has been focused on Luther's own conversion experience, as his *Turmerlebnis,* or "tower experience," is commonly considered to be. Why, then, has the concept of conversion in Luther's theology remained unstudied? The answer does not lie with the unavailability of the sources. Thanks to Johannes Ficker's publication in 1908 of a preliminary version of Luther's own copy of the *Lectures on Romans* (1515–1516) and the publication by Emanuel Hirsch and Hanns Rückert in 1929 of Luther's *Lectures on Hebrews* (1517–1518), scholarly attention was directed toward his early exegetical works.[4] Luther's revised *Lectures on Galatians* of 1519 was published in the second volume of the *Weimar Ausgabe* in 1884.[5] His first biblical commentary, the *Dictata super Psalterium* (1513–1515), was made available in print in a very defective edition well before the end of the nineteenth century.[6]

The absence of an analysis of conversion in Luther's early theology is clearly not due to the unavailability of the sources. The more disturbing question then arises of whether the concept has not been considered because it is merely peripheral to the main themes of his thought. Certainly other themes in Luther's theology have received extensive and exhaustive consideration. One need only mention the debate surrounding the theme of justification by faith and the question of when Luther first "discovered" it. This issue became even more complex when Luther's "reformatory breakthrough" came to be equated with his *Turmerlebnis.* Studies on both the *Dictata* and the *Lectures*

[3]Ritschl, *Theologie der deutschen Reformation,* pp. 157–183.

[4]Ficker's final edition of the *Lectures on Romans* appeared in 1938 as vol. 56 of WA. Ficker published the edition of the *Lectures on Hebrews* in 1939 as pt. 3 of vol. 57 of the WA. The edition of Hirsch and Rückert was published as *Luthers Vorlesung über den Hebräerbrief nach der vatikanischen Handschrift* (Berlin and Leipzig: Walter de Gruyter, 1929).

[5]*In epistolam Pauli ad Galatas M. Lutheri commentarius,* ed. J. A. F. Knaake, was published as part of WA 2.

[6]*Dictata super Psalterium,* ed. Gustav Kawerau, was published in vol. 3 of the WA in 1885 and in vol. 4 in the following year.

on Romans differ drastically in their assertions as to when Luther
made his decisive evangelical discovery. The results of these
myriad studies have often been hampered by a tendency to look
at the young Luther through the more clearly defined theology
of the older man. As one perceptive scholar has noted, there is
no reason why Luther could not use the same terminology in
both his early and his later theology and mean quite different
things.[7]

The debate regarding Luther's discovery of justification by
faith has continued into recent scholarship. In his controversial
book *Fides ex auditu* (1958), Ernst Bizer claimed that in his *Lectures on Romans* Luther still understood justification as obtained
through faith *and* humility.[8] This conclusion led to a major debate between Bizer and Heinrich Bornkamm and stimulated a
renewed study of Luther's earliest writings.[9] This debate was
paralleled by the efforts of Uuras Saarnivaara, Otto Pesch, and
others to distinguish between the development of Luther's reform theology and his *Turmerlebnis*.[10] As a result, new attention

[7]"Es muss bis auf die von der Alternative 'reformatorisch-unreformatorisch'
freie Interpretation der Texte völlig offen bleiben, ob in die Aussagen der
frühen Zeit schon der Sinn späterer Aussagen zu legen ist. Es könnte ja gerade
in der Frühzeit unter gleichen oder fast gleichen Formeln sich noch ein ganz
anderer Sinn verbergen" (Matthias Kroeger, *Rechtfertigung und Gesetz: Studien zur
Entwicklung der Rechtfertigungslehre beim jungen Luther*, Forschungen zur Kirchen-
und Dogmengeschichte, vol. 20 [Göttingen: Vandenhoeck & Ruprecht, 1968], p.
29).

[8]Ernst Bizer, *Fides ex auditu: Eine Untersuchung über die Entdeckung der
Gerechtigkeit Gottes durch Martin Luther*, 3d rev. ed. (Neukirchen-Vluyn: Neukirchner Verlag, 1966).

[9]Heinrich Bornkamm, "Zur Frage der Iustitia Dei beim jungen Luther, Teil
I," *ARG* 52 (1961), 16–29, and "Zur Frage der Iustitia Dei beim jungen Luther,
Teil II," *ARG* 53 (1962), 1–60. For an excellent summary of responses to Bizer's
thesis, see Otto Pesch, "Zur Frage nach Luthers reformatorischer Wende," in
Der Durchbruch der reformatorischen Erkenntnis bei Luther, ed. Bernhard Lohse, Wege
der Forschung, vol. 123 (Darmstadt: Wissenschaftliche Buchgesellschaft, 1968),
pp. 453–489.

[10]Uuras Saarnivaara, *Luther Discovers the Gospel: New Light upon Luther's Way
from Medieval Catholicism to Evangelical Faith* (St. Louis: Concordia, 1951); Pesch,
"Zur Frage nach Luthers reformatorischer Wende," pp. 497–501. Also Lowell
Green, "Faith, Righteousness, and Justification: New Light on Their Development under Luther and Melanchthon," *Sixteenth Century Journal* 4, no. 1 (1973),
65–86. Green discusses the influence of Melanchthon in helping Luther to
arrive at his understanding of faith and justification in *How Melanchthon Helped
Luther Discover the Gospel: The Doctrine of Justification in the Reformation* (Fallbrook,
Calif.: Verdict Publications, 1980).

has been directed to Luther's 1545 account of his decisive conversion experience.

Our question about the possibly peripheral character of conversion in Luther's theology becomes the more pressing when one notes the formidable number of recent studies dealing with a variety of concepts in Luther's theology and going beyond the traditional preoccupation with such themes as justification by faith. The works of Michael Baylor on *conscientia,* Rudolf Damerau on *humilitas,* Werner Jetter on baptism, Günther Metzger on *affectus,* Karl-Heinz zur Mühlen on the formula *nos extra nos,* Martin Seils on *cooperatio,* and Reinhard Schwarz on the relation among *fides, spes,* and *caritas* constitute only a few examples among many.[11] But though a fresh appraisal has been given to Luther's early writings in their late medieval context and a variety of studies have been done on concepts besides those originally viewed as central to Luther's reformatory breakthrough, the concept of conversion has remained unexamined.[12]

[11]Michael G. Baylor, *Action and Person: Conscience in Late Scholasticism and the Young Luther,* Studies in Medieval and Reformation Thought, vol. 20 (Leiden: E. J. Brill, 1977); Rudolf Damerau, *Die Demut in der Theologie Luthers,* Studien zu den Grundlagen der Reformation, vol. 5 (Giessen: Wilhelm Schmitz, 1967); Werner Jetter, *Die Taufe beim jungen Luther: Eine Untersuchung über das Werden der reformatorischen Sakraments- und Taufanschauung,* Beiträge zur historischen Theologie, vol. 18 (Tübingen: J. C. B. Mohr [Paul Siebeck], 1954); Günther Metzger, *Gelebter Glaube: Die Formierung reformatorischen Denkens in Luthers erster Psalmenvorlesung, dargestellt am Begriff des Affekts,* Forschungen zur Kirchen- und Dogmengeschichte, vol. 14 (Göttingen: Vandenhoeck & Ruprecht, 1964); Karl-Heinz zur Mühlen, *Nos extra nos: Luthers Theologie zwischen Mystik und Scholastik,* Beiträge zur historischen Theologie, vol. 46 (Tübingen: J. C. B. Mohr [Paul Siebeck], 1972); Martin Seils, *Der Gedanke vom Zusammenwirken Gottes und des Menschen in Luthers Theologie,* Beiträge zur Forderung christlicher Theologie, vol. 50 (Gütersloh: Gerd Mohn, 1962); Reinhard Schwarz, *Fides, Spes und Caritas beim jungen Luther,* Arbeiten zur Kirchengeschichte, vol. 34 (Berlin: Walter de Gruyter, 1962).

[12]Leif Grane, *Contra Gabrielem: Luthers Auseinandersetzung mit Gabriel Biel in der Disputatio contra Scholasticam Theologiam,* Acta Theologica Danica, vol. 4 (Gyldendal, 1962); Heiko A. Oberman, "Facientibus Quod in se est Deus non Denegat Gratiam: Robert Holcot O.P. and the Beginnings of Luther's Theology," *HTR* 55 (1962), 317–342; Oberman, *The Harvest of Medieval Theology: Gabriel Biel and Late Medieval Nominalism,* 2d rev. ed. (Grand Rapids, Mich.: William B. Eerdmans, 1967); Oberman, "'Iustitia Christi' and 'Iustitia Dei': Luther and the Scholastic Doctrines of Justification," *HTR* 59 (1966), 1–26; Oberman, "Simul Gemitus et Raptus: Luther und die Mystik," in *The Church, Mysticism, Sanctifica-*

It is my contention that far from being peripheral to Luther's theology, conversion was very much on Luther's mind in the years before and immediately following his break with the church of Rome.[13] Indeed, by tracing Luther's changing treatment of conversion through his various writings we are able to attain a new vantage point from which to survey Luther's road to his own conversion. Without understanding Luther's concept of conversion we are at a disadvantage in assessing his perception of his own experience. Perhaps no concept is more crucial for understanding and evaluating the description of conversion that Luther offers his readers in his 1545 Preface.

Especially in his first two commentaries, the *Dictata* and the *Lectures on Romans*, Luther devotes considerable attention to the

---

tion and the Natural in Luther's Thought: Lectures Presented to the Third International Congress on Luther Research, ed. Ivar Asheim (Philadelphia: Fortress Press, 1967), pp. 20–59; Oberman, "'Tuus sum, salvum me fac': Augustinréveil zwischen Renaissance und Reformation," in *Scientia Augustiniana: Festschrift für Adolar Zumkeller OSA*, ed. Cornelius Petrus Mayer and Willigis Eckermann (Würzburg: Augustinus, 1975), pp. 349–394; Steven E. Ozment, *Homo Spiritualis: A Comparative Study of the Anthropology of Johannes Tauler, Jean Gerson, and Martin Luther (1509–16) in the Context of Their Theological Thought*, Studies in Medieval and Reformation Thought, vol. 6 (Leiden: E. J. Brill, 1969). Recent scholarship has drawn attention to the influences of nominalism and late medieval Augustinianism on Luther, although debate continues as to precisely how the latter should be defined (Heiko A. Oberman, "Headwaters of the Reformation: *Initia Lutheri—Initia Reformationis*," in *Luther and the Dawn of the Modern Era: Papers for the Fourth International Congress for Luther Research*, ed. Oberman, Studies in the History of Christian Thought, vol. 8 [Leiden: E. J. Brill, 1974], pp. 40–88). David C. Steinmetz cogently surveys the problems in defining the term "Augustinian" in its late medieval context in "Luther and the Late Medieval Augustinians: Another Look," *Concordia Theological Monthly* 44 (1973), 245–260. He has also focused special attention on Johannes von Staupitz, Luther's mentor and superior in the Augustinian order. See further *Misericordia Dei: The Theology of Johannes von Staupitz in Its Late Medieval Setting*, Studies in Medieval and Reformation Thought, vol. 4 (Leiden: E. J. Brill, 1968). In his latest work, *Luther and Staupitz: An Essay in the Intellectual Origins of the Protestant Reformation*, Duke Monographs in Medieval and Renaissance Studies, no. 4 (Durham, N.C.: Duke University Press, 1980), Steinmetz spells out the differences between Luther's Word-based theology and that of Staupitz on such key theological questions as the nature of grace, as well as the differences between Luther and Augustine and between Luther and the Ockhamist theologians.

[13]General references to the concept of conversion without further explication of Luther's understanding are made by Saarnivaara, *Luther Discovers the Gospel*, p. 15, and Fredrik Brosché, *Luther on Predestination: The Antinomy and the Unity Between Love and Wrath in Luther's Concept of God*, Acta Universitatis Upsaliensis, Studia Doctrinae Christianae Upsaliensis, vol. 18 (Uppsala, 1978), p. 188.

concept of conversion. His concern manifests itself in several ways. He is deeply concerned with the problem of preparation for conversion to faith and righteousness, with the nature of conversion as it occurs in baptism and penitence, and with how the Christian perseveres in conversion to the attainment of final and perfect righteousness. That his statements are often ambiguous, sometimes contradictory, and occasionally unclear demonstrates his struggle to formulate his own understanding of conversion. Both in his struggle for intellectual understanding and in the process of his own conversion, the Psalms and Paul's Letter to the Romans play roles of special importance. Although I shall frequently offer interpretations of Luther's statements, I shall make no attempt to resolve internal contradictions or to erase ambiguities. In other words, I do not seek to improve upon Luther himself, a temptation that besets any scholar who seeks to write a coherent analysis of Luther's early theology.

The word *conversio* occurs infrequently in the commentaries on Hebrews and Galatians. Nevertheless, in these works, too, Luther is very much involved with questions related to conversion, in particular with preparation for faith and righteousness, the nature of repentance, and the character of daily life in Christ. Throughout the writings of these years to 1519, Luther is deeply concerned with the idea of transformation, from sinner to saved, from guilty to forgiven, from a life lived under wrath and fear to one under grace and hope. The themes in his commentaries and writings of these years not surprisingly mirror his own questioning and seeking. It was, as Luther himself later notes in his 1545 Preface, a long and arduous process. The experience he describes in that famous self-revelation was the culminating event in a long process of discovery and conversion. It was a process in which Luther came to perceive how God converts man—without his aid, indeed, even without his arriving at a passively receptive state of humility. This issue of humility as preparation for grace was to haunt and obsess Luther's early efforts to understand how a person is converted to God, or, in the terms he uses and scholars after him have consistently followed, how a person comes to be justified before God.

I shall examine Luther's concept of conversion and demonstrate why this concept is so important for understanding both his developing theology and his personal transition from obsession with his own unworthiness before God and fear of Him to trust in God's mercy and reliance on His saving act in Christ. As early as the *Dictata*, Luther emphasizes the incarnation as the decisive conversion event in history. Man's conversion occurs only after and because of God's conversion to man in the incarnation. When we push to the very center of Luther's perception of conversion, we encounter the incarnated Christ on the Cross. To understand fully Luther's *theologia crucis* we must consider his concept of conversion.

I shall take into consideration Luther's pre-1513 writings, but I shall concentrate on those from the *Dictata* to 1519. By that date he had reached those fundamental understandings that characterize his mature theology. From November 1517 onward, as a result of the unanticipated reaction to his *Ninety-five Theses,* Luther was thrust from pulpit and podium onto center stage in Germany. It was in the very midst of turmoil and confrontation that Luther arrived at full clarity regarding conversion.

A preview of the method and content of the book may prove helpful. Chapters 2 through 4 examine the major biblical commentaries of the years 1513–1519. In the *Dictata* and *Lectures on Romans,* Luther is concerned with the question of preparation for conversion. In both commentaries, although less so in *Romans,* there are ambiguities in his response to this question. In *Romans* his concern shifts from the question of preparation to that of how the Christian is to persevere in conversion. Both questions are related to Luther's understanding of faith and humility, and thus frequent references will be made to these ideas. In the commentaries on Hebrews and Galatians (1519), references to the word "conversion" seldom occur, yet both works discuss questions intimately connected to conversion, such as preparation for faith. Further, these commentaries are of special importance because they parallel in time Luther's first reform writings.

Chapter 5, on Luther's early writings, covers in essence the same time period as that of the *Dictata* and *Lectures on Romans*, while Chapter 6, on the reform writings, parallels Luther's work on Hebrews and Galatians. In these various writings Luther employs the concept of conversion in various contexts, including sermons, letters, theses, and tracts. The similarities and differences to be found in his understanding of the concept in these writings and in his major commentaries merit close analysis. Chapter 7 examines Luther's 1545 account of his road to reform. Since no one has as yet analyzed his description of the tower experience on the basis of his writings about conversion, important new evidence is brought to the ongoing debate regarding the dating and authenticity of this event. Chapter 8 surveys the results of this study and discusses their importance.

A brief outline of the ways in which Luther employs the word *conversio* may serve as background for discussion of the concept. Luther occasionally refers to the *conversio*, the acceptance of the tenets of the Christian faith, by Jews and heretics.[14] Far more frequently, however, he speaks of *conversio* as consisting of one of the following: (1) the unrepeatable entrance into the Christian life, that is, baptism; (2) a repeatable event, that is, contrition or penitence; (3) an event, that is, a dramatic personal transformation, as with Paul and Augustine, or the instance of God becoming man in the incarnation.[15] I shall concentrate on the first two of these usages, since Luther speaks most frequently

[14]To cite one example, "Ego autem miror, inde probari possit Iudaeorum universalis conversio, ut multi hic dicunt, quum Christus aperte dicat 'Non peribit generatio haec, donec omnia fiant'" (*WA* 3 [*Dictata*], 329, 26–28 [gloss to Ps. 58:15]).

[15]The following passage from Luther's scholion to Rom. 8:26 includes the interpretation of *conversio* as both unrepeatable and repeatable (uses 1 and 2): "Primam gratiam eam voco, Non que in principio conversionis infunditur, sicut in baptismo, contritione, compunctione, Sed omnem aliam sequentem et novam, Quam nos gradum et augmentum gratie dicimus" (*WA* 56, 379, 10–12). An instance of the third usage occurs in the interpretation of Rom. 9:3 with respect to Paul's conversion: "Et sexto, Quod optat solum anathema esse a Christo, quod est mitius. Sed ante Conversionem potius optabat Christum et omnes suos anathema esse a toto mundo et non ipse se a Christo, Sed Christum a se et omnibus alienum fiere" (*WA* 56, 389, 28–390, 2). In his *Dictata* exegesis of Ps. 84:7 Luther describes *conversio* in the incarnation: "Sed conversio ista dei maxima et prima est, qua unitus est nostre nature" (*WA* 4, 8, 9–10).

and at greatest length about them. Both, however, are connected to, indeed dependent on, Luther's fundamental understanding of *conversio* as the event of God becoming man in the incarnation. As a term and of much lesser importance for Luther, *conversio* may mean (1) a mundane turning to an unspecified object or goal; (2) man's negative act of turning toward the lesser instead of the higher good; and (3) a turn of phrase, a rhetorical usage.[16] None of these ways of using the word is unique to Luther. Yet we cannot proceed with a discussion of his theological understanding of conversion without knowing the basic ways in which he defines the term.

Nor can we adequately understand Luther's concept of conversion without some general background on the ways in which the word *conversio* was defined in the medieval period and the contexts in which it was used. To comprehend the concept and the ways Luther intertwined conversion with other concepts, such as faith and humility, we must have some sense of the tradition of usage to which Luther was heir. As monk, theologian, student of mysticism, Luther must have been well acquainted with the various meanings of the word *conversio*. From these meanings and usages at his disposal, he chose to retain, emphasize, and build on some while virtually ignoring others in his early works. As I have already noted, he chose to see the

---

[16]An example of the first meaning is this passage from the interlinear gloss to Ps. 45:3: "*et transferentur* dimissis Iudeis se convertendo ad gentes *montes* Apostoli et discipuli . . ." (*WA* 3 [*Dictata*], 265, 11–12). For the second, the following passage from the scholion to Rom. 4:7: "Ut sit iniquus propter aversionem et peccator propter conversionem, ibi a bono, hic ad malum, ibi per omissionem, hic per commissionem pollutus" (*WA* 56, 277, 16–18). For the third, the following passage from the *Operationes in Psalmos* of 1519–1521 demonstrates the use of *conversio* to mean a turn of phrase or reversal of the roles of two words in a figure of speech: "Nunc videamus verba. Primum est: Loquimini in cordibus vestris, hoc est: secum bene meditentur nec irae obtemperent, quae praeceps est et verbum habet in lingua, non in corde iuxta illud Ecclesiastici xxi. 'In ore fatuorum cor illorum, et in corde sapientium os illorum', pulchra et egregia conversio sententiae. Hoc idem et hic versus monet, ut os ad cor vertamus, non effundamus statim quicquid tentatio suggerit. Hoc enim est cor in ore habere, imprudenter loqui, quod maxime faciunt irati: os in corde habere, prudenter loqui, quod faciunt quieti et mites. Quare possemus eandem conversionem emulari hoc loco et dicere: Loqui in cordibus et cogitare in oribus (ut sic dixerim) esse contraria, illud sapientium, hoc stultorum" (*WA* 5, 113, 16–26 [Ps. 4:5]).

fundamental meaning of *conversio* to be the act of God becoming man in the incarnation. From this perception he further developed his concept of conversion and fixed its place in his theology, but he did not do so, we may safely assume, without realizing which earlier meanings of the term he was following and which he was not.

Let us survey some of the areas where the idea of conversion plays a significant role. Indeed, from its very beginnings, conversion was an essential component of the Christian way. Jesus urged people to "repent" and "follow me" (Matt. 4:17 and 19).[17] In the early days of the Christian sect, conversion meant a change of belief to the acceptance of Jesus as the Messiah and a transformation of one's life so that one acted in accordance with his precepts and the model of his life. To become a Christian meant to be converted. It meant renouncing one's old way of life, confessing monotheism, and accepting Jesus as one's savior. Conversion to the Christian way included definite and concrete ways of acting in the world. One could no longer observe the emperor cult or offer sacrifices to pagan deities.[18] For the convert certain professions were immediately foreclosed. For example, no longer could one be a soldier or magistrate.[19] By refusing to swear loyalty to the emperor, Christians invited the charge

[17]In his important study about conversion in early Christianity, first published in 1933, Arthur Darby Nock distinguished between conversion and adhesion to a religion. Motivating adhesion was the world view that suggested that the more rites one observed and the more cults to which one belonged, the more secure was one's position in the world. Nock wrote: "By conversion we mean the reorientation of the soul of an individual, his deliberate turning from indifference or from an earlier form of piety to another, a turning which implies a consciousness that a great change is involved, that the old is wrong and the new is right. It is seen at its fullest in the positive response of man to the choice set before him by the prophetic religions" (*Conversion: The Old and New in Religion from Alexander the Great to Augustine of Hippo* [London: Oxford University Press, 1972], p. 7).

[18]Ibid., p. 227. For a description of conversion from paganism to Christianity, see pp. 212–253.

[19]Ibid., p. 227. On the question of Christians serving in the Roman army, E. R. Dodds writes in *Pagan and Christian in an Age of Anxiety: Some Aspects of Religious Experience from Marcus Aurelius to Constantine* (New York: W. W. Norton, 1970), p. 114: "There were already Christians in the army by the beginning of the third century, if not earlier; by the end of it there were so many that Diocletian felt obliged to institute a purge. By Porphyry's time the charge of lack of patriotism was out of date, and was apparently dropped." The "thundering legion" recruited from among Christians in Egypt has proved to be a controversial point for pacifist readings of early Christianity.

of political sedition, which gained in popularity after the Christians were blamed in A.D. 64 for the burning of Rome. Above all, conversion to Christianity implied a willingness to witness in its behalf and, if necessary, to face death for one's beliefs.[20]

The most famous account of early Christian conversion is that of the apostle Paul. The stories in Acts and from Paul himself in Galatians leave many questions unanswered and pose various problems, but they dramatically portray conversion from one way of life to another.[21] His conversion is described as an unexpected event, not as the culmination of a long process. Indeed, Paul's account, with its emphasis on suddenness and confrontation with the divine, provides the touchstone for other descriptions of conversion in the tradition.

At this juncture a problem arises in defining "conversion." On the one hand, we have Paul's account, in which human initiative is described as playing no role. Paul was "turned" by the divine power, which acted upon him, and his only responses were awe and obedience. On the other hand, some accounts describe conversion to Christianity as a process. The conversion of Justin Martyr in the second century provides a good example.[22] The

[20]Nock, *Conversion*, pp. 192–197. For a full discussion of the place of the martyr in the early church, see W. H. C. Frend, *Martyrdom and Persecution in the Early Church: A Study of Conflict from the Maccabees to Donatists* (Garden City, N.Y.: Anchor Books, Doubleday, 1967).

[21]Gal. 1:11–17; Acts 9:1–22, 22:3–16, 26:4–18. For a discussion of the psychology of conversion, see William James, *The Varieties of Religious Experience: A Study in Human Nature* (New York: New American Library, 1958), pp. 140–206. On Paul and his conversion, see Ernst Benz, *Paulus als Visionär: Eine vergleichende Untersuchung der Visionsberichte des Paulus in der Apostelgeschichte und in den paulinischen Briefen*, Abhandlungen der Geistes- und Sozialwissenschaftlichen Klasse, Jahrgang 1952, no. 2 (Wiesbaden: Akadamie der Wissenschaften und der Literatur in Mainz, Franz Steiner Verlag, 1952), esp. pp. 85–88 and 97–102; Josef Blank, *Paulus und Jesus: Eine theologische Grundlegung*, Studien zum Alten und Neuen Testament, vol. 18 (Munich: Kosel, 1968), pp. 185–248; Johannus Munck, *Paul and the Salvation of Mankind* (Richmond: John Knox Press, 1959), esp. pp. 11–35; Hans Joachim Schoeps, *Paul: The Theology of the Apostle in the Light of Jewish Religious History* (Philadelphia: Westminster Press, 1961), esp. pp. 53–58; Krister Stendahl, *Paul among Jews and Gentiles and Other Essays* (Philadelphia: Fortress Press, 1976). Stendahl prefers to speak in terms of Paul's call, rather than in terms of conversion (pp. 7–23).

[22]Justin, *Dialogue with Trypho, A Jew*, in *The Ante-Nicene Fathers*, vol. 1: *The Apostolic Fathers with Justin Martyr and Irenaeus*, ed. Alexander Roberts and James Donaldson, rev. A. Cleveland Coxe (Grand Rapids, Mich.: W. B. Eerdmans, 1975), pp. 194–270. See also Nock, *Conversion*, pp. 255–257.

courage of the Christians in facing torture and death may initially have inspired many conversions such as Justin's.[23]

The most influential conversion in Latin Christianity was that of Augustine of Hippo, who in his *Confessions* left a dramatic account of his own road to conversion. It was to the order bearing Augustine's name that Luther attached himself in 1505. It was also to Augustine that Luther frequently appealed in the defense of his reform theology. Thus Augustine's understanding of conversion is of special importance for the study of Luther. In looking at the idea of conversion in Augustine, we shall direct our attention specifically to the *Confessions*, since in this story of his own experience Augustine employed the concept in various ways. He highlighted the contrast between conversion to God and aversion to Him, imagery that is paralleled by that of the two cities or the two churches, *ecclesia ab Abel* and *ecclesia a Cain*.[24] Man may be either turned to God by humble piety or turned away from Him by lifting up the horn of false liberty.[25] Once man is converted to God, he does not simply occupy a stable, unchanging position, but begins to travel the arduous road of pilgrimage. *Conversio* transforms *peregrinatio* from an undirected movement of aimless wandering into a directed movement of hopeful pilgrimage toward rest in God.[26]

In the later books of the *Confessions*, in which Augustine interprets the opening verses of Genesis, conversion plays a central role. Augustine affirms that spiritual creatures were removed from chaos through their conversion to the *Verbum*.[27] Man as spiritual creature was created and then turned to God.[28]

---

[23]Dodds, *Pagan and Christian*, pp. 132–133.

[24]Augustine, *Confessiones*, in *PL* 32, II, 6, 14, col. 681, ll. 11–13.

[25]Ibid., III, 8, 16, col. 690, ll. 41–45.

[26]Ibid., X, 5, 7, col. 782.

[27]Ibid., XIII, 2, 3, col. 845, l. 46–col. 846, l. 2.

[28]With reference to Augustine's *De Trinitate*, David J. Hassel has discussed the relation between conversion and creation in the following way: "This formation of the creature is achieved when the *Verbum* calls the creature into form and into existence in imitation of His own substantial, formative union with the Father. Only by being converted or turned to the light, in answer to this call, can the creature be illuminated and thereby formed or created. For, if the creature remains averted from this sapiential light, it remains unformed" ("Conversion-Theory and *Scientia* in the *De Trinitate*," *Recherches Augustiniennes* 2 [1962], 384).

26

Conversion also occurred on a prior level of creation, when matter itself was created; this *conversio* preceded *reformatio*, since it was only through *conversio* that matter received form.[29] The alternative to the form achieved through conversion would have been for matter to remain in a state that Augustine termed *vagabunda deliquia*"[30]—a state of wandering want—and the same would have held for man the spiritual creature if he had not been converted to God.

Man as converted spiritual creature is able within his individual history to avert himself from God. Such aversion occurred in the Fall, and it continues on an individual basis throughout history. The angel fell; the soul of man flowed downward; together they demonstrated the abyss for the whole of spiritual creation in the utter darkness that could be transformed only by God's words "Let there be light."[31] The result of the Fall was man's disquietude as his soul settled into the miserable restlessness of fallen spirit—a dissatisfaction and restlessness that remained until he began his pilgrimage, his return, to God. When man acts *aversus Deum*, Augustine wrote, he is no longer whole, a fragmented being. Only as man begins the process of return does God collect him from dispersion.[32] Thus, on the negative side of man's condition, before *conversio*, Augustine wrote of *aversio, dispersio, defluxus*. In one of the most powerful passages in the *Confessions*, Augustine wrote of his earlier days: "I went away from Thee, my God, in my youth I strayed too far from Thy sustaining power, and I became to myself a barren land."[33]

For Augustine the possibility of man's second conversion is

---

[29]On this point Gerhart Ladner has written: "But within an act of *creatio ex nihilo* there can be no *reformatio* because there has been no *forma*, there can only be *formatio* of a still *informis creatura;* this *formatio* consists of *revocatio* to God of a creature which, when it was drawn out of nothingness, found itself outside of God and in the *conversio* of that creature to Him" (*The Idea of Reform: Its Impact on Christian Thought and Action in the Age of the Fathers* [New York: Harper & Row, 1967], p. 169).

[30]*PL* 32, XIII, 5, 6, col. 847, ll. 13–14.

[31]Ibid., 8, 9, col. 848, ll. 11–13.

[32]Ibid., II, 1, 1, col. 675, ll. 22–23.

[33]Ibid., 10, 18, col. 682, ll. 51–53; *The Confessions of St. Augustine*, trans. F. J. Sheed (New York: Sheed & Ward, 1965), p. 37.

rooted in God's mercy, in the sending of His Son to earth. Even as the conversion of creation was accomplished through the *Verbum aeternum,* so is man's conversion from his fallen state to pilgrimage in grace made possible by the incarnation of the *Verbum.* Through the *Verbum* man now has that hope to accompany him on his pilgrimage which promises him that he will be saved.[34]

The concept of conversion occupies a key position in the *Confessions,* linking together Augustine's account of his own life and his exegesis of the opening verses of Genesis. One scholar has argued that the *Confessions* is drawn together by its preoccupation with a vision of man: "A theory of man, indeed; man as Prodigal, lost sheep, soul in odyssey, *peregrinatio,* ambiguous term which can mean 'wandering' or 'pilgrimage,' depending on the direction of its movement, away from or back to God."[35]

With regard to Augustine's own conversion, it has been argued that each transition he described was a conversion.[36] These conversions included his decision to pursue the search for wisdom after reading Cicero's *Hortensius,* his later decision to join the Manichees, and his turn to orthodox Christianity.[37] In the broader sense of the word, that is an accurate analysis. For

[34]*PL* 32, XIII, 14, 15, col. 851, ll. 39–44.

[35]Robert J. O'Connell, *St. Augustine's Confessions: The Odyssey of a Soul* (Cambridge: Belknap Press of Harvard University Press, 1969), p. 186.

[36]In his survey of literature concerning Augustine's conversion, Jens Nörregard mentions Otto Scheel, *Die Anschauung Augustin über Christi Person und Werk,* as a proponent of the view that the real turning point or conversion was not that described by Augustine but rather his adherence to Neoplatonism: "Die sogenannte 'Bekehrung' war kein entscheidendes Moment, da Augustins theologisches und philosophisches Denken dadurch keine durchgreifende Wandlung erfahren hat. Der wirkliche Wendepunkt war die Bekanntschaft mit dem Neuplatonismus" (Jens Nörregard, *Augustins Bekehrung,* trans. A. Spelmeyer [Tübingen: J. C. B. Mohr (Paul Siebeck), 1923], pp. 6–7; see also pp. 1–19). On Augustine's conversion, see also Vernon Bourke, *Augustine's Quest of Wisdom: Life and Philosophy of the Bishop of Hippo* (Milwaukee: Bruce, 1945), esp. pp. 48–66; Romano Guardini, *The Conversion of Augustine,* trans. Elinor Briefs (Westminster, Md.: Newman Press, 1960); John J. O'Meara, *The Young Augustine: The Growth of St. Augustine's Mind up to His Conversion* (London: Longmans, Green, 1954), esp. pp. 173–190.

[37]See further Pierre Courcelle, *Recherches sur les Confessions de Saint Augustin* (Paris: E. de Boccard, 1950), especially his assessment of the *Confessions* on p. 258.

those who read Augustine's *Confessions* or heard his story told, however, the real "conversion" took place with his emotional affirmation of Christianity during his famous garden experience. In Augustine's own eyes, each earlier transition only served to bring him to a new level of crisis, culminating in his acceptance of Neoplatonism, which held that once man had reached intellectual insight, he would be able to act according to that knowledge. But that was precisely what Augustine was unable to do. In opposition to his intellect, he turned from the ladder leading to God and faced toward the world of the corporeal. "Yet I did not stably enjoy my God, but was ravished to You by Your beauty, yet soon was torn away from You again by my own weight, and fell again with torment to lower things. Carnal habit was that weight."[38] His frustration at his failure to be directed toward higher things was tempered by his self-satisfaction with the magnitude of his knowledge. "I did not weep for my state, but was badly puffed up with my knowledge. Where was that charity which builds us up upon the foundation of humility, which is Christ Jesus?"[39]

According to Augustine's own description, the ultimate moment of crisis came when his intellect was committed to what he knew he should do but his will continued to be torn in two directions. He heard the command "Cast yourself without fear, He will receive you and heal you," but it was exactly this "casting," this "turning," that Augustine himself could not accomplish.[40] It was only as he responded to the half-understood words "tolle lege, tolle lege," picked up the Epistles of Paul, and read the words of Romans 13:13 that he felt his will to be freed to act and knew himself to be converted to Christ.[41] Through his conversion Augustine perceived himself to have been turned away from a life of concupiscence to one of continence.[42] Con-

---

[38]*PL* 32, VII, 17, 23, col. 744, ll. 52–55; *Confessions of St. Augustine*, p. 149.
[39]*PL* 32, VII, 20, 26, col. 747, ll. 7–9; *Confessions of St. Augustine*, p. 152.
[40]*PL* 32, VIII, 11, 27, col. 761, ll. 33–35; *Confessions of St. Augustine*, p. 177.
[41]*PL* 32, VIII, 12, 28–30, cols. 761–764.
[42]Nock noted that in contrast to the conversions of earlier pagans to Christianity, Augustine lived in a world in which Christian ideas were very much present: "Christianity is throughout presupposed and present in the subject's

version for Augustine was not, as it was for Paul, the acceptance
and affirmation of new beliefs. It was rather the resolution of an
inner battle that resulted in the unity of will and intellect. With
Augustine the stage setting of conversion moved from the realm
of outward confession to that of inner resolution of conflict. A
new and important emphasis was given to conversion.[43]

The following are the fundamental characteristics of Augustine's conversion according to his account in the *Confessions*.
First, conversion was preceded by struggle, by an uncertain
movement of return to God which could not become pilgrimage
until he was converted by God. Second, from the account Augustine gave in Book 8—the way in which he wanted his readers
to perceive his conversion—it was an event, part of a chain consisting of the conversions of Antony, Ambrose, and Alypius.
Although there had been a long process of preparation, conversion itself was described as the sudden, dramatic action of God
on the individual's personal history, similar in this respect to the
experience of Paul on the road to Damascus. Conversion
brought Augustine from disintegration, a character at war within itself, to integration, a unity that allowed him to enter with full
intensity on the path of pilgrimage. From an intellect and a will
divided, he was transformed into a whole person, no longer lost
in a confused search for knowledge but firmly directed toward
wisdom. Conversion was the point that separated the time of
wandering from that of pilgrimage.

Both the context of conversion and the meaning of the term
itself underwent important changes as Christianity became the
official religion of the Roman Empire and as more and more
people were born into Christianity. Augustine stood at the end

---

subconsciousness . . . ; it is a progress in a continuous line; it is like a chemical
process in which the addition of a catalytic agent produces a reaction for which
all the elements were already present" (*Conversion*, p. 266).

[43]The question of conversion and its place in Augustine's theology could be
explored in various contexts relevant to Luther's subsequent ideas, for example,
with respect to his predestinarian views. See Gotthard Nygren, *Das Prädestinationsproblem in der Theologie Augustins: Eine systematisch-theologische Studie*, trans.
Christa-Maria Lyckhage, Studia Theologica Lundensia, vol. 12 (Göttingen: Vandenhoeck & Ruprecht, 1956).

of the period in which conversion preceded baptism for most Christians. Mass conversions of conquered peoples continued to occur, although these conversions bore the marks of adhesion more than the signs of conversion. Beginning in the fifth century, however, conversion also referred to an event that occurred after baptism. Conversion in this context was a change not from a non-Christian to a Christian life, but from Christianity to a stricter following of its precepts, involving the taking of a vow. Conversion was equated with entering a monastic community, following a new manner of life, and separating oneself from the life of the secular world.[44] Monastic life also came to be called the *vita apostolica*. For a time, from the fifth to the seventh centuries, conversion referred also to the act of those members of the laity who did not take monastic vows but pledged themselves to a stricter observance of Christianity within the context of their lives in the world.[45] While not renouncing their married state, such persons observed continence, practiced penitence daily, and devoted themselves to good works.[46] The Council of Orange and others designated these people as a separate class, distinct from both monks and ordinary laity. By the end of the seventh century, however, these unofficial lay communities were forbidden. Such people then often attached themselves to monasteries as lay brothers. Indeed, in many monastic communities

[44]Paul Galtier, "Conversi," *Dictionnaire de spiritualité*, vol. 2, pt. 2 (Paris: Beauchesne, 1953). "Sans doute ce passage se trouve-t-il appelé *conversio:* on y fait profession d'adopter la *conversatio* monastique. Aussi les mots *conversus, convertens* sont-ils d'usage courant dans le langage monastique pour désigner ceux qui demandent à embrasser ce genre de vie" (col. 2218).

[45]"Mais, à cette époque, 5ᵉ–7ᵉ siècles, ce mot sert également à désigner des fidèles, qui, sans quitter le monde et tout en continuant à y remplir leurs obligations sociales, ont renoncé a ses vanités . . ." (ibid.).

[46]"Ils ont pour trait caractéristique leur application aux observances d'une vie profondément religieuse. Ni clercs, ni moines, restant engagés dans les liens du mariage, leur conduite générale, leur *conversatio*, comme on dit, jusqu' à l'austérité de leurs vêtements, les font reconnaître comme particulièrement adonnés à une vie réglée, pieuse et pénitente. On ne saurait dire qu'ils constituent une classe à part dans l'Église: tout au moins, n'y ont-ils pas de statut juridique exactement défini. On les trouve qualifiés de 'religiosi'; mais ce mot n'es pris, alors, qu'au sens générique d'une personne attentive à ses devoirs religieux: . . . Leur 'conversio' toutefois leur donne un droit tout particulier à être ainsi qualifiés, car la 'conversatio' qui en résulte tranche assez sur celle du commun des fidèles pour les faire désigner couramment par le nom de *conversi*" (ibid.).

they exercised considerable power in daily activities, particularly in the conduct of economic affairs. Directly or indirectly these lay people participated in a more intense form of Christianity while still retaining their secular status.

Nonetheless, the "converted" in the early Middle Ages were not primarily members of voluntary lay associations, which were eventually forbidden, but members of monastic orders. In this sense, conversion constituted the entrance into the religious life. At the same time, it meant following the life of a lay religious, since in the beginning most monks were laymen. By the twelfth century the term *conversi* was used to designate lay brothers as distinct from choir monks and priests. This terminology continued into the later Middle Ages, among the mendicants as well as the monks. In a letter of May 16, 1519, Luther referred to the *conversi,* the lay brothers, of a certain cloister.[47]

The *Regula Benedicti,* described by Luther in 1516 as "*regula approbatissima,*"[48] was of great significance in establishing the meaning of conversion as entrance into the monastic community. It brought to fruition what was begun by Pachomius, Cassian, Caesarius of Arles, and others, and presented both a principle for monastic organization that was general enough to meet the demands of varying times and places and a code that was specific enough to deal with individual violations and to offer a stable framework for the governance of community life.[49]

In his rule, Benedict referred ten times to *conversatio morum.*[50]

---

[47]"Conversi illic iam dudum regnant" (*WA Br* 1, 399, 9). We note that the editor of the *Br* found the term *conversi* not to be self-evidently clear. In n. 5, p. 400, he adds: "Laienbrüder, nicht: Bekehrte-Lutheraner. . . ."

[48]*WA* 4, 556, 17 (*Praelectio in librum Iudicium*).

[49]See Herbert B. Workman, *The Evolution of the Monastic Idea from the Earliest Times Down to the Coming of the Friars* (Boston: Beacon Press, 1962), pp. 139–180.

[50]Justin McCann has listed these in his edition of the Rule: "Prol. Processu vero conversationis et fidei; C. 1 Non conversationis fervore novicio; C. 1 De quorum omnium horum miserrima conversatione; C. 21 Fratres boni testimonii et sanctae conversationis; C. 22 Lectisternia pro modo conversationis . . . accipiant; C. 58 Noviter veniens quis ad conversationem; C. 58 Promittat de . . . conversatione morum suorum; C. 63 Ut conversationis tempus . . . discernit; C. 73 Ut . . . initium conversationis nos demonstremus habere; C. 73 Ceterum ad perfectionem conversationis qui festinat" (*The Rule of St. Benedict* [Westminster, Md.: Newman Press, 1952], p. 203).

The exact meaning of this phrase continues to be a matter of debate. Indeed, it apparently became problematic relatively soon after the composition of the rule, since in later manuscripts it was frequently changed to the more readily understandable *conversio morum.*[51] Benedict appears to be using the term *conversatio* in a twofold sense, one of which refers to the act of becoming a monk, the change from secular to religious life; the other "denotes the monastic life as an established discipline and a regular observance."[52] As Justin McCann has suggested, the two meanings cannot easily be separated: "Becoming a monk passes into being a monk; but there is the constant factor of the monk and his purpose. It may be said, indeed, that his whole life is, or ought to be, a prolongation in time of his original "conversion'; which is, I believe, the fundamental meaning of St Benedict's second vow."[53] A dual understanding of the term allows for an interpretation of *conversatio* as both the moment of transformation and the following of the monastic discipline to which one committed oneself as a result of *conversio/conversatio.* The important text in Chapter 58 embodies this twofold meaning: "Now this shall be the manner of his reception. In the oratory, in the presence of all, he shall promise stability, conversion of his life, and obedience; and this before God and his Saints."[54] The goal of the rule is to lead one from the *initium conversationis* to *perfectionem conversationis.*

[51]"*Conversatio* morum telle est certainement la leçon authentique du passage cité de la règle. C'est la version qu' offrent notamment les manuscrits A*BXOSV. Très tôt, cependant, elle fut remplacée par le mot *conversio* morum suorum (mss AcTK); les manuscrits cassiniens les meilleurs contiennent *conversio,* ainsi que tous les commentateurs du moyen âge, y compris les plus anciens. Et c'est *conversio morum* que, jusqu' à ces derniers temps, on lisait sur toutes les chartes de profession dans l'ordre de Saint-Benoît" (Philibert Schmitz, "Conversatio (conversio) morum," *Dictionnaire de spiritualité,* vol. 2, pt. 2, col. 2206). For further discussion of the controversy regarding *conversatio morum–conversio morum,* see Basilius Steidle, "'De conversatione morum suorum' zum philologischen Verständnis von Regula S. Benedicti, cap. 58, 17," in *Regula Magistri: Regula S. Benedicti,* ed. Basilius Steidle (Rome: Herder, 1959); O. Lottin, "Le voeu de 'conversatio morum' dans la Règle de Saint Benoît, *Recherches de Théologie ancienne et médiévale* 26 (1959), 5–16; and the older treatment by John Chapman, *Saint Benedict and the Sixth Century* (London: Sheed & Ward, 1929), pp. 207–233.

[52]McCann, ed., *Rule of St. Benedict,* p. 168n.

[53]Ibid., p. 168.

[54]Ibid., p. 131.

Two points remain to be mentioned with regard to Benedict and the rule. In spite of the difficulty in understanding *conversatio* (later *conversio*) *morum,* it clearly denoted a process of discipline characterized by *compunctio,* "pain of the spirit, a suffering resulting simultaneously from two causes: the existence of sin and our own tendency toward sin . . . and the existence of our desire for God and even our very possession of God."[55] Conversion as a process was constantly marked by compunction as one realized one's sinfulness. At the same time, however, conversion continued to refer to the event of entrance into the monastic life. Gregory the Great gave an excellent example of this meaning in his dedicatory letter to Leander, accompanying his *Expositio in beatum Iob seu Moralium libri xxxv.*[56] There is a marked similarity between Gregory's description of his entrance into the monastic life and Augustine's of his road to Christian faith, but with Gregory conversion received a new context. For him one effected conversion by leaving the secular world with all its garb and customs for the life of the monastery.

The second point that deserves mention concerns the reception of oblates into the Benedictine community. In the fifty-ninth chapter of his rule Benedict made provision for receiving the sons of both wealthy and poor families.[57] This provision, important as it came to be in feudal society, also laid the basis for the undermining of the concept of a spiritual conversion that led one to join a monastic community. In its beginnings Christian baptism was received as a result of conversion by adult believers, although it remains a matter of debate whether or not whole households were baptized after the conversion of their masters. As Christianity became the official religion of the empire, bap-

---

[55] Jean Leclercq, O.S.B., *The Love of Learning and the Desire for God: A Study of Monastic Culture* (New York: Fordham University Press, 1977), pp. 37–38.

[56] Gregorius I, *Moralia in Iob Libri I–X* in *Corpus Christianorum,* Series Latina, vol. 143 (Turnholti: Brepols, 1979), pp. 1–2. English translation in George E. McCracken, ed., *Early Medieval Theology,* Library of Christian Classics, vol. 9 (Philadelphia: Westminster Press, 1957), pp. 183–184.

[57] "Si quis forte de nobilibus offert filium suum Deo in monasterio, si ipse puer minori aetate est, parentes ejus faciant petitionem quam supra diximus; et cum oblatione ipsam petitionem et manum pueri involvant in palla altaris, et sic eum offerant" (McCann, ed., *Rule of St. Benedict,* p. 134).

tism was increasingly administered to infants as a matter of course. Thus one was born a Christian without experiencing the conversion to which baptism originally testified. In monastic usage, *conversatio* (*conversio*) was the renunciation of the world for the life of the cloister, but those who joined the monastery as young children were trained in the *conversatio morum* without ever experiencing the conversion that had previously led adults to become monks.

In the subsequent tradition, from Gregory the Great onward, *conversatio* (*conversio*) *morum* as ongoing penance was emphasized at the expense of *conversio* as event or decisive experience. The event proved to be less important than the ongoing experience of daily conversion that was shared by those who had grown up within the community as oblates and had become full members of the community as well as by those who had experienced conversion to the monastic life as adults. In other words, initial *conversio* no longer proved essential to a life of *conversatio morum*/*conversio mentis*.

By the time of Gregory's death, at the beginning of the seventh century (604), conversion had several meanings: the turning from paganism and Judaism to Christianity, the change from secular to monastic life as a following of the *vita apostolica*, and equation with *compunctio*—what Jean Leclercq has aptly defined as pain of the spirit—in the context of penance.[58] In this connection, and increasingly in the period up until Bernard of Clairvaux, conversion to the monastic life was defined in terms less of a change of heart or mind than of a change to and the following of a new way of life.

With the exception of the northern and eastern frontiers of Christian Europe, where missionary activity was continued, from the seventh to the eleventh centuries conversion referred primarily to this change in manner of life which led one to separate from the world and follow the cloistered life. Occasionally it meant the substitution of one monastic rule or customary for another. Beginning with the eleventh century there was a

---

[58]Leclercq, *Love of Learning*, p. 37.

shift back to seeing conversion as the decisive event that led an adult Christian to join a monastic order. Reinhold Seeberg has called the eleventh century "a period of *maturata conversio.*"[59] Unlike the oblates, who experienced no such mature conversion, these new monks underwent a change of heart that led them to separate themselves from the world. The example that comes quickly to mind is that of Bernard of Clairvaux, who joined the newly formed Cistercian order with thirty of his companions and rapidly transformed the struggling community into an enormously successful organization comprising many houses.

Seeberg has suggested that with Bernard there was a "new subjectivism" that was closer to the theology of Augustine.[60] Belief was essential, but it also had to be accompanied by an experience that established the truth in one's heart. Within the monastic context, this experience issued in a life of ongoing penance. In his *Sermons on the Song of Songs* Bernard referred to contrition as belonging to the beginning of conversion: "Here, then, is one ointment which the sinful soul should provide at the beginning of its conversion and to apply to its still smarting wounds."[61] Bernard linked contrition at the beginning of conversion to the work of those who publicly and fully did penance; in other words, to those who had left the secular life and joined the monastic one.[62] He referred to monastic life as the *ordo poenitentium*, since one completed there the satisfaction for sins which had been only partially accomplished within the sacrament of penance.[63] Although monastic life was characterized as

[59]Reinhold Seeberg, *Lehrbuch der Dogmengeschichte,* vol. 3: *Die Dogmenbildung des Mittelalters,* 6th ed. (Basel: Benno Schwabe, 1960), p. 128. See also Jean Leclercq, *Monks and Love in Twelfth-Century France: Psycho-Historical Essays* (Oxford: Oxford University Press, 1979), pp. 8–26, on adult recruitment and its psychological implications.

[60]Seeberg, *Lehrbuch der Dogmengeschichte,* vol. 3, p. 131.

[61]Bernard of Clairvaux, *The Works of Bernard of Clairvaux,* vol. 2: *On the Song of Songs I,* trans. Kilian Walsh, O.C.S.O., Cistercian Fathers Series, no. 4 (Spencer, Mass.: Cistercian Publications, 1971), p. 64; *Sancti Bernardi opera,* vol. 1: *Sermones super Cantica Canticorum 1–35,* ed. J. Leclercq, C. H. Talbot, and H. M. Rochais (Rome: Editiones Cistercienses, 1957), Sermo 10, IV, 5, pp. 50, 29–51, 1.

[62]Reinhard Schwarz, *Vorgeschichte der reformatorischen Busstheologie,* Arbeiten zur Kirchengeschichte, vol. 41 (Berlin: Walter de Gruyter, 1968), p. 92.

[63]Ibid., p. 97.

one of ongoing penance, Bernard also termed full monastic life the *vita contemplativa*. At a lower level on the ladder of monastic life, penance was given a place as the particular characteristic of the novice.[64] Thus the experience of contrition joined to conversion constituted the entire life of the monk and had a place of special importance for the novice.

This emphasis on adult experience was reflected in the rules or charters of the several new monastic orders that specified that no children were to be accepted. The rules drawn up for the Carthusians by Guy, the fifth prior of the Greater Charterhouse, forbade the reception of boys.[65] The new monastic/military order of the Templars reflected Cistercian influence in its refusal to allow boys to join its ranks.[66] With the reemphasis on voluntary adult entry into the monastic life in the eleventh century, the early medieval interpretation of conversion as a mature change of heart leading to acceptance of the monastic vocation was given renewed meaning. Inner experience and decision, not political or family considerations, were regarded as the only appropriate reasons for entering the new monastic orders.

In his *Sermons on the Song of Songs* Bernard wrote of his own experience of conversion. He confessed: "I am not ashamed to admit that very often I myself, especially in the early days of my conversion, experienced coldness and hardness of heart."[67] Still, Bernard continued to seek God and to love Him. Yet despite his efforts, he remained separated from Him. Although he linked this experience of separation from God to the commencement of his conversion, Bernard also saw it as a recurring state: "Many of you, too, I feel, have had similar experiences, and have them even still. In what light then must we view them? I hold that through them our pride is shown up, our humility guarded,

[64]Ibid., p. 98.

[65]Watkin Williams, *Saint Bernard of Clairvaux*, Historical Series of the University of Manchester, no. 237; Historical Series no. 69 (Manchester: Manchester University Press, 1935), p. 33.

[66]"Ut pueri, quamdiu sunt parvi, non accipiantur inter fratres Templi" (*Regula Pauperam Commilitionum Christi Templique Salomonis*, par. 14, cited in Williams, *Saint Bernard of Clairvaux*, p. 237).

[67]Bernard of Clairvaux, *On the Song of Songs I*, p. 102; *Sermones super Cantica Canticorum 1–35*, Sermo 14, IV, 6, p. 79, 19–20.

brotherly love fostered and good desires aroused."[68] In another
of the sermons, Bernard affirmed that a person can do the good
only when the Word is present in him.[69] For Bernard, conversion is preceded by a knowledge of God which then instructs
one's will. This knowledge, however, is in turn dependent on
God's act in giving it to one. Although he described conversion
as an individual's act of the will, it is an act that depends on God's
work within the soul.[70]

In his *Sermon to the Clergy on Conversion* Bernard addressed
himself to the danger that clerics might fall away from God and
divine wisdom through the pursuit of mundane knowledge.[71]
In his *Vita* Gaufridus wrote that Bernard urged his listeners to
be converted from useless studies to the worship of true wisdom,
synonymous in this context with entry into the monastic life.[72]

The several facets of Bernard's understanding of conversion
can now be summarized. First, conversion is the experience of
being turned by God away from the world and toward the monastic life. The emphasis on leaving the world is well expressed
by the efforts of the Cistercians and Premonstratensians to
found their cloisters in the most lonely and secluded of places.
Second, the monastic life itself is seen as one of continuous contrition and satisfaction and thus of *conversio morum*. Third, in his

[68]Bernard of Clairvaux, *On the Song of Songs I*, p. 103; *Sermones super Cantica
Canticorum 1–35*, Sermo 14, IV, 6, p. 80, 15–18.
[69]Bernard of Clairvaux, *Sermones super Cantica Canticorum 1–35*, Sermo 32,
III, 7, p. 230, 21–24.
[70]In his study *The Mystical Theology of Saint Bernard* (New York: Sheed & Ward,
1940), Etienne Gilson describes *conversio* as the "movement of the will from
proper to common"; in other words, from self-concern to selflessness and true
love of the other for the sake of God (p. 135).
[71]Bernard of Clairvaux, *Sermo ad clericos de conversione*, in *S. Bernardi opera*, vol.
4: *Sermones I*, ed. J. Leclercq and H. Rochais (Rome: Editiones Cistercienses,
1966), pp. 69–116. Debate continues over the precise dating of the sermon and
hence its context. Williams (*St. Bernard of Clairvaux*) places it before the Council
of Sens, which condemned Abelard in June 1140. Leclercq and Rochais place the
sermon in late 1139 due to textual references to the Christmas liturgy (pp. 61n
and 62n). Leif Grane describes the sermon as "an undisguised attempt to take
his (Abelard's) students away from him," even though Abelard is not mentioned
by name (*Peter Abelard: Philosophy and Christianity in the Middle Ages*, trans. Frederick and Christine Crowley [New York: Harcourt, Brace & World, 1970], p. 129).
[72]*Admonitio* preceding *Sermo ad clericos de conversione*, in *PL* 82, cols. 833–834.
Jean Leclercq discusses this sermon in *Bernard of Clairvaux and the Christian Spirit*,
trans. Claire Lavoie, Cistercian Studies Series, no. 16 (Kalamazoo: Cistercian
Publications, 1976), pp. 38–39.

Sermon to the Clergy Bernard described conversion as a person's turn away from worldly knowledge to divine wisdom, which he equated with the turn to the monastic life. Fourth, although Bernard wrote of conversion as an individual's act of the will, he also insisted that conversion is not a human achievement. The conversion of souls is a work of the divine, not the human voice, even though God may use man as his instrument.[73]

Bernard also wrote of the conversions of Christians who were taking vows not as monks but as crusaders. In Bernard's view this positive event was shadowed only by the fact that the Devil was thwarting the conversion of the infidels. For Bernard, God was at work in the Crusades, converting those who had strayed from the fold. But the Devil responded by raising up the Slavs, since he feared "the conversion of the pagans, when he heard that their tale was to be completed, and that the whole of Israel was to find salvation."[74] Bernard urged Christians to join together for the purpose of the "complete wiping out or, at any rate, the conversion of these peoples."[75]

It would be inaccurate to see the Crusades to Jerusalem and the Near East as primarily directed to the conversion of the infidels. Many motives were at work, but there was far more emphasis on the destruction of the pagans and the securing of their lands for Christian nobles than on their religious conversion. At the same time, however, the Crusades did focus new attention on conversion to Christianity. For example, Bernard's remarks definitely showed a desire to effect the conversion of the Jews in Christian Europe. Rupert of Deutz wrote a *Dialogue Between Christianity and Judaism* around 1126.[76] His contemporary Rudolph of St. Truiden frequently engaged in disputations

[73]Bernard of Clairvaux, *Sermo ad clericos de conversione*, p. 71, 6–7.

[74]Bernard of Clairvaux, *The Letters of Saint Bernard*, trans. Bruno Scott James, pp. 466–468, cited in James A. Brundage, *The Crusades: A Documentary Survey* (Milwaukee: Marquette University Press, 1962), p. 94.

[75]Brundage, *Crusades*, p. 94.

[76]McCracken, ed., *Early Medieval Theology*, p. 254. Rupert's *Dialogue* forms part of a large body of apologetic literature from the late eleventh and early twelfth centuries including the efforts of such men as Gilbert Crispin and Peter Abelard. See further G. R. Evans, *Anselm and a New Generation* (Oxford: Clarendon Press; New York: Oxford University Press, 1980), pp. 34–68, and esp. pp. 59–62, on conversion.

with Jews while he was abbot of St. Pantaleon in Cologne.[77] The fascinating autobiographical account of Hermannus of Scheda described a debate with Rupert which presaged Hermannus' conversion from Judaism to Christianity.[78] Indeed, Hermannus experienced conversion in the most complete medieval sense, not only turning from Judaism to Christianity and exchanging his name of Judah ben David ha-Levi for that of Hermannus, but also turning from the secular life of a money lender to the monastic vocation of the rigorous Premonstratensians.[79] The confrontation with Islam also focused attention on the means for converting Moslems and on the understanding of conversion itself. Both Thomas Aquinas and Raymond Lull devoted them-selves to the question of converting Moslems, and Lull per-formed the important task of training missionaries in Arabic and educating them concerning the precepts of Islam.

By the twelfth and thirteenth centuries conversion had a vari-ety of connotations, including both the turning from Judaism or Islam to Christianity and the turning within Christianity from a secular to a monastic life. The term *conversi* no longer described only those adults (in contrast to oblates) who joined the monas-tery at a mature age, but was also used by the Cistercians and others to designate the lay brothers who were admitted to the order and were chiefly responsible for keeping the monastery running on a daily basis.[80] With the Cistercians and other new

[77]Hermannus Quondam Judaeus, *Opusculum de conversione sua*, ed. Gerlinde Niemeyer, Monumenta Germaniae historica, die deutschen Geschichtsquellen des Mittelalters, 500–1500. Quellen zur Geistesgeschichte des Mittelalters, vol. 4 (Weimar: Hermann Böhlaus Nachfolger, 1963), "Einleitung," p. 5, Evans, *An-selm and a New Generation*, pp. 36–37.

[78]Hermannus Quondam Judaeus, *Opusculum*, pp. 76–84 (pts. 3 and 4).

[79]Ibid., p. 1. Niemeyer discusses the blend of rationalism and mysticism in Hermannus' account; see p. 8.

[80]Williams, *St. Bernard of Clairvaux*, p. 22, See also S. Hilpisch, "Conversi," *New Catholic Encyclopedia*, vol. 4 (New York: McGraw-Hill, 1967), p. 285, and J. Bond-uelle, "Convers," *Dictionnaire de droit canonique*, vol. 4 (Paris: Librairie Letouzey et Ané, 1949), col. 566. At this stage the term *conversi* had several meanings. First, it was used to describe those who joined the monastery and became monks by taking a vow; second, it was also used (and this we see to be particularly the case at Cîteaux) to refer to those lay people who associated themselves with the life of the monastery, took a simple vow, but were distinguished from the choir monks. These *conversi* performed the manual work necessary to run the monastery but

orders, conversion to the religious life was understood as inner experience rather than outward exchange of one way of life for another. It is this aspect of conversion that provides the context for both Dominic and Francis, the founders of the two great mendicant orders.

By the time of Francis of Assisi, the idea of voluntarily following a life of evangelical poverty within the world was already a significant force. The success of Francis and his order represented the establishment as religiously orthodox of the voluntary pursuit of this ideal in the world. Francis followed here in the steps of those earlier proclaimed as heretics for their views, notably the Waldensians.[81]

The biographies of Francis by Bonaventura and Thomas of Celano differ in their portrayals of the young Francis and his conversion. Bonaventura saw Francis' conversion as a major vocational change, but the young, preconversion Francis was described as virtually sinless. Thus there was no sense of conversion as a radical break to transform Francis from sinner to saved.[82] From his youth, according to Bonaventura, Francis was filled with love for the poor and with horror for the evils of

did not (at least in the beginning; see further in the *Dictionnaire de droit canonique* article for subsequent developments) sleep within the cloister. Thus by the twelfth century the term may refer either to an adult (in contrast to an oblate) who joined the monastic order or to a lay person who affiliated himself with a monastery while not taking full vows or living within the cloister.

[81]See Herbert Grundmann, *Ketzergeschichte des Mittelalters*, vol. 2, pt. G (1), of *Die Kirche in ihrer Geschichte: Ein Handbuch,* ed. Kurt Dietrich Schmidt and Ernst Wolf (Göttingen: Vandenhoeck & Ruprecht, 1963); *Religiöse Bewegungen im Mittelalter: Untersuchungen über die geschichtlichen Zusammenhänge zwischen der Ketzerei, den Bettelorden und der religiösen Frauenbewegungen im 12. und 13. Jahrhundert und über die geschichtlichen Grundlagen der deutschen Mystik,* 2d rev. ed. (Hildesheim: Georg Olms, 1961); Kurt-Victor Selge, *Die ersten Waldenser,* vol. 1: *Untersuchung und Darstellung,* Arbeiten zur Kirchengeschichte, vol. 37/1 (Berlin: Walter de Gruyter, 1967).

[82]Bonaventura, *Opera omnia,* vol. 8: *Legenda Sancti Francisci,* pp. 505–507 (see also his *Legenda minor S. Francisci* [Quarrachi, 1898], pp. 565–579, esp. pp. 565–567); Thomas of Celano, *St. Francis of Assisi According to Brother Thomas Celano,* which includes the *Tractatus primus super vitam Sancti Francisci de Assisii seu Legenda Gregorii auctore Thomas de Celano,* ed. H. G. Rosedale (London; J. M. Dent, 1904). English translations of Bonaventura and Celano may be found in Marion Habig, ed., *St. Francis of Assisi: Writings and Early Biographies,* 3d rev. ed. (Chicago: Franciscan Herald Press, 1973).

money.[83] Celano, in contrast, described Francis as not only being at one with his companions in sin, but in fact excelling them.[84] Celano's presentation, with its stress on Francis' ongoing struggle and uncertainty and its Augustinian reversal from sinner to repentant convert, demonstrated that Francis was personally altered by his conversion. According to both accounts, Francis' conversion was to a life of penance, poverty, and prayer in which the danger of falling back into the ways of the world always remained. It is poverty that provides the center around which all the other themes in Francis' postconversion life revolve. In its symbolic sense, poverty reminds the brothers of the order that they are pilgrims and exiles.[85] Pilgrimage is the appropriate way of life for the Christian in the world. With Francis as with Augustine, *conversio* changes *peregrinatio* from wandering into pilgrimage. As pilgrimage was the way of Christ and those who followed Him, so is idle wandering the way of those who either have not been converted or have rejected their conversion.[86] In its most specific sense, pilgrimage is equated with obedience to the rule of the order; wandering is equated with disobedience. At the same time, Francis saw pilgrimage as mission directed toward the conversion of others. The best example was Francis' own efforts to convert the sultan.[87]

Even during Francis' lifetime the adherence to apostolic poverty came under attack within the order. In addition there was debate concerning whether a vocation of study and teaching was

[83]Bonaventura, *Legenda Sancti Francisci*, p. 506, 9–15; Habig, ed., *St. Francis of Assisi*, p. 635.

[84]Thomas of Celano, *Tractatus primus*, I, p. 7, 17–36; Habig, ed., *St. Francis of Assisi*, pp. 230–231.

[85]Paul Sabatier, ed., *Le Speculum perfectionis ou Mémoires de Frère Léon*, vol. 1 (Manchester: Manchester University Press, 1928), p. 18; Habig, ed., *St. Francis of Assisi*, p. 1132.

[86]"But if any of the brethren are unwilling to observe them [duties imposed by the Rule], I do not regard them as Catholics or as friars of mine, and do not wish to see them or speak to them until they have done penance. I say the same of all others who wander about as they please and reject the discipline of the Rule . . ." ("A Letter Sent Toward the End of His Life to the Chapter General and All the Friars," in *St. Francis of Assisi: His Life and Writings as Recorded by His Contemporaries*, trans. Leo Sherley-Price (New York: Harper, 1959), p. 191.

[87]Bonaventura, *Legenda Sancti Francisci*, p. 531, 39–42; Habig, ed., *St. Francis of Assisi*, p. 701.

permitted under the rule. Francis saw grave dangers in a life of study. He feared that his friars would forget their first vocation of following apostolic poverty, would become puffed up with knowledge and inwardly cold and unreformed. Nonetheless, the Franciscans, like the Dominicans, became the most prominent scholars within the church, and they were soon joined by the Austin Friars. W. A. Pantin has written: "When St. Bernard had preached on conversion to the scholars of Paris, his preaching, if successful, would have emptied the schools. To the friars, on the contrary, conversion meant an intensification of the life of the schools."[88] Even though Francis clearly opposed this change, its roots lay in his own conception of conversion as leading to a life of preaching and service in the world. To preach successfully, to bring about the conversion of the heretics, Jews, and Moslems, it became necessary that conversion to the mendicant orders be followed by intensive study of the scriptural and theological sources of the Christian tradition, and thus that new intellectual weapons for the war of polemics be forged. In some instances, academic study became its own end, and wrangling between the various orders took the place of total devotion to the original goal of scholarship.

The idea of conversion also played a significant role within two areas quite different from those we have previously considered. One area is sacramental theology; the other is mysticism. Although we will not dwell long on either area, the shades of meaning that the idea acquired in these two contexts could not have remained unknown to Luther. For example, we know that he carefully prepared for his ordination as a priest and for the offering of his first mass. In preparing for that occasion he came to be familiar with the use of the word *conversio* as *transubstantiatio* in the works of the major medieval theologians. Although it remains a matter of debate as to precisely how familiar Luther was with the works of Thomas himself, and with Thomas' eucharistic theology, he knew something of Thomas directly and

---

[88]W. A. Pantin, *The English Church in the Fourteenth Century* (Cambridge: Cambridge University Press, 1955), p. 150.

much more through later Thomists. We do know that Luther prepared for the priesthood by working his way through the *Canonis misse expositio* of Gabriel Biel.[89] We know that Luther was acquainted with the works of Jean Gerson and Johannes Tauler, both of whom employ the term "conversion" in their mystical writings but understand it quite differently.

Thomas, on the one hand, and Ockham and Biel, on the other, proposed two different interpretations of conversion in the eucharist.[90] For Thomas, conversion as transubstantiation is a production. The bread and wine are "turned into" the body and blood of Christ; conversion is one act. For Ockham and Biel, conversion is not a simple and direct change; it is a more compli-cated dual act involving the annihilation of the first substance and its replacement by the second. This is a complex theological issue, and our task is not to explore the interpretations of the eucharist proposed by Thomas and Biel. Their differing in-terpretations of eucharistic conversion, however, have impor-tant implications for the way man's conversion is described. Thomas and Biel offer two different models: Is the new brought forth or produced from the old, or must the old first be annihi-lated and then replaced by the new?

Conversion is an important concept in two other sacraments besides the eucharist: baptism and penance. When Thomas wrote of baptism, he referred to it less in connection with con-version than in relation to regeneration and renovation.[91] When

---

[89]Gabriel Biel, *Canonis misse expositio*, 4 vols., ed. Heiko A. Oberman and William J. Courtenay, Veröffentlichungen des Instituts für europäische Geschichte, Mainz (Wiesbaden: Franz Steiner, 1963–1967).

[90]See Thomas Aquinas, *Summa theologiae*, vol. 58: *The Eucharistic Presence*, trans. William Barden, O.P. ([Cambridge ?], Eng.: Blackfriars, 1965). On Ockham and Biel, see Gabriel Buescher, *The Eucharistic Teaching of William of Ockham*, Franciscan Institute Publications, no. 1 (St. Bonaventure, N.Y.: Fran-ciscan Institute, 1950), and Rudolf Damerau, *Die Abendmahlslehre des Nomi-nalismus insbesondere die des Gabriel Biel*, Studien zu den Grundlagen der Reforma-tion (Giessen: Wilhelm Schmitz, 1963). See also the discussion by William J. Courtenay, "Cranmer as a Nominalist—*Sed Contra*," *HTR* 57, no. 4 (October 1964), 367–380.

[91]Thomas Aquinas, *Summa theologiae*, vol. 57: *Baptism and Confirmation*, trans. James J. Cunningham, O.P. [Cambridge?], Eng.: Blackfriars, 1975), pp. 75 and 83.

he discussed the question of who should receive baptism and whether it should ever be delayed, however, Thomas affirmed that "perfect turning [conversion] to God is accomplished by those who are reborn in Christ through baptism."[92] In this context, he distinguished between the baptism of infants and that of adults. He insisted that with infants baptism should definitely not be delayed, since "fuller conversion cannot be expected of them"; with adults, however, "baptism should not be conferred . . . as soon as they are converted but it should be put off until some fixed time."[93] The baptism of adults should be delayed so that they may have the opportunity to receive further instruction in the teachings of the church and may also demonstrate that their way of life coincides with the Christian way.[94] In the instance of adult baptism the sacrament retains its early meaning of testimony to a conversion already at least begun.

Further light is shed on Thomas' understanding of conversion in the section of the *Summa* where he discussed penance. He traced the movement of penitence, of sorrow for sins, to its origin in God's conversion of the heart. From this conversion follows man's cooperative action involving faith, servile fear, hope, charity, and filial fear, which culminates in his full conversion. By himself man cannot initiate this process of penitential conversion. Even the fear of punishment or servile fear follows upon God's act in converting the heart.[95] For man to achieve God's full pardon in the sacrament of penance, however, he too must act. He must convert fully to God and renounce his former act of aversion, and he can do so only when he is filled with the virtue (dependent on grace) of penitence.[96] Thomas also described remission of sins as conversion, occurring either instantaneously or over a period of time: "So also spiritually, sometimes he converts the heart of man with such great force

[92]Ibid., p. 89. On Thomas' understanding of baptism, see also Jetter, *Taufe beim jungen Luther*, pp. 67–68.
[93]Thomas Aquinas, *Summa theologiae*, vol. 57, p. 89.
[94]Ibid., pp. 89 and 91.
[95]Ibid., vol. 60: *Penance*, trans. Reginald Masterson, O.P., and T. C. O'Brien, O.P. ([Cambridge?], Eng.: Blackfriars, 1966), p. 65.
[96]Ibid., p. 79.

45

that in an instant he attains perfect spiritual health, with not only pardon for sin, but also with the eradication of all sin's remnants, as was the case with Mary Magdalene. Sometimes, however, he first forgives sin through operating grace; and afterwards, through co-operating grace, he takes away sin's after-effects little by little."[97]

Thomas also discussed conversion in connection with justification. When he addressed himself to the question of whether a movement of faith is required for the justification of the ungodly, he argued that such a movement is necessary, that man can act by free will, but that the conversion of the soul that makes possible this movement of faith is accomplished by God.[98] Thomas described man's first conversion as "imperfect." Only as the soul gradually increases in charity does conversion become perfect.[99] The same ideas concerning conversion and will are presented more fully in Thomas' discussion of the angels.[100]

Aquinas is important for our survey of the concept of conversion in the medieval period less for his development of any new interpretations of conversion than for his systematic interrelating of different meanings in a number of contexts. Conversion as God's act of turning or transforming man's heart is essential to man's justification and salvation. Conversion as man's turning to God by free will and grace is constitutive for his entire life, but it occupies a place of special importance within the sacrament of penance. For Thomas, then, conversion is both an act and a process. Conversion as God's act constitutes the necessary beginning for man's acquisition of faith and the virtue of penitence.[101]

[97]Ibid., pp. 93 and 95.

[98]Ibid., vol. 30: *The Gospel of Grace,* trans. Cornelius Ernst, O.P. ([Cambridge?]), Eng.: Blackfriars, 1972), p. 175.

[99]Ibid., p. 199.

[100]Ibid., vol. 9: *Angels,* trans. Kenelm Foster, O.P. ([Cambridge?], Eng.: Blackfriars, 1968), pp. 246–251.

[101]"The first source of such acts [of penitence] is God's operation converting the heart. . . . The second act is a movement of faith. The third is a movement of servile fear. . . . The fourth is a movement of hope. . . . The fifth is a movement of charity whereby sin itself is displeasing, and not in view of punishment. The sixth is a movement of filial fear whereby a person freely offers amendment to God out of reverence for him" (ibid., vol. 60, p. 65). Note e, p. 65, offers the

For Thomas, God's initial act of conversion turns man's heart to Him; it is only through this act that man acquires faith and reaches repentance. The nominalist theologian Gabriel Biel placed conversion at a different point in relation to penance. He affirmed that the *prima gratia,* first grace, which results in man's justification, comes after his own best efforts.[102] In comparison with Thomas, Biel both limited conversion, restricting it to the last movement in Thomas' progression, and conceived of it as a result of man's own action, stemming from his doing what is within him. Conversion from *amor sui* to *amor dei* thus provides the last stage before the reception of first grace or justification.

For Thomas conversion as God's act makes possible the acquisition of faith as the ungodly are transformed into believers. For Biel this was not the case. He affirmed that man by his own efforts can attain the *fides acquisita,* "the habit of faith acquired by natural means through the *facere quod in se est.*"[103] Man is born with a natural disposition to hear those truths of the faith that are preached to him; to this faith that man has attained is then added *fides infusa,* which is joined to hope and love but plays a less significant role than *fides acquisita.*[104] Conversion is not God's act of turning man's heart, since in Biel's theology

---

following explanation: "In 1a2ae. 112, 2 ad 1 & 2 the text makes it clear that this process of conversion may be understood either as a series of progressing dispositions, or as elements in the complex act of complete conversion. The 'act of repentance' here, then, may be understood in either sense. It is the response as it springs from charity and from filial fear that is complete repentance. A person may approach the sacrament of Penance with only imperfect dispositions, but when the sacrament is received effectively, with the bestowal of grace, the act of repentance is completed." For a detailed discussion of penance and justification in Thomas and Luther, see the excellent study by Otto Hermann Pesch, *Theologie der Rechtfertigung bei Martin Luther und Thomas von Aquin,* Walberger Studien der Albertus-Magnus-Akademie, Theologische ser., vol. 4 (Mainz: Matthias Grünewald, 1967).

[102]Heiko Oberman has summarized Biel's position in this way: "Whether justification, the reception of the *gratia prima,* takes place before or at the moment of confession, in both cases man has 'to do his very best' with the intention to confess at his earliest convenience. This *facere quod in se est* is the necessary disposition for the infusion of grace and implies a movement of the free will, which is at once aversion to sin and love for God. . . . Conversion is the transition of the *amor sui* to *amor dei*" (*Harvest of Medieval Theology,* p. 152).

[103]Ibid., p. 468.

[104]Ibid., pp. 71–72.

man can attain the first *fides* through his own efforts. Conversion has a place only when man has lost the *prima gratia* of baptism and fallen into *amor sui;* conversion then comprises the shift—by man himself—from *amor sui* to *amor dei*. When this conversion occurs, so does the infusion of *prima gratia*. Conversion should not be understood, however, as constituting sufficient cause for the reception of *prima gratia*.[105]

As we move on in the following chapters to Luther's early biblical commentaries, we shall find that the question of man's responsibility for his conversion is very much on Luther's mind, and that it is at the very center of his own struggle to learn how one attains righteousness before God. In his days of struggle Luther turned his attention not only to the Bible but to the writings of several mystics. During 1515–1516 he devoted himself to writing marginal comments on the sermons of Johannes Tauler, and in these comments he refers his readers to Jean Gerson's *De mystica theologia*. As he pondered the works of these two mystics, he found that they, too, wrote frequently about conversion, and he no doubt added their perceptions to his own understanding of the term. Yet, as we shall see, Gerson and Tauler also speak of conversion in quite different and distinct ways.

For a full discussion of Tauler's concept of conversion it would first be necessary to consider his anthropology, most particularly his notion of the *Grund* or ground of the soul and the relation between the *Grund* and the *gemuete,* perhaps best defined as the powers within the soul which serve to draw the person back to his divine origin.[106] With the same intensity as Augustine, Tauler spoke of the way in which nature and most especially mankind has fallen away, averted itself, from God and its original purpose. Nonetheless, man has the opportunity to engage in battle against the desires of his corrupted will. He can cease his "wandering" and convert inwardly to the *Grund,* the

---

[105]According to Oberman, "there is no ultimate and sufficient disposition which temporally precedes the infusion; genuine love for God is not a previous but a concomitant disposition for the infusion of grace" (ibid., pp. 152–153).

[106]Ozment, *Homo Spiritualis*, p. 22.

basis for a covenant with God. This conversion away from sin, which involves man's active inner effort, is followed by God's response of forgiveness.[107] A new stage now occurs and a new conversion results, which one scholar has described in this way: "If resignation and will-lessness are the most comprehensive descriptions of the strategic way, the realization of a 'divine form' is the ultimate goal of Tauler's order of salvation. He describes the third and final historical stage of the order of salvation as the 'passing over into a God-formed being, into the oneness of the created spirit in the essential spirit of God, which one may call a substantive conversion (*weseliche ker*).'"[108]

At its initial level, the conversion Tauler describes appears to be the entering into and following of the *via purgativa*, which involves renunciation of the will and the attainment of resignation. It is the turn inward to the *Grund*. Although this conversion is both spiritual and inner, it reflects itself in one's outer way of life. Of the various interpretations of conversion we have considered, it perhaps most resembles a highly internalized version of the monastic *conversio morum*. The end of the *via purgativa* is a full conversion away from sin, followed by God's turning toward man in forgiveness. This stage is then followed by a higher conversion, parallel to eucharistic transformation, in which "the purified and clarified spirit sinks completely into the divine darkness, into a still silence and an inconceivable and inexpressible unity."[109] Man's own action in conversion is superseded by the conversion of his spirit into the uncreatedness of God. Several of Tauler's sermons demonstrate his blending of mystical and eucharistic imagery in his concept of conversion.[110]

Jean Gerson deliberately rejected the equating of conversion with transubstantiation. We shall return to this issue, but first let

---

[107]Ozment describes this process in ibid., p. 29.

[108]Ibid. See also Ignaz Weilner, *Johannes Taulers Bekehrungsweg: Die Erfahrungsgrundlagen seiner Mystik*, Studien zur Geschichte der kath. Moraltheologie, vol. 10 (Regensburg: Friedrich Pustet, 1961).

[109]Ozment, *Homo Spiritualis*, p. 38, citing Johannes Tauler, *Die Predigten Taulers*, ed. Ferdinand Vetter, Deutsche Texte des Mittelalters, vol. 11 (Berlin: Weidmannsche Buchhandlung, 1910), p. 117.

[110]*Predigten Taulers*, pp. 292–298, 310–316.

us see some of the contexts in which Gerson employed the concept of conversion. He gave the concept a place not only in his mystical works but in his writings advocating academic reform. As Louis Pascoe has explained at some length in his study of Gerson's reform program, he called for a *conversio ad studium* to be fostered by the high example set by the clerical and academic authorities.[111] The failure to implement this academic conversion contributed directly, in Gerson's view, to the disintegration of the spiritual stability and welfare of the church.[112] Parenthetically, Gerson constitutes a fine example of those teachers and pastors who were greatly concerned with the adequate training of clerics and the dispensing of good pastoral care long before Luther brought these issues to public attention.

Gerson also discussed conversion in connection with the study of canon law. According to Pascoe, "Given the various types of law that comprise the body of canon law, Gerson contends that for the perfect study of canon law there is needed a threefold *conversio: retrorsum, introrsum,* and *deorsum.*"[113] It is only by this threefold conversion that divine, natural, and positive law can be distinguished and later correctly applied within concrete circumstances. Thus conversion as this threefold turning of the mind provides the absolutely essential basis for the study and application of canon law.[114]

In Gerson's theology, penitence, conversion, and mysticism are intimately related. In *Contra curiositatem studentium* he stressed that the clear and wise understanding of what is believed from the Gospel, which is called mystical theology, is to be sought through penitence rather than through human reason

---

[111]Louis B. Pascoe, *Jean Gerson: Principles of Church Reform,* Studies in Medieval and Reformation Thought, vol. 7 (Leiden: E. J. Brill, 1973), pp. 124–125. Pascoe refers to *Scriptum est melius* in Jean Gerson, *Oeuvres complètes,* ed. P. Glorieux (Paris: Desclee, 1960–1968), vol. 2, pp. 112 and 116 (p. 124n).

[112]Pascoe, *Jean Gerson,* p. 124.

[113]Ibid., p. 62, citing Gerson, *Conversi estis nunc ad pastorem,* in *Oeuvres complètes,* vol. 5, pp. 177–178.

[114]Pascoe, *Jean Gerson,* p. 63, citing Gerson, *Conversi estis nunc ad pastorem,* pp. 177–178.

alone.[115] In another text, Gerson indicated that mystical theology or penitential mysticism constitutes a process of conversion.[116] Through his penitential way of life (similar to the monastic *conversio morum*), man becomes "like" God to the point of enjoying a mystical, volitional union, of which affective knowledge is very much a part.[117] Steven Ozment has summarized in these terms the results of mystical union for Gerson: "There is no removal of man's *esse realis* in the *unio mystica*. He is 'like' God through an approximation of Adamic, not pre-creaturely, manhood; or, stated another way, he is like his *esse idealis* as Adam was like his *esse idealis* before the Fall. Thus, while both Tauler and Gerson, *mutatis mutandis*, conceive the union with God as the point of maximum similitude and intimacy with God, Gerson cautiously removes language which would suggest a substantive union."[118]

A selection from Gerson's *De mystica theologia: Tractatus primus speculativus* is especially worthy of our attention since it focuses directly on his rejection of conversion as synonymous with transubstantiation in describing mystical union:

> There were others who wanted to render this spiritual union or transformation more understandable through the use of concrete natural analogies. They said that the soul is united with God and transformed into Him like a drop of water released into a bottle of strong wine. In the wine the water loses its own being and is

[115]James L. Connolly, *John Gerson: Reformer and Mystic* (Louvain: Librairie Universitaire, 1928), pp. 284–285, citing Gerson, *Contra curiositatem studentium*, in Jean Gerson, *Opera omnia*, ed. Du Pin (Antwerp, 1706), vol. 1, p. 106. On the theme of *curiositas*, see Heiko A. Oberman, *Contra vanam curiositatem: Ein Kapitel der Theologie zwischen Seelenwinkel und Weltall*, Theologische Studien 113 (Zurich: Theologischer Verlag, 1974). On Gerson, see pp. 34–37.

[116]Connolly, *John Gerson*, pp. 259–279, citing Gerson, *De monte contemplationis*, in *Opera omnia*, ed. Du Pin, vol. 3, pp. 531–579.

[117]Ozment, *Homo Spiritualis*, pp. 77 and 79–82.

[118]Ibid., p. 83. For further discussion of Gerson's mysticism, see Johann Stelzenberger, *Die Mystik des Johannes Gerson*, Breslauer Studien zur historischen Theologie, vol. 10 (Breslau: Müller & Seiffert, 1928), and Walter Dress, *Die Theologie Gersons: Eine Untersuchung zur Verbindung von Nominalismus und Mystik im Spätmittelalter* (Gütersloh: C. Bertelsmann, 1931).

changed completely into another being. The way in which food is converted into nutriment through the digestive process was also an analogy instanced in connection with Augustine's description of the Lord, when he writes: 'I am the food of the strong; come forward and you shall eat me. You will not, however, change me into yourselves as with carnal food, but you will be changed into me.' I remember having once read that during a sermon in which this example of the soul's union with God was presented, a certain devout woman became so overheated and inwardly inflamed that, like new wine that has been vacuum sealed, she was unable to contain herself after she had received the Spirit and consequently ruptured her arteries and nerves and died.[119]

Gerson also wrote: "For the same reason, the analogy drawn from the transubstantiation which occurs in the blessed sacrament is ill-suited to explain the transformation of the one who loves into the beloved, God."[120] In Gerson's opinion, this interpretation of conversion leads to the obliteration of the distinction between the creature and the creator. For him, conversion was above all the turn toward the Word, sometimes understood primarily in an intellectual sense and at other times seen as encompassing the entire being of a person, which can bring him to the point of mystical union and rest in God.[121] For Gerson, in contrast to Tauler, conversion carried none of the eucharistic characteristics of transformation, but rather the marks of a new directedness, analogous to Augustine's understanding of conversion.

We have now seen that the concept of conversion had a rich and varied set of meanings and contexts during the medieval period. Perhaps its most predominant meaning until the later Middle Ages was in reference to the change of life from secular to monastic. In the subsequent period, as in the case of Francis of Assisi, conversion meant less an outward change, certainly no

[119]*Jean Gerson: Selections from "A Deo exivit," "Contra curiositatem studentium," and "De mystica theologia speculativa,"* ed. Steven E. Ozment, Textus minores, vol. 38 (Leiden: E. J. Brill, 1969), p. 53.

[120]Ibid., p. 55.

[121]Ibid., pp. 61 and 63.

longer one necessarily involving a departure from the world, and more a change of the heart that allowed one to pursue the *vita apostolica* in the world. In differing contexts, conversion meant the redirectedness or transformation of the individual. This conversion could be to Christianity itself, to monasticism, to the mendicant orders, to mystical union. The concept also occupied an important place within sacramental theology, most especially in the eucharist, but also within baptism and penance.

All of these meanings must have been familiar to the young monk and teacher Martin Luther. As he developed his theology and agonized over his own relationship with God, his concept of conversion changed and matured until at last understanding and experience became one. To that story—and that struggle—we now turn.

[2]

Dictata super Psalterium
(1513–1515)

Beginning in August 1513 and through the following months, probably until late October 1515, Luther lectured twice a week on the Psalms. It was an enterprise for which he carefully prepared himself, and in the process he confronted those questions that were central to his own life: Can one prepare for faith or pave the way for conversion by one's own efforts? Does God at the very least expect one to attain a level of humility in which one recognizes one's unworthiness? It would be a mistake, however, to think of Luther at age thirty as a retiring scholar who devoted himself entirely to his lecture preparation and the examination of his own soul. Even at this relatively early point in his career he had attained some prominence, and with prominence came responsibility. In May 1512 he had become subprior of the Wittenberg monastery and regent of the monastery school. In May 1515 he was promoted to district vicar, with the heavy responsibility of overseeing eleven monasteries in Saxony and Thuringia. Besides these duties, he was often called upon to preach to his fellow monks and to larger congregations in the City Church.

On October 19, 1512, he received the degree of *doctor in biblia* and assumed the chair of biblical studies at the University of Wittenberg. In the later, difficult days of the reform movement, when he frequently felt himself to be standing alone against the world, he sustained himself with the thought that he had been called against his own inclination to become a doctor and professor of theology, and that God had thereby called him to this work. But now we are moving ahead of our story, for when Luther chose to offer his first biblical lectures on the Psalms, he was seeking to teach not only his students but himself, to answer on the basis of a close study of his beloved Psalms many of his own concerns about the relationship between God and man. As we shall see, the idea of conversion, turning to God, occurs again and again in the Psalms and in Luther's exegesis of them.

The intimate relation between Luther's exegesis and his personal religious preoccupation is well illustrated by such a passage as the following:

> Hence to be before God and before the face of God means to enter into the sanctuary of God. This entrance has nothing to do with space, as I have said, but with attitudes and morals, that is, conversion to spiritual and divine things. For before one is converted in this way, he is unholy and before the world and himself, because he sees and has in view only his own affairs and those of the world. Thus he is outside the sanctuary of God and going away. The sanctuary of God is nothing but the soul spiritually converted to God, for the soul is the seat of wisdom, and it promises that it will dwell in the midst of the people (that is, in their hearts).[1]

A change of heart means entrance into the sanctuary of God; to leave behind the earthly and visible is to enter into the presence of God. In this text Luther expresses his understanding of conversion and describes those who are unconverted. The passage leaves unanswered, however, the question of precisely how conversion occurs. Does man through his own efforts prepare for conversion, or is his conversion entirely the work of God? One's answer to this question depends in large part on one's

---

[1] *WA* 3, 479, 16–23 (Ps. 72:16–17); *Luther's Works*, vol. 10: *First Lectures on the Psalms I*, ed. Hilton C. Oswald, trans. Herbert J. A. Bouman (St. Louis: Concordia, 1974) (hereafter cited as *LW* 10), pp. 418–419. Copyright © 1974 Concordia Publishing House. Used by permission.

understanding of Luther's concepts of humility (*humilitas*) and of doing the best that is in one (*facere quod in se est*), matters of debate among Luther scholars. In the *Dictata* we do not find either a single, clearly defined concept of conversion or a systematic, entirely consistent theology. If Luther's theological development at this early stage in his career is to be accurately presented, inconsistencies cannot be glossed over or a theological synthesis anticipated.[2] Our examination of the texts concerning conversion will be divided into three major sections: first, the nature and extent of man's preparation for conversion, the most complex and disputed question; second, the character of conversion itself; and third, the constitution of man's postconversion life. At this point, I suggest, Luther understands conversion primarily in two ways. First, conversion is the shift from unfaith and unrighteousness to faith and righteousness *coram Deo*, before God. The postconversion person is one who has undergone this transition. Second, conversion constitutes the turning to God of the repentant Christian. It must be stressed, however, that it is often difficult to distinguish to which conversion Luther is referring in a particular text.[3]

[2]Reinhold Weier notes: "Etwa ab 1518 erwies sich in unserer Untersuchung als möglich, die Entwicklung von Luthers Theologieverständnis einigermassen systematisierend darzustellen. Eine entsprechende Möglichkeit besteht für die frühesten Ansätze dieses Theologieverständnisses nicht in demselben Masse. Da ist alles zu sehr in Bewegung: auftauchend, wieder abschwellend" (*Das Theologieverständnis Martin Luthers*, Konfessionskundliche und kontroverstheologische Studien, vol. 36 [Paderborn: Bonifacius Druckerei, 1976], p. 135). Also Lennart Pinomaa: "Nun ist allerdings zu beachten, dass bekanntlich die erste Psalmenvorlesung kein einheitliches theologisches System mit klaren Linien darstellt, sondern als blosse Materialsammlung für Luthers Vorlesungen verschiedene, einander überschneidende Betrachtungsarten in sich aufnimmt" (*Der existenzielle Charakter der Theologie Luthers: Das Hervorbrechen der Theologie der Anfechtung und ihre Bedeutung für das Lutherverständnis* [Helsinki, 1940], p. 25). Bernhard Lohse has also remarked on the difficulty of and problems within the *Dictata* text (*Martin Luther: Eine Einführung in sein Leben und sein Werk*, Beck' sche Elementarbücher [Munich: C. H. Beck, 1981], p. 133).

[3]My understanding of Luther's concept of conversion agrees in many respects with that of Otto Ritschl, who has presented the fullest discussion I have found. I do not see as clear a distinction as he does between *Bekehrung* and *Busse* in the early Luther (*Dogmengeschichte des Protestantismus*, vol. 2: *Orthodoxie und Synkretismus*, pt. 1: *Die Theologie der deutschen Reformation*, pp. 170–171). In the following text Ritschl also admits the problem of a firm distinction: "Und nur wer noch gar nicht den rechten Glauben hat oder ihn eingebüsst hat, muss das

What preparations does Luther believe one can make for conversion, and to what extent is one capable by one's own efforts of
achieving or preventing conversion? Luther appears to propose
two separate and indeed contradictory answers to this question.
In some passages he suggests that a person can attain humility, a
nonmeritorious disposition, before conversion and justification.[4] In terms of justification, Luther's position in this instance
is terminologically consistent with nominalist theology.[5] To the

---

opus alienum Gottes in seiner ganzen Schrecklichkeit an sich erfahren, um seine
Bekehrung dann doch allein dem hinreissenden Eindruck der Güte Gottes zu
verdanken. Immerhin sind die Grenzen zwischen den beiden Klassen der in
ihrer Sünde schwachen Gläubigen und der noch glaubenlosen Sünder fliessend"
(p. 171).

[4] "Quare a nullo iustificatur, nisi ab eo, qui se accusat et damnat et iudicat.
Iustus enim primo est accusator sui et damnator et iudex sui. Et ideo deum
iustificat et vincere ac superare facit. Econtra impius et superbus primo est
excusator sui ac defensor, iustificator et salvator" (*WA* 3, 288, 30–33 (Ps. 50:6);
LW 10, 236). Whether or not man's confession of his sins is itself the result of
grace, Luther does not indicate. "Et ideo humiliantur et non inflantur. Quia
nemo per fidem iustificatur nisi prius per humilitatem sese iniustum confiteatur.
Hec autem est humilitas" (*WA* 3, 345, 28–30 [Ps. 69:8]; *LW* 10, 290). In large
part I agree with Damerau's stress on the significance of humility in Luther's
early theology in *Demut in der Theologie Luthers*. On this passage, see p. 75. He
argues that in this and similar texts Luther is describing man's own act of judging
and humbling himself (p. 76). He writes: "Noch ist Luthers Gerecht-
igkeitsbegriff in die vom Synergismus fundierte mönchische Theologie einge-
baut; er muss also von daher analysiert werden, um nicht reformatorische Ele-
mente hineinprojizieren" (p. 78). He discusses at length how Luther moves
from a synergistic understanding of righteousness to one that emphasizes humility as an "*a-meritorische Disposition*" (p. 165) for grace. Damerau relates Luther's
concept of humility particularly to monasticism and suggests the influence not
only of Augustine but of Benedict and Bernard of Clairvaux, among others.

[5] "Hinc recte dicunt Doctores, quod homini facienti quod in se est, deus infalli-
biliter dat gratiam, et licet non de condigno sese possit ad gratiam preparare,
quia est incomparabilis, tamen bene de congruo propter promissionem istam dei
et pactum misericordie" (*WA* 4, 262, 4–7 (Ps. 113:1); *Luther's Works*, vol. 11: *First
Lectures on the Psalms II*, ed. Hilton C. Oswald, trans. Herbert J. A. Bouman (St.
Louis: Concordia, 1976) (hereafter cited as *LW* 11), p. 396. On the theology of
Gabriel Biel, see Oberman, *Harvest of Medieval Theology*. On the relation between
Luther and nominalism, see Grane, *Contra Gabrielem*, esp. pp. 297–301, where
he discusses this text. He argues that in spite of Luther's terminology, he has
broken with Biel's concept of a disposition preparatory to grace: "Das bedeutet
nämlich, dass das Dasein des Menschen immer Vorbereitung ist" (p. 299). See
also Oberman, "Facientibus Quod in se est Deus non Denegat Gratiam," *HTR* 55
(1962), 317–342. Oberman, unlike Grane, sees this passage to be within the
framework of nominalism, theologically as well as terminologically; see pp.
131–132. On the important concept of *pactum* in scholastic theology, see Berndt
Hamm, *Promissio, Pactum, Ordinatio: Freiheit und Selbstbindung Gottes in der scholas-

person who does what is in him (*facere quod in se est*), God does not deny his grace (*Deus non denegat gratiam*).[6]

In other passages Luther argues that man cannot even attain humility until he is converted by God's grace and filled with a holy light.[7] The self-knowledge that makes humility possible is given to man by God. Some texts suggest that Luther in fact

---

tischen Gnadenlehre, Beiträge zur historischen Theologie, vol. 54 (Tübingen: J. C. B. Mohr [Paul Siebeck], 1977). Reinhard Schwarz discusses *pactum* in the *Dictata* in his book *Vorgeschichte der reformatorischen Busstheologie*, pp. 249–257. Bizer discusses the relation between righteousness and humility, but he does not consider the role of humility in preparing for conversion in his monograph *Fides ex auditu*. On the relation between humility and grace in the *Dictata*, see Axel Gyllenkrok, *Rechtfertigung und Heiligung in der frühen evangelischen Theologie Luthers*, Uppsala Universitets Arrskrift 1952:2 (Uppsala: A.-B. Lundequistska Bokhandeln; Wiesbaden: Otto Harrassowitz, 1952), pp. 38–51, and Albrecht Peters, *Glaube und Werk: Luthers Rechtfertigungslehre im Lichte der heiligen Schrift*, Arbeiten zur Geschichte und Theologie des Luthertums, vol. 8, 2d ed. (Berlin and Hamburg: Lutherisches Verlagshaus, 1967), pp. 34–40.

[6]The most convincing study of this nominalist terminology in the *Dictata* I find to be that of Ozment, *Homo Spiritualis*. In contrast to such scholars as Vogelsang and Jetter, Ozment finds the problem of Luther's understanding of preparation for grace—and I would include conversion—to be of real significance and complexity: "The issue of a highly refined Pelagian *facere quod in se est* and *meritum de congruo* is something more than a straw man. Not only does one find the systematic content of these *termini technici* of nominalist covenant theology in the *Dictata*, but one also finds that these terms are explicitly employed to define the relationship between human preparation and God's granting grace. This fact makes it impossible to dismiss this issue by simply concluding that 'mournful waiting and praying' are the only forms of preparation for the advents of Christ [Vogelsang, *Anfänge von Luthers Christologie*, p. 71]; . . . that preparation for grace is 'already the work of grace' [Jetter, *Taufe beim jungen Luther*, p. 279]; or that man's disposition for grace is 'nothing other than God's "Disposition"' [Link, *Ringen Luthers*, p. 55]" (pp. 159–160). Although I find Luther's statements on preparation for grace and conversion to be less consistent and more contradictory than does Ozment (see p. 150, for example, on the causal relation between *intellectus* and *affectus*, on the one hand, and *confessio*, on the other), I agree with his conclusion that Luther strips the *meritum de congruo* of its content of *bonitas* and does not view it as a *necessary* antecedent to grace (p. 181). He concludes: "And as John the Baptist 'precedes' Christ, so humility 'precedes' God's gracious presence with man in Christ. This is not as antecedent and consequent, but as expectation and fulfillment, the former *needing*, not demanding, the latter to empower and justify its presence" (pp. 182–183). Unfortunately, Ozment does not discuss *humilitas* in relation to the *facere quod in se est* as fully as one would wish. See also Steinmetz, *Luther and Staupitz*, p. 88.

[7]"Igitur Non qui sibi humillimus videtur, sed qui sibi fedissimus et turpissimus videtur, hic est speciosissimus coram deo. Et ratio est, quia suam feditatem nunquam videret, nisi esset intime illustratus lumine sancto, sed habens tale lumen est speciosus, et quanto clarius, tanto speciosior" (*WA* 3, 290, 31–35 [Ps. 50:7]; *LW* 10, 239).

equates conversion with this illuminating knowledge of one's true identity before God.[8] Only by God's action in converting man does he come to see himself as the sinner he is. Grounded in self-love and self-righteousness before his conversion, he is incapable of taking a step toward God. The apostle Paul provides an excellent example of a person who knew himself to be misguided and in error only after his dramatic conversion.

In the comments on Psalm 41 there are two passages that do not specifically mention conversion but that refer to either "natural" and preconversion man or the penitent Christian. Luther writes: "Tropologically, however, anyone who is in sins and desires to repent and seek the grace of God can pray this psalm." This passage could refer to the Christian after conversion, who continues to recognize that he sins and is in need of God's grace; in the text that follows, however, there are indications that Luther is referring to man at the point of his conversion:

> For such a one is in Egypt, indeed, already in the exodus from Egypt, disquieted in himself and about himself and angry with himself, and therefore he seeks to remember God in the land of Jordan. Thus the literal intent of the psalm is about the departure from the synagog into the church, from Egypt and sins into grace, and about the longing of those who are going this way. And such a longing is natural in human nature, because the synteresis and desire for the good is inextinguishable in man, although it may be hindered in many. And for such synteresis and in his person this psalm was written: God surely hears the desire and above all an-

[8]"Moraliter: A carne adversaria spiritus quis liberabit? Nunquid ego vel homo? Non, quia hinc video, quod errat qui seipsum vult salvare, et est homo mendax. Sed gratia dei per Ihesum Christum liberat triumphatque nos ab isto Pharaone. Et hinc fit, ut etiam quod ait 'Credidi', se a domino habere dicat. Quia fidem nullus homo ex se habet, sed est mendax." (*WA* 4, 269, 3–7 [Ps. 115:11]; *LW* 11, 403). See the excellent discussion of this complex passage by Karl-Heinz zur Mühlen, *Nos extra nos,* pp. 54–66. Hedwig Thomas compares Luther's interpretation of Ps. 115:11 with those of older exegetes in the tradition, including Augustine, Cassiodorus, and Lyra, and concludes: "Diese Nebeneinanderstellung zeigt, wie einzigartig Luthers Deutung des excessus als Glaubenserkenntnis ist; denn für die älteren Exegeten besteht der excessus entweder in dem pavor mentis in persecutione oder in mystischer Kontemplation" (*Zur Würdigung des Psalmenvorlesung Luthers von 1513–1515* [Weimar: Hermann Böhlaus Nachfolger, 1920], pp. 45–46).

swers it after Christ has made Himself the Mediator for such a person.[9]

The *synteresis* is active in each person and pushes him in the direction of conversion, but conversion also depends on the work of Christ as mediator.[10] Luther's comments on Psalm 69

[9]WA 3, 238, 6–15 (Ps. 41:8); LW 10, 197. See Ozment, *Homo Spiritualis*, pp. 151–152.

[10]Both the precise nature of the *synteresis* in medieval thought and its role in Luther's theology are difficult to define. For a study of the origin of the term and its place in the works of various medieval theologians, see M. W. Hollenbach, "Synderesis," *New Catholic Encyclopedia*, vol. 13, p. 882. See also Baylor, *Action and Person*, who outlines the relation between *synteresis* and conscience in medieval theology. In spite of significant differences between such theologians as Thomas Aquinas and Bonaventura in the period of high scholasticism, there was agreement that the *synteresis* was the inextinguishable spark that directed a person toward the good. For reasons that cannot be discussed here, the nominalist theologian William of Ockham rejected the notion of the *synteresis* as a habit (*habitus*). However, his follower Gabriel Biel reintroduced the concept into the idea of conscience. Since Biel followed Ockham in maintaining that the will is free and knows no necessity, the *synteresis* could not be placed there; instead, Biel located it in the reason. Accordingly, "he defined the *synteresis* as the 'inborn potency or faculty (*potentia*) to assent naturally to a practical principle, evident from its terms, which dictates or signifies in universal terms that some action is to be sought or avoided'" (Baylor, *Action and Person*, p. 95).

Luther's fullest discussion of the *synteresis* occurs in a sermon preached on December 26, 1514, the Feast of St. Stephen (*WA* 1, 30–37). Although his usage is not entirely consistent, Luther speaks of a two-fold *synteresis, synteresis voluntatis et rationis* (*WA* 1, 36), a spark directing both the will and the reason. In a sense, the *synteresis* constitutes what Walther von Loewenich, among others, has termed an *Anknüpfungspunkt* between God and man (*Luthers Theologia Crucis*, 5th ed. [Witten: Luther-Verlag, 1967], p. 54). To relate our comments specifically to Ps. 41, it is clear that the *synteresis* directs a person toward salvation. Yet even at this early point in his theology, Luther insists that God hears the cry man utters through the *synteresis* only when it is mediated by Christ. As Ozment has correctly noted, "although this Christological interjection is hardly indicative of a Christological exclusivity, it does introduce a . . . significant qualification of the soteriological potential of the *synteresis*" (*Homo Spiritualis*, p. 151). Thus, although it is clear that Luther at this point still affirms that there is a remnant, a spark, within man which directs him to the good and toward salvation, it is unclear precisely how great a role it plays. What is important in relation to conversion is that at this point Luther still affirms that there is a spark within man which contributes to his turning to God. Luther's anthropology is certainly not yet constituted by an understanding of man as total sinner, unable to make a move toward God until he receives grace. Man is still a participant in preparing for his conversion and in attaining righteousness. For a further discussion of the concept of *cooperatio* in Luther's theology, see Seils, *Gedanke vom Zusammenwirken Gottes*, esp. pp. 25–61. On the *synteresis*, see Gordon Rupp, *The Righteousness of God: Luther Studies* (London: Hodder & Stoughton, 1953), pp. 150–154. On the *synteresis* in the 1514 sermon preached on the Feast of St. Stephen, see Grane, *Contra Gabrielem*, pp. 290–293, and von Loewenich, *Luthers Theologia Crucis*, pp. 54–63.

suggest that people can prevent their conversion: "Therefore killing those who are stricken in their heart is the reason why they cannot be converted and saved. Yet they might be converted if they would stop."[11] The person who chooses to be unrighteous puts his own intellect and will above God.[12] Luther aims his criticism at Jews, heretics, and all those who, though seemingly humble, do not let their spiritual pride be overcome by faith.[13]

Two other passages may also refer to the condition of man before conversion and the need for that conversion if a person is to attain salvation. In the first Luther writes: "But why does he say 'my countenance'? Because seeing is the whole reward, and because God is not saving except to those who turn their face to Him and their back to temporal things. But those who seek salvation in temporal things want to make God helpful to their back, because they turn their face to temporal things and their back to God, since it is not possible to serve two masters."[14] Salvation depends on man's turning or conversion to God and his turning away from or aversion to temporal matters and even to his own intellect and will. Perhaps the strongest statement in favor of man's ability to prevent conversion occurs in the comments on Psalm 1: "The 'three transgressions' are all sins, namely, sins of weakness against the Father, sins of ignorance against the Son, and sins of evil or concupiscence against the Holy Spirit. But the 'four transgressions' means to add to the sins already mentioned excuses with regard to them and to refuse to confess them. These cause the person to 'stand in [his own] way' with a very stiff neck. And therefore he is not converted and cannot be converted, because he directly shuts the door of mercy to him-

---

[11]*WA* 3, 438, 3–4 (Ps. 68:27); *LW* 10, 380.

[12]*WA* 3, 331, 20–23 (Ps. 58:1); *LW* 10, 274. Luther stresses that man can turn his will and intellect against God despite the *synteresis*. Baylor notes: "But Luther did not equate the *synteresis* with either the entire reason or the entire will. Consequently, the presence of the *synteresis* did not establish for him a complete or even a general conformity between human nature and God" (*Action and Person*, p. 159).

[13]*WA* 3, 331, 29–34 (Ps. 58:1); *LW* 10, 274. See Ulrich Mauser, *Der junge Luther und die Häresie*, Schriften des Vereins für Reformationsgeschichte, no. 184 (Gütersloh: Gerd Mohn, 1968).

[14]*WA* 3, 236, 12–16 (Ps. 41:6); *LW* 10, 195.

self and resists the Holy Spirit and forgiveness for himself."[15] What is required is that man not resist grace or, phrased more positively, that he recognize his sinfulness and confess it. Man can act to foreclose the possibility of conversion. Thus these passages show that to attain to conversion man must either maintain a passive and receptive state or actively recognize his own need.[16] This suggests that it is necessary for one to reach a degree of humility and self-knowledge before conversion.

The issue of self-knowledge is raised again in Psalm 50, in connection with salvation. Luther comments: "Therefore the one who is most attractive in the sight of God is not the one who seems most humble to himself, but the one who sees himself as most filthy and depraved. The reason is that he would never see his own filthiness, unless he had been enlightened in his inmost being with a holy light."[17] Luther's reference in this passage may be to the conversion of the sinner, for he bases his whole in-

---

[15]WA 55[2], 211, 4, 6–8 (Ps. 1:1); LW 10, 12.

[16]Leif Grane has discussed the problem of preparation for grace, with particular reference to Ps. 115. He suggests: "Es scheint also klar zu sagen, dass Luther über eine menschliche Vorbereitung zur Gnade nichts zu sagen hat. Trotzdem existiert das Problem, jedenfalls terminologisch. Erstens als ein Problem, das in der *Dictata* überall in Verbindung mit dem *humilitas*-Begriff auftritt. Nur der Demütige kann gerecht werden. Bedeutet das, dass *humilitas* eine menschliche Vorbereitung für das gottliche Zuteiling von *iustitia* ist? . . . Man Luthers Gedankengang falsch versteht, wenn man *humilitas* als eine menschliche Leistung auffasst" (*Contra Gabrielem*, p. 295). The problem of ascertaining the role of *humilitas* is also intimately connected with knowing precisely how much power Luther assigns to the *synteresis* in directing man toward salvation and thereby also bringing him to humility. For Grane's discussion of the *synteresis*, see esp. pp. 290–293. Gordon Rupp writes: "There are passages where Luther seems to conceive of humility as a kind of predisposition for grace, a human achievement which makes a man 'apt' for salvation. . . . The tension within Luther's use of 'humilitas' continues in his Lectures on Romans. . . . There, too, is the thought that humility is a pre-requisite of grace. As in the Psalms, it is a mark of the humble that they are ready to hear the Word of God. Humility is finally replaced by faith, not in the sense that the word drops out of Luther's vocabulary, or ceases to have meaning for him as a Christian virtue, but that the conception of man's passive waiting upon God is taken up into the word 'Faith,' as the means whereby man abandons his own self-righteousness and apprehends the righteousness of God" (*Righteousness of God*, pp. 149–150). See also on *humilitas* Pinomaa, *Existenzielle Charakter der Theologie Luthers*, pp. 21–37. Pinomaa describes the transition from an anthropocentric to a theocentric concept of *humilitas;* see esp. pp. 28–29.

[17]WA 3, 290, 31–35 (Ps. 50:7); LW 10, 239.

terpretation of this psalm on Paul, Romans 3. The person who does not know himself as a sinner makes God a liar and passes judgment on Him. The righteous person is the one who accuses and condemns himself, but it is only because of God's having turned to him and filled him with the light of knowledge that he is able to recognize himself as a sinner. This righteousness is grounded in God's covenant with man: "Yes, even faith and grace, through which we are today justified, would not of themselves justify us if God's covenant did not do it. It is precisely for this reason that we are saved: He made a testament and covenant with us that whoever believes and is baptized shall be saved."[18]

Before continuing the discussion of preparation for conversion, it is necessary to consider briefly Luther's concept of God's conversion. We have already noted that he affirms that God has made a covenant, *pactum Dei,* with man. Behind this idea is the nominalist concept of God as Will. Without the sure presence of a covenant, even with faith and grace, man might still be uncertain of God, and God himself might choose not to justify man.[19] The incarnation testifies to the covenant that God has made with man. Indeed, the basis for all of God's acts of conversion, every turn he makes toward man in mercy, lies in His own conversion in the incarnation. In a marginal gloss to Psalm 84:7 Luther

[18]WA 3, 289, 1–4 (Ps. 50:7); *LW* 10, 236–237. Jetter discusses Luther's understanding of baptism in the *Dictata* on pp. 211–254 of *Taufe beim jungen Luther.* Among several points: "Das heilsgeschichtliche Faktum des Menschwerdung Christi aus der Jungfrau geschieht 'mystisch' weiter in der Christwerdung des Menschen aus Wasser und Geist. Indem er in uns geboren wird, werden wir in ihm geboren, entsteht das neue Glaubensvolk" (p. 224). In its nature baptism or spiritual rebirth (*Wiedergeburt*) "ist also nicht, wenigstens nicht primär, Wesensveränderung, Wesenserneuerung. Sie ist eher Ortsveränderung, Erneuerung der Sicht" (p. 225). On this view, see also p. 228.

[19]Berndt Hamm offers a comprehensive study of the relation between God's *pactum* and His freedom as interpreted in scholastic theology in *Promissio, Pactum, Ordinatio.* See esp. pp. 377–390 for a discussion of Luther's understanding of preparation for righteousness. Kenneth Hagen offers a study of Luther's covenantal theology in his *Lectures on Hebrews* in *A Theology of Testament in the Young Luther: The Lectures on Hebrews,* Studies in Medieval and Reformation Thought, vol. 12 (Leiden: E. J. Brill, 1974). Luther's understanding of testament will be considered in Chapter 5. Steinmetz discusses covenant in relation to grace (*Luther and Staupitz,* p. 86).

explains that the two words *converte* and *conversus* in the text indicate God is converted and converts us; He assumes our nature and we by faith assume His nature.[20] This passage calls forth the mystical image of the reciprocal exchange between the soul and Christ or the Bride and Bridegroom. Luther may have come into contact with this imagery through his mentor in the order, Johannes von Staupitz, or even earlier.[21] During this period Luther was reading the sermons of Johannes Tauler, with whose theology he was greatly impressed.[22] Even in 1520, after

[20]*WA* 4, 2, 24–26 [Ps. 84:7].

[21]For a discussion of the influence of mysticism on Luther, see Bengt Hoffman, *Luther and the Mystics: A Re-examination of Luther's Spiritual Experience and His Relationship to the Mystics* (Minneapolis: Augsburg, 1976). Hoffman considers in general terms parallels and divergencies between Luther and various mystical traditions. Wilhelm Link discusses the mysticism that Luther encountered and his responses to its many aspects in *Das Ringen Luthers um die Freiheit der Theologie von der Philosophie*, 3d ed. (Darmstadt: Wissenschaftliche Buchgesellschaft, 1969), pp. 315–350. Arthur Rühl, "Der Einfluss der Mystik auf Denken und Entwicklung des jungen Luther," dissertation, Philipps-Universität Marburg, 1960, and Friedrich Ruhland, *Luther und die Brautmystik nach Luthers Schriftum bis 1521* (Giessen: Otto Kindt, 1938), specifically discuss the question of Luther's sources. On the relation between Staupitz and Luther and the influence of mysticism on Staupitz, see also Ernst Wolf, *Staupitz und Luther: Ein Beitrag zur Theologie des Johannes von Staupitz und deren Bedeutung für Luthers theologischen Werdegang*, Quellen und Forschungen zur Reformationsgeschichte, vol. 9 (Leipzig: M. Heinsius Nachfolger Eger & Sievers, 1927); Steinmetz, *Misericordia Dei*, esp. pp. 152–171. Steinmetz gives special consideration to Luther's understanding of religious ecstacy, *excessus mentis*, in "Religious Ecstasy in Staupitz and the Young Luther," *Sixteenth Century Journal*, 11, no. 1 (Spring 1980), 23–37. Steinmetz concludes: "Luther joins ecstasy and justification by faith, exaltation and humiliation, hiddenness and revelation, incarnation and ascent, *excessus mentis* and *pavor mentis*, cognition and silent astonishment in a dizzingly original combination. Like Staupitz and unlike Gerson, Luther is concerned to develop an understanding of the central role of religious ecstasy in the justification of the sinner. Like Perez and unlike Staupitz, Luther is fascinated with the illumination of the mind which takes place in ecstasy. Unlike Staupitz, Gerson, and Perez, Luther associates religious ecstasy with faith rather than with love" (p. 37). In *Luther and Staupitz* Steinmetz clarifies the differences between Luther and Staupitz on terms such as *humilitas;* see pp. 68–95.

[22]Some aspects of Tauler's use of the term *conversio* were discussed in Chapter 1. At several points in his notes Luther employs the concept of conversion, although he differs markedly from Tauler in his understanding of how an individual reaches conversion and salvation. Steven Ozment argues that scholars have too often spoken of Tauler's influence on Luther without adequately stressing the ways in which Luther breaks with Tauler ("An Aid to Luther's Marginal Comments on Johannes Tauler's Sermons," *HTR* 63 [1970], 305). Although there is a certain vagueness in Luther's comments which suggests that he is using the sermons as a springboard for working out his own understanding of conversion to God, it is nonetheless clear that conversion for Luther is not what it is for

Tauler, a turning within oneself by one's own efforts to find that *Grund* which will link one to God. Luther is much more at home with the alternative image in Tauler, which asserts that when man empties himself (and this applies most especially to the spiritual goods he has achieved) God will fill him, but for Luther even this emptying comes to be regarded as God's work. Ozment argues: "All plans which man can fashion through the interaction of his own powers and the objects present to him in the world are shown to be incapable of 'substantiating' him before God and in the face of sin and death. A 'vacuum' emerges, and Luther agrees with Tauler and Augustine that its persistence is simply not possible. But how is it filled for Luther? It is not filled with a *Seelengrund* in substantive unity with the uncreated Ground, but with 'sheer' and 'naked' faith in God alone, i.e. in the 'plan' of God, i.e. in the 'passion of Christ'" (*Homo Spiritualis*, p. 205). See also Steven Ozment, "Luther and the Late Middle Ages: The Formation of Reformation Thought," in Robert M. Kingdon, ed., *Transition and Revolution: Problems and Issues of European Renaissance and Reformation History* (Minneapolis: Burgess, 1974), pp. 109–152, esp. pp. 145–146. For another assessment of Luther's early understanding of the *synteresis*, see Baylor, *Action and Person*, pp. 157–208, esp. pp. 162–165.

Luther used the term "conversion" in his discussion of the three kinds of myrrh in Tauler's sermon "Accipe puerum et matrem eius et vade in terram Israhel" (Vetter, *Predigten Taulers*, pp. 12–16). He describes the first myrrh as "aversio a bonis male delectantibus," the second as "passiones in conversione ad bona spiritus." The first bitterness is an active turning away from the delights of the world and the second is an active turning toward spiritual goods, an even more bitter experience than the first (*WA* 9, 99, 1–2 and 17–20). In both instances aversion and conversion appear as man's own action and within the context of progress in reaching a higher spiritual level as a Christian. That these two movements occur within the context of grace is made clear by Luther's interpretation of the third myrrh, "tercia myrrha suspensio gratiae et spiritus" (*WA* 9, 99, 29). Thus conversion seems to refer not to a turning to faith or a turning in penitence but to a movement toward a higher spiritual level.

Luther speaks again of conversion in his comments on the sermon "Ascendit Jhesus in naviculam que erat Symonis" (Vetter, *Predigten Taulers*, pp. 170–176). God gives people spiritual goods, but some fail to use these goods correctly and instead rest in them and seek their own glory in them. God wills that they turn inward so that He may give them something better, namely Himself (*WA* 9, 101, 23–26). Particularly in this passage conversion is joined to the mystical experience of God in which man is able to play an active role. In his following comments on this sermon, the most lengthy of his notes, Luther emphasizes the importance of *resignatio* and *fides*. He compares God's transformation of man to that of a craftsman who destroys the substantial form of his material in order to give it a new one. It is not man's place to dictate to God how He should go about His work, but rather he should respond with resignation and a naked faith (*WA* 9, 102, 9–17). Although Luther emphasizes God's work in man, he also leaves a place for man's act of resignation (parallel to humility in the *Dictata*). What remains unclear is the extent to which resignation is truly man's own work. These notes, like the *Dictata*, show the lines along which Luther's theology is developing—the emphasis on faith, the naked mercy of God—but it is still a matter of new wine in old wineskins as Luther continues also to affirm the power of the *synteresis* (for example, *WA* 9, 103, 25–27) and to speak of conversion within the context of spiritual progress as movement from a lower to a higher level. For a brief comparison of Tauler and Luther, see von Loewenich, *Luthers Theologia Crucis*, pp. 174–183, esp. pp. 182–183, for a summary.

he had decisively turned away from mystical theology, Luther used the image of the Bride and Bridegroom to describe one of the benefits of faith, by which the soul as Bride takes on the righteousness of Christ the Bridegroom and the Bridegroom accepts as His dowry the sins of the soul.[23]

In his exegesis of Psalm 84 Luther joins three instances of conversion. The first refers to the conversion enacted in the incarnation. This passage is the most systematic and complete account of Luther's understanding of conversion in the *Dictata:*

> *'Thou wilt turn [conversus], O God, and revive us; and Thy people shall rejoice in Thee.'* A verse very much like this is 'When the Lord restored [*convertendo*] the captivity of Zion, we became like men comforted' (Ps. 126:1). 'Therefore we died before Your turning [*conversionem*], and Your turning away [*aversio*] is our death. But Your turning [*conversio*] to us becomes our life.' How can the soul live (it is of such life that he is here speaking) from which God has turned away [*aversus est*]? It is God who is the life of the soul as the soul is the life of the body. But that turning [*conversio*] of God by which He was united with our nature is the greatest and first. The second is that by which He is united spiritually with our spirit through faith and love. The third is through the clear vision. Thus He is one flesh with us, and we are one spirit with Him. But the second and third are rather our conversion [*conversio*], by which we are converted [*convertimur*] to Him, while the first one is peculiar to Him and unspeakable, by which He is turned [*conversus est*] to us. Thus He says (Zech. 1:3): 'Return [*convertimini*] to me (this happens through the Spirit), and I will return [*convertar*] to you' (this happens through the Incarnation). In the Song of Solomon (Song of Sol. 1:1) we read: 'Oh, that He would kiss me with the kiss of His mouth.' Thus by his turning [*conversus*] He gives life to all who cling to Him. The fact that he says 'turn' ['*conversus*'] no doubt suggests that before He was turned away [*aversus*] by His wrath and indignation, by which we are dead. Now, however, He has turned [*conversus est*] through love and goodness, by which we live again. . . . But the verse is not yet fully explained. If He gives life,

[23]WA 7, 25, 26–26, 12 (*Von der Freiheit eines Christenmenschen*).

then He first kills. For He kills those who live ill so that He might give life to those who have been put to death.[24]

To summarize, the first conversion occurs with God in the incarnation, and it is of decisive importance for mankind; the second occurs when man experiences conversion through faith and love; and the third occurs when man experiences conversion through clear vision, an experience in the future life in which he will see God *facie ad faciem*, face to face.

As Luther emphasizes, conversion is fundamentally Christocentric. There is no conversion to God the Father without conversion to the Son, by whom many have been and are offended: "They were unwilling to be converted and to acknowledge Him, because He was a man and hidden. So also now many are offended at the truth. . . . They all need to be converted by the Lord. But this is a conversion of the mind and the will; the mind turned away through ignorance and too much wisdom, the will through the inclination toward his own feeling and his own mind, a condition that pride causes in Jews and heretics."[25] Two points are especially important in these comments on conversion: first, that conversion involves fully both the mind and the will—the intellectual and emotional aspects of the individual—and second, that conversion can be obstructed by both ignorance and an abundance of human wisdom paralleled by a will com-

[24]*WA* 4, 8, 3–24 (Ps. 84:7); *LW* 11, 158–159. Copyright © 1976 Concordia Publishing House. Used by permission. Ruhland links this passage to Luther's references to marriage or bridal mysticism: "Wichtig ist, dass Luther die *conversio* vom Hohenlied aus beleuchtet. Sie ist in diesem angedeutet mit dem Wort: *Osculetur me osculo oris sui.* Wenn wir diese Belegstelle beachten, kommen wir bei der Analyse dieser Stelle aus der Psalmenvorlesung zu folgenden Ergebnis. Die grosse unbegreifliche Heimsuchung Gottes ist die Inkarnation. Diese verknüpft Luther mit den Gedanken der Brautmystik" (*Luther und die Brautmystik*, pp. 19–20). In his scholion to 84:11 Luther associates the reception of righteousness and peace with God's conversion (*WA* 4, 14, 1–3 [Ps. 84:11]; *LW* 11, 166).

[25]*WA* 4, 7, 12–18 (Ps. 84:5); *LW* 11, 157. See Gerhard Ebeling, *Lutherstudien*, vol. 1 (Tübingen: J. C. B. Mohr [Paul Siebeck], 1971), pp. 54–61, and Reinhold Seeberg, *Lehrbuch der Dogmengeschichte*, vol. 4, pt. 1: *Die Lehre Luthers*, 2d and 3d rev. eds. (Leipzig: A Deichertsche Verlagsbuchhandlung, Werner Scholl, 1917), p. 101.

mitted to one's own senses and mind instead of the "foolishness" of the Cross. Conversion means not only the acceptance of Christ and of divine wisdom but the rejection of one's own plan for attaining salvation based on human knowledge.

The reference to God's conversion in the incarnation leads to the question of whether God engaged in acts of conversion before that event. The answer is yes. Nonetheless, for two reasons, Luther does not engage in a discussion of conversion before the incarnation. First, Christ is at the center of the Psalms for Luther, and most passages he interprets as either reflecting or prefiguring the conversion of the Jews or Gentiles to Christ.[26] Second, Christ is God's right hand and the one through whom He created the world; thus, with some exceptions, God's acts of conversion before the incarnation refer equally to those of the Second Person of the Trinity. The scholion to Psalm 73:11 provides an excellent example of this equivalence. Luther writes that God corrects with His left hand for the sake of salvation and bestows favor with His right hand. With the left hand He turns man from sin and with the right He converts man to himself. But God may also choose to hide His right hand—to deny, in other words, His grace—which leads to the destruction of those who are deprived of His help. Luther adds: "For the right hand of God is the Son of God, and He is Himself in the bosom of the Father. Therefore, hiding His right hand in the midst of His bosom means to conceal His Godhead in the Father from them, so that they do not regard the Son but only the Father as God, and the Son only as man." The complexity of Luther's understanding of the relation between God's act of conversion and man's own efforts is demonstrated in the passage that follows: "But He would not do this to them unless they had first turned away His right hand into His bosom, had forced the spirit into the letter, and had hidden the faith before God. Therefore, as they did to Him, so is He doing to them."[27] Luther emphasizes both that man can prevent his conversion by stubbornly turning

[26]WA 55¹, 6, 25 and 8, 1 (*Praefatio*); LW 10, 7. See Vogelsang, *Anfänge von Luthers Christologie*, pp. 16–30 and 62–87.

[27]WA 3, 502, 24–27, 30–37 (Ps. 73:11); LW 10, 445.

away from God and that there is no road to salvation except through conversion to Christ.[28]

One final example may be given of conversion in the incarnation with its consequence of an exchange of goods between God and the sinner. In the marginal gloss to Psalm 103:29 Luther claims that God takes the spirit of sinners and gives them His spirit when He converts them.[29] Then those who have been converted return to dust, that is, to the recognition that they are dust. Conversion itself leads people to true self-knowledge. They are then renewed and made into new creatures.

With this passage we return to the question of preparation for conversion, or, more specifically, whether knowledge of oneself as a sinner in need of God's grace occurs before conversion, simultaneously with it, or as its consequence. In his remarks on Psalm 69:4 Luther suggests that before conversion people must recognize the error of their ways. Heretics who feel themselves to have outstripped others in Christian wisdom and righteousness have in fact made the least spiritual progress. Thus Luther affirms that "one's wish must be that they be turned backward and be turned away from their own understanding and be directed toward the beginnings of salvation. Let them be turned away from their own thought and opinion, so that they may be converted in Christ when they shall have blushed because of their pride and shall have understood that their progress was not progress but a turning away from Christ." It appears that the heretics must first understand the error of their ways before they are converted: "Let them understand themselves and acknowledge that they were turned away from Christ."[30] As Luther maintains in another passage: "For no one is justified by faith except one who has first in humility confessed himself to be unrighteous."[31] However, while this passage establishes a con-

---

[28]On conversion and Christ in relation to both Jews and Gentiles, see the scholion to the words *Converte nos* of Ps. 59:4: *WA* 3, 608, 1–8; *LW* 11, 97.

[29]*WA* 4, 171, 21–25 (Ps. 103:29).

[30]*WA* 3, 444, 1–10 (Ps. 69:4); *LW* 10, 387.

[31]*WA* 3, 345, 29–30 (Ps. 59:8); *LW* 10, 290. Günther Metzger gives a helpful overview of how Luther's understanding of *humilitas* in the *Dictata* has been interpreted by a number of major scholars (*Gelebter Glaube*, p. 154n). The lack of

agreement as to whether *humilitas* is a disposition, part of the process of justification, or a work of God is indicative of the difficulty of the problem (Adolf Hamel, *Der junge Luther und Augustin: Ihre Beziehungen in der Rechtfertigungslehre nach Luthers ersten Vorlesungen 1509–1518 untersucht*, vol. 1 [Gütersloh: C. Bertelsmann, 1934], pp. 40–71). Albert Brandenburg has formulated very well the nature of the difficulties one encounters: "Welches ist der Beitrag der humilitas zum Geschehen der fides? Und wie ist die humilitas ihrerseits bestimmt als Ineinander von göttlicher und menschlicher Tätigkeit? Gibt es eine Mittätigkeit des Menschen in der humilitas? Die Ermittlung der Antworten auf diese Fragen ist ungemein schwer. Der Leser bekommt den Eindruck einer nicht leicht definierbaren Vieldeutigkeit des Wortes humilitas. Zahlenmässig erscheint der Begriff humilitas etwa so haüfig wie das Wort iudicium" (*Gericht und Evangelium: Zur Worttheologie in Luthers erster Psalmenvorlesung*, Konfessionskundliche und kontroverstheologische Studien, vol. 4 [Paderborn: Bonifacius Druckerei, 1960], pp. 59–60). Brandenburg himself characterizes *humilitas* as "ein Begriff des Übergangs" in Luther's theology (p. 64), and links it to *iudicium* and *iustitia:* "In demütigen Hören vernehmen wir oder sollen wir vernehmen Gottes Gerichtswort. Man muss also diesen doppelten Akt sehen. Erstens, es geschieht unser Heil im Evangeliumswort, also die Gerechtigkeit, indem unter dem Gerichtswort uns in unseren Glauben hinein die Gerechtigkeit, welche Christus ist, geschenkt wird. Zweitens soll der demütige Menschen vom Gerichtswort als solchem getroffen werden. Das Gerichtswort soll ihn zur Selbstverleugnung, zur Selbstanklage, zum Selbstgericht rufen. Das versteht Luther unter humiliatio: Gott ruft uns zum Selbstgericht, zum Bekenntnis unserer Sünde auf. Lassen wir diesen Gerichtsruf Gottes wirksam werden, geschieht die von Gott bewirkte (humiliatio) als Selbstdemütigung, dann ist eben im Menschen die humilitas da. . . . Die beiden Geschehnisse, also Ereignis der Gerechtigkeit unter dem Gerichtswort und der Anruf Gottes zum Selbstgericht, stehen in Wechselwirkung miteinander. Das eine bedingt das andere. Gerichtswort kann nur Evangelium werden da, wo das von Gott bewirkte und von uns vollzogene Selbstgericht ist. Gerechtigkeit, durch das Evangelium verkündet, und Demut als Selbstanklage durchdringen sich, ja die Demut wird zum Bestandteil der Gerechtigkeit" (p. 65). According to this interpretation, *humilitas* is the cooperative work of man under grace with God, linked to the *humiliatio* worked by God in man. Brandenburg leaves open to question the precise role of the penitential disposition in relation to justification: "Wieweit Bussgesinnung konditional oder gar verdienstlich zur Gerechtwerdung beiträgt, kann hier bei dem Luther der Psalmenvorlesung letztlich nicht entscheiden werden" (p. 66). Albrecht Peters writes: "In der ersten Psalmenvorlesung malt Luther seinen Hörern die Demut als rechte Disposition zum Empfang der Gnade vor Augen; die Proportion zwischen der Tiefe unserer resignatio und unserer Erhöhung durch Gott bleibt gewahrt; doch weiss er bereits; rechte Demut ist nicht das Produkt menschlicher Bemühung, sie ist das Geschenk der göttlichen Gnade" (*Glaube und Werk*, p. 36). Peters points accurately to both dimensions of Luther's understanding, but not all passages in the *Dictata* demonstrate that Luther sees *humilitas* as God's gift. For other interpretations, see Gyllenkrok, *Rechtfertigung und Heiligung*, pp. 20–51, esp. p. 35, with its discussion of *humilitas* as *iudicium:* "und somit ein gutes Werk Gottes und ein Teil seiner Erlösungstat, d. h. Evangelium. Andererseits jedoch ist das iudicium auch eine Erfahrung des Christen und identisch mit der Tugend der Demut, und zwar dann, wenn Luther zur humilitas mahnen will und betont, dass sie tatsächlich eine unerlässliche Vorbedingung der Rechtfertigung, d. h. Gesetz, ist." On Ps. 59:8, see p. 46. On the relation between grace and humility, Gyllenkrok summarizes Luther's *Dictata* understanding on pp.

nection between humility and justification, it does not explicate the relation between conversion and humility.

The problem of self-knowledge is closely related to that of whether or not God's grace is operative in man before his conversion. The question may also be interpreted as one of determining how helplessly man is enmeshed in his sinfulness before the reception of *prima gratia* and of whether or not the *synteresis* is of decisive influence in the preconversion individual. With regard to the *facere quod in se est,* according to Biel, the person who does the best that is in him does not for that reason earn or merit first or justifying grace or achieve the level of *meritum de condigno,* real merit before God; the most he can achieve is *meritum de congruo,* what one scholar describes as "half merits or merits in a metaphorical sense."[32] In this way God's sovereignty is protected. God gives the individual *prima gratia* only because He has established a covenant in which He has freely agreed to do so. By his own law of grace, God agrees not to desert the person "who does what is in him, 'facit quod in se est,' and this means 'uti ratione per quam potest comprehendere deum esse et invocare adiutorium deo.'"[33] Throughout the *Dictata* Luther

47–51. On humility and justification, he concludes: "Luther sieht sich vor die Forderung, sich zu verändern, gestellt, so dass sein eigentliches Verlangen nach Rechtfertigung, sich unter der Form des Verlangens nach Demut verbergen muss" (p. 50). See also von Loewenich, *Luthers Theologia Crucis,* pp. 150–157; Regin Prenter, *Der barmherzige Richter: Iustitia dei passiva in Luthers Dictata super Psalterium 1513–1515,* Acta Jutlandica, Aarsskrift for Aarhus Universitet 33, 2, Teologisk ser. 8 (Aarhus: Universitetsforlaget I; Copenhagen: Ejnar Munksgaard, 1961), pp. 131–140; zur Mühlen, *Nos extra nos,* pp. 39–45. As I have indicated in this chapter, *humilitas* often appears as either a disposition or as man's expectation preceding justification; at the same time, Luther is strongly moving away from the position that man can by his own effort contribute to his justification.

[32]Heiko A. Oberman, ed., *Forerunners of the Reformation: The Shape of Late Medieval Thought Illustrated by Key Documents,* translations by Paul L. Nyhus (New York: Holt, Rinehart & Winston, 1966), p. 129.

[33]Oberman, *Harvest of Medieval Theology,* p. 53 (citing Biel, II *Sent.* d 22 q 2 art. 3 dub. 1 N). Ozment describes the basic Ockhamist position in the following way: "Ockhamists asked: If God rewards good works done in a state of grace with eternal life as a just due, could He not also be expected to reward good works done in a state of nature with an infusion of grace as an appropriate due? Had God not in fact promised to do precisely that? Ockham and Biel answered these questions in the affirmative: in accordance with God's gracious goodness (*ex liberalitate Dei*), he who does his best in a state of nature will receive grace as a

is struggling with this question of preparing for conversion or reception of the *prima gratia*.[34]

Although several problems remain concerning Luther's understanding of preparation for conversion, there is no ambiguity about the nature of conversion itself. Conversion as the initial turning of man by grace to faith is God's work, part of the *opus dei*. Luther discusses this work at length in his exegesis of Psalm 76.[35] He writes that God's works are threefold: first, the works of creation; second, those "wonderful works shown to the people of Israel in Egypt"; and third, "the spiritual works of redemption and justification, for these above all have been committed to all Christians."[36] The individual who has been converted confesses that this change [*mutatio*] of the Lord has occurred in his life and gives thanks for His works.[37] Change, in turn, is often preceded by humiliation: "First the moral Egypt must be stung and humbled and destroyed, and then, finally, follows the change of the right hand of the Most High."[38] Yet Luther also joins together humiliation leading to remorse and the change that leads to new life. In his scholion to Psalm 76:11 Luther writes: "But neither do I have this remorse [*compunctionem*] of myself, for it has changed me into a different man; it has

fitting reward (*meritum de congruo*). . . . Ockham and Biel did not consider this Pelagian; it was a part of the arrangement God himself had freely willed for man's salvation, God's very covenant. Absolutely considered, it was not human activity, either outside or within a state of grace, that determined man's salvation; it was rather God's willingness to value human effort so highly. Ockhamist theologians were convinced, however, that God meant for men to acquire grace as semi-merit within a state of nature and to earn salvation as full merit within a state of grace by doing their moral best. All the subtle and important qualifications notwithstanding, in this theology men could in fact initiate their salvation" ("Luther and the Late Middle Ages," in Kingdon, ed., *Transition and Revolution*, pp. 118–119).

[34]On *prima gratia* in the context of baptism, see Jetter, *Taufe beim jungen Luther*, pp. 229 and 231–233, where he discusses Luther's and Biel's similar understanding but concludes: "Und doch ist Luther im Grund viel weiter; denn er, aber nicht der Tübinger Nominalist, denkt von der persönlichen Gnade aus. Gnade ist nicht Gnadeninfluxus, sondern quottidianus adventus per gratiam tam in incipientibus quam proficientibus (4,305,32f)."

[35]*WA* 3, 526–549 (Ps. 76); *LW* 11, 10–37.

[36]*WA* 3, 530, 10–24 (Ps. 76); *LW* 11, 10.

[37]*WA* 3, 535, 16–18 (Ps. 76:11); *LW* 11, 17.

[38]*WA* 3, 535, 26–27 (Ps. 76:11); *LW* 11, 17.

enlightened me so that I know myself. If this change were of men, then it could be for all. Therefore, 'Now I have begun.' From this we are taught that no one can begin the new life unless he repents of the old, unless he has burned in this remorse, as this psalm teaches."[39] Affirming the radical nature of man's sinfulness, he stresses that remorse is necessary to change an old sinner into a new person. No one can begin a new life unless he has repented of the old, but remorse is possible only as a gift of God. We may rightly see remorse as an initial part of man's experience of conversion, painful but necessary. As this passage indicates, remorse is also related to *illuminatio mentis*, the spiritual insight mediated by God in which a person recognizes himself as a liar and sinner. Although the connections are not developed explicitly, Luther links this illumination to the reception of faith. In his exegesis of Psalm 50:7 Luther affirms that one knows oneself to be a sinner only through God's change wrought in one: "Therefore the one who is most attractive in the sight of God is not the one who seems most humble to himself, but the one who sees himself as most filthy and depraved. The reason is that he would never see his own filthiness, unless he had been enlightened in his inmost being with a holy light."[40] In this instance, conversion as illumination brings about the individual's true knowledge of himself.

Luther speaks more directly about conversion in his final comments in the *Dictata:* "But it can be said that the word directs to Christ, who turns back [*convertit*] and is turned back [*convertitur*] in His members. For when we are turned back [*convertimur*] as a stream, He is and does all this through faith in us. Therefore He turns us back [*convertit*] as a stream, because of His turning [*conversione*], which He does in us, we are His stream."[41]

Conversion, whether it occurs in baptism or after one has lost one's faith or transgressed against God, is Christ's action—it is the very conversion of Christ within a person that makes him a member of the Body of Christ and causes Christ to go forward

[39]*WA* 3, 541, 14–19 (Ps. 76:11); *LW* 11, 25.
[40]*WA* 3, 290, 31–34 (Ps. 50:7); *LW* 10, 239.
[41]*WA* 4, 414, 12–16 (Ps. 125:5); *LW* 11, 553.

73

in him.[42] Yet conversion is not the gift of an ongoing state. As Luther writes about baptism, it is not the end but the beginning of the struggle to grow in faith and love.

We may now turn to a more general description of the postconversion life. In Psalm 83 Luther writes: "A lonely sparrow on the housetop is bound to make a mournful sound, and so also the turtledove, for we must always be in the groaning of penitence, for blessed are they who mourn. . . . We must praise God and bewail our sins at the same time; praise because we have been saved, groan because we have sinned and are in the evils and dangers of this life."[43] There is no secure resting place for the Christian. The dual characteristics of this life are thanksgiving for God's saving action and remorse for the sins one continues to commit. Luther does not conceive of penitence as only an act done at a specific moment but as a way of life. The call to be penitent exceeds the demand on the Christian to perform the sacrament of penance. In the *Dictata* there is evidence that Luther is transferring the monastic ideal of a life of ongoing penitence—*conversio morum*—from the cloister to the everyday life of all Christians.[44]

Christian life constitutes a constant battle between flesh and spirit, faith and concupiscence. Although Luther does not explicitly draw these connections, it appears that a person after baptism, and thus after reception of *prima gratia*, can stray so far from God that he can be brought back to the fold only by God's act of conversion.[45] At the same time, however, Luther sees

[42]WA 3, 545, 30–33 (Ps. 76:20); LW 11, 32. See Metzger, *Gelebter Glaube*, p. 195.

[43]WA 3, 644, 32–36 (Ps. 83:4); LW 11, 139. On *gemitus*, see Oberman, "Simul Gemitus et Raptus: Luther and Mysticism," in Ozment, ed., *Reformation in Medieval Perspective*, pp. 237–239. Steinmetz discusses Luther's understanding of *duplex* confession, which is "the confession of sin and the confession of praise. The two acts of confession imply and require each other. Confession of sin without confession of praise is characteristic of the despair of a convict on the gallows, while confession of praise without confession of sin is pharisaical and leads to religious hypocrisy" (*Luther and Staupitz*, p. 79).

[44]For an excellent study of penance and sacramental confession, see Thomas N. Tentler, *Sin and Confession on the Eve of the Reformation* (Princeton: Princeton University Press, 1977).

[45]Ritschl, *Dogmengeschichte des Protestantismus*, vol. 2: *Orthodoxie und Synkretismus*, pt. 1: *Theologie der deutschen Reformation*, pp. 170–171.

Christian life as one of real spiritual progress, even though man constantly needs grace. One scholar has suggested that Luther lifts the nominalist idea of *facere quod in se est* out of the context of preparation for *prima gratia* and into one of lifelong preparation, more properly, ongoing preparation for sanctification.[46] He argues that for Luther in the *Dictata* the Christian never proceeds beyond the stage of *dispositio ad gratiam*. To substantiate his interpretation, he refers particularly to Psalm 118:76 and 78.[47] In the scholion to Psalm 118:59 Luther also articulates his perception of an ongoing disposition or preparation for grace: "But as he said above (v. 26), 'I have declared my ways, and Thou hast heard me,' our errors and defection from God must be confessed. They are then more fully thought about, when the face of the Lord shines upon us. And thus another life is begun anew, or advance is made toward a newer life, which is a certain conversion and beginning, nonetheless."[48] With this statement we see once again that in the *Dictata* the concept of conversion is very vital to Luther's exegesis and developing theology.

Along with the constancy of the *dispositio ad gratiam*, it is important to note that Luther also sets out specific steps of progress in Christian life. The following passage from Psalm 118 expresses his views on this subject:

> Wisdom is most properly the first step also of the beginners, when someone is newly given the knowledge and enlightenment of Christian truth and spiritual grace. After this wisdom has been

---

[46]Grane, *Contra Gabrielem*, p. 301: "Mann kann deshalb feststellen, dass Luther mit der traditionellen Terminologie, deren Unanwendbarkeit er noch nicht entdeckt hat, etwas anderes ausdrückt als die übliche Lehre über *facere quod in se est:* Das Leben auf dieser Erde ist in allen seinen Stadien Vorbereitung, und immer eine Vorbereitung, die das nächste Stadium nicht vollgültig verdient."

[47]WA 4, 344, 12–15 and 345, 31–35; *LW* 11, 469 and 471. Grane, *Contra Gabrielem*, p. 301: "Damit ist der entscheidende Unterschied zwischen dem vorbereitenden Stadium und dem Stand der Gnade, der für die scholastische Lehre von *dispositio ad gratiam* so wichtig ist, im Grunde aufgehoben worden. Wenn man die Worte: *sed bene congrue*, die anscheinend für einen Anschluss an die bielsche Lehre über *dispositio* sprechen, in diesem Zusammenhang stellt, werden sie zu einem Beweis dafür, dass der Mensch niemals über das vorbereitende Stadium hinaus gelangt; dieser Gedanke zeigt, dass die Gnade grundsätzlich anders verstanden wird als in der Scholastik."

[48]WA, 4, 334, 32–36 (Ps. 118:59); *LW* 11, 456.

obtained as a foundation, then follows the understanding of those things which he would not have been able to understand without a teacher. . . . But now wisdom brings light to him and so he is moved from glory to glory, and he accepts grace for grace and wisdom for wisdom, which comes about through understanding. Then, at length, comes counsel (*consilium*), which teaches how to apply both correctly for doing the good and avoiding the evil, so that he may not sin but do good, which is extremely difficult in the midst of so many dangers. . . . In the fourth place, comes strength (*fortitudo*) for putting these things into practice and fearing no one's resistance. What good does it do for counsel to decree rules and a way of acting . . . if laziness and fear of the world do not permit them to come about? Then, in the fifth place, comes knowledge (*scientia*), that is, a sure insight gained by experience, that what wisdom and understanding teach in faith is true. For none are experts in the spiritual and Christian life except those who have put their wisdom and understanding to the test in counsel and strength. Then, at length, in the sixth place, he can also be of benefit to others through godliness (*pietas*).[49]

In the *Dictata* Luther characterizes Christian life as life in the middle. In the following passage he expresses an understanding of that life which he will more fully develop in the *Lectures on Romans:* "And there is no one, not even the best one, who does not have some evil. Hence he can deservedly be called evil before God. . . . As Rev. 22:11 says: 'He who is righteous, let him be justified still.' So also he who is good, let him be made good still. Therefore, since there is such a mixture among us, if we say that we are good and have no sin, the truth is not in us (I John 1:8), since only God is good, righteous, and truthful." To this statement he then adds: "Therefore we are always in the middle between the goodness which we have from God and the evil which we have of ourselves, until in the future all evils are swallowed up and God alone is all in all (I Cor. 15:28), so that we are not our own but God's, and He is ours."[50] Perfection is not a possibility in this life, since evil always remains in a person. Yet

[49]*WA* 4, 327, 1–5, 9–13, 16–23 (Ps. 118:35); *LW* 11, 445.
[50]*WA* 4, 336, 15–20, 22–25 (Ps. 118:65); *LW* 11, 458.

perfection is the goal toward which a person must always strive.[51] The Christian's recognition that he lives in the middle, between his own evil and the goodness he receives from God, should not lead him to stop making progress. At the same time, this progress brings one back to the beginning: "And He gives continually to all who are progressing not according to merit but according to the mercy by which He struck a covenant with us, to give gratis to us who ask and beg. But He gives in a far greater manner to the beginners. And, as has often been said, to make progress is nothing else than always to begin."[52] This return to the beginning consists in continuing to recognize oneself as a liar and unrighteous *coram Deo*. Luther also distinguishes between having knowledge of the Christian faith and making progress in faith.[53] The distinction is between living according to the letter or the spirit. The person who is enlightened in what may be termed matters of faith has only the letter as long as he does not show forth in his life what he has understood. The good tree, the person converted by God, bears the responsibility of producing good fruit, works of faith.

The relation between humility and the individual's life before conversion has already been discussed at some length. Humility also occupies an important place in the daily life of the Christian. In Psalm 77 Luther presents a moral interpretation of the plagues sent by God to the Egyptians. His exegesis is especially noteworthy for its complex interrelating of contrition (*contritio*) and remorse (*compunctio*).[54] In a summary statement he emphasizes the following: "And our food should be locusts, so that our

---

[51] *WA* 4, 345, 31–35 (Ps. 118:79); *LW* 11, 471.
[52] *WA* 4, 350, 12–15 (Ps. 118:88); *LW* 11, 477; Grane, *Contra Gabrielem*, pp. 300–301.
[53] *WA* 4, 320, 37–40 (Ps. 118:25); *LW* 11, 436. On this passage and also on Ps. 118:105, see Metzger, *Gelebter Glaube*, pp. 115–121. On *fides* and *affectus* in Ps. 118:105 see also zur Mühlen, *Nos extra nos*, pp. 68–69.
[54] *WA* 3, 593, 20–25 (Ps. 77:46); *LW* 11, 83–84. On Luther's use of *compunctio* and *contritio*, Schwarz writes: "Luther zieht den Begriff *compunctio* dem Begriffe *contritio* vor. Das darf als ein Zeichen dafür genommen werden, dass er sich mehr in den Bahnen der patristisch-monastischen Theologie als in denen der scholastischen Theologie bewegt" (*Vorgeschichte der reformatorischen Busstheologie*, p. 272).

place in which we should dwell with God (that is, conscience), the bridegroom with the bride, might be burned and destroyed by the constant anger of remorse. . . ."[55] In line with monastic interpretation, remorse (*compunctio*) appears to be a constant or way of life, while contrition assumes the character of a specific event, though Luther does not always maintain a precise distinction between the two in his *Dictata* exegesis.[56] Contrition involves both the understanding and the heart, the intellectual and emotional sides of the person. Remorse, constant anger at and disappointment with oneself for one's sins, is the way of life that prepares the conscience to become the dwelling place of Christ. It is possible to see humility and remorse as opposite sides of the same coin. Humility is openness to correction by God and awareness of one's need for grace; remorse is confrontation with oneself as one realizes the sins one has committed and the good one has failed to do.

Humility excludes the possibility of resting on one's achievements: "Therefore wanting to remain always in the course and desire of making progress, this is true humility, which truly says, 'My soul has coveted to desire Thy ordinances at all times.' The proud and slothful, who seek to be holy or at ease, covet a quick end to work and an arrival at the top. Therefore they do not covet the desire and a constant zeal of progressing. . . . Let us, therefore, covet this, that we may always be able to progress and not pause at any time or have reached perfection. One who lives in the spirit does this."[57] Perfection is an illusion, since in reality

---

[55]*WA* 3, 593, 28–30 (Ps. 77:46); *LW* 11, 84.

[56]In the following passage *contritio* seems to be a constant process, similar to *compunctio* in the passage previously cited: "Alio modo de conversis ad Christum, qui tabescunt bene et salubriter per contritionem semper seipsos destruentes et carnem peccati inutilem ad malum reddentes" (*WA* 3, 223, 16–18 [Ps. 38:12]; *LW* 10, 186). This passage also shows that *contritio* remains a constant after conversion to Christ.

[57]*WA* 4, 315, 34–39; 316, 1–3 (Ps. 118:20); *LW* 11, 428–429. In his scholion to Ps. 76:12–13 Luther writes of the *perfectus homo*, who advances beyond the benefits of his own meditation to share his gifts with others (*WA* 3, 535, 5–8). It is apparent that Luther writes about perfection in various ways. Perfection as the attainment of sinlessness he sees to be impossible; perfection as the fruit of meditation and as that stage in which a person's vision encompasses as fully as human nature allows both creation and the Creator he sees as possible.

the Christian stands constantly in need of grace, as the humble person recognizes. Phrased differently, through humility and remorse one comes to hate one's own soul. This attitude is derived from God's work within the individual.[58] Hatred of oneself as a sinner—rooted in the conversion recognition of oneself as a liar before God—leads to a life of perpetual crucifixion, a continuous struggle by the new man in Christ against the old man in Adam.[59]

Meditation occupies an important place in Christian life. Humility brings the awareness that one sins and is in need of grace. Meditation brings the realization that there is always something more to understand about Scripture and spiritual matters.[60] As Luther writes: "For there is no one so perfect that he need not still be perfected in something, no one so enlightened that he need not be further enlightened, kindled, purified, and humbled, and so with regard to all virtues. . . . Thus he always needs illumination and kindling more and more, so that he who has made a beginning may make progress."[61] The person who meditates makes progress by being changed into what is taught in the Scriptures themselves: "And note that the strength of Scripture is this, that it is not changed into him who studies it, but that it transforms its lover into itself and its strengths."[62] This description resembles the imagery of eucharistic transformation or transubstantiation of Thomas Aquinas and Johannes Tauler. The passage also calls forth the image of the spiritual marriage with the exchange between the Bride and Bridegroom. In this instance, however, the exchange is not reciprocal. The reader takes on the virtues depicted in Scripture, but Scripture is itself not changed. Indeed, Luther emphasizes that it is the special power of Scripture not to be changed by the one who

---

[58]*WA* 3, 594, 12–13 and 15–16 (Ps. 77:50); *LW* 11, 84 and 85.

[59]Von Loewenich discusses life under the Cross in *Luthers Theologia Crucis*, pp. 129–193.

[60]*WA* 4, 319, 27–30 and 32–38 (Ps. 118:24); *LW* 11, 434. For a brief but excellent overview of Luther's understanding of *meditatio* in the *Dictata*, see Metzger, *Gelebter Glaube*, pp. 120–121.

[61]*WA* 4, 320, 14–17 and 22–23 (Ps. 118:25); *LW* 11, 435.

[62]*WA* 3, 397, 9–11 (Ps. 67:14); *LW* 10, 332.

studies it. Behind this statement is Luther's understanding not only of the power of the Word but of the manner by which exegesis occurs. A direct line may be drawn from this early statement in the *Dictata* to Luther's later self-understanding. In his view, not he but the Word is the reformer of the church; it is the Word, not Luther, that slays and converts.

Luther is aware of the danger in confusing divine with satanic illumination. The devil is quite capable of appearing in the guise of an angel of light. Illumination is to be tested by its fruits; if it leads to pride rather than to renewed humility, then it originates in the devil. The learned or contemplative, Luther warns, is particularly susceptible to the sin of pride, and often mistakes the devil's illusion for God's insight.[63] Closely related to this warning is Luther's statement that the heretics and ungodly may often appear to perform God's commandments with ease and to be righteous and holy, while those who are truly faithful are left to struggle with difficulties and appear to themselves as un-righteous. Although it may not seem so, God is in fact giving his special care to those who find themselves continually struggling so that they may remain in humility and "might overcome and know that wisdom is stronger than everything."[64]

The idea of spiritual progress is a recurring theme in Luther's description of postconversion life. The Christian is always in motion and may never allow himself to stop and savor the taste of righteousness.[65] Thus Luther writes: "Hence he who in the present moment trusts that he is righteous and stands in that opinion has already lost righteousness, as is clear likewise in motion: That which is the goal in the present moment is the starting point in the next moment. But the starting point is sin,

---

[63]*WA* 3, 408, 24–28 and 409, 1–4 (Ps. 67:36); *LW* 10, 348 and 349. Luther contrasts the illumination of the devil with the insight of the Holy Spirit. On the role of the Holy Spirit in Luther's theology, see Regin Prenter, *Spiritus Creator,* trans. John M. Jensen (Philadelphia: Muhlenberg Press, 1953).

[64]*WA* 3, 334, 23–24 (Ps. 59:13); *LW* 10, 278.

[65]*WA* 4, 364, 14–18 (Ps. 118:122); *LW* 11, 496. For a discussion of the Christian as *homo viator,* see Metzger, *Gelebter Glaube,* pp. 187–195. On *profectus,* see Prenter, *Barmherzige Richter,* pp. 140–148. Ozment discusses how Luther redefines the philosophical concept of *motus* in a theological context and the role of *motus* in Christian life and progress (*Homo Spiritualis,* pp. 130–138).

from which we must always be going; and the goal is righteousness, to which we must always be going. Therefore I have correctly said that the preceding righteousness is always wickedness
with regard to the next, as is the letter to the spirit, emptiness to
fullness. . . ."[66] Although Luther does not believe that man can
merit righteousness, he emphasizes the importance of his action.
Righteousness can be lost in a moment when a person stands still
and trusts that he has arrived at his goal.

Luther links to the concept of Christian life as progress the
image of birth: "If we are the children of God, we must always
be in the process of birth. Hence it is said, 'He who is born of
God does not sin' (1 John 3:9), but his birth from God preserves
him. As the Son is always in God from eternity and is born into
eternity, so we also must be born, renewed, and reborn."[67] This
passage and its references to birth and rebirth relate to the second conversion of Psalm 84. There is one definite moment that
transforms a person and puts him on the path of pilgrimage.[68]
But the person who is "saved" continually asks for salvation as
he strives to live according to God's will. Thus "we are always
saved with respect to the things which we have and which we
have accomplished by beginning. But with respect to the things
which are before us and toward which we have to be stretched
out by making progress we are not yet saved, but weak, captive,
and wretched. Therefore here, too, we must always cry for salvation."[69] For Luther, Christian life is defined as ongoing seeking
and need rather than as resting and security.

[66]*WA* 4, 364, 18–24 (Ps. 118:122); *LW* 11, 496.
[67]*WA* 4, 365, 14–18 (Ps. 118:125); *LW* 11, 497.
[68]On baptism and its relation to spiritual progress, see Jetter, *Taufe beim jungen
Luther*, pp. 175–254, esp. pp. 223–254.
[69]*WA* 4, 375, 1–4 (Ps. 118:146); *LW* 11, 511. Gerhard Rost discusses Luther's
comments on predestination in the *Dictata* in pp. 93–96 of *Der Prädestinationsgedanke in der Theologie Martin Luthers* (Berlin: Evangelische Verlagsanstalt,
1966). On man's will in relation to predestination he offers this analysis of
Luther's position: "Der Mensch hat seine Seele in seiner Gewalt und kann sie in
der Freiheit des Willens entweder verderben oder erretten, indem er das Gesetz
Gottes entweder verwirft oder erwählt. Er ist frei zu beidem!" (pp. 94–95). Rost
points out that in some instances Luther emphasizes grace and the absence of
merit, but that he also continues to articulate the power of man's will: "Wenn sie
ihren Willen ändern, wenn sie sich bekehren würden, dann würde der Fluch von

81

Closely related to the idea of man's spiritual progress are the concepts of God's judgment and justice. I merely outline some aspects of the complex picture that Luther develops concerning God's judgment and granting of righteousness and man's own self-judgment. The Christian is called upon to judge himself and by grace is enabled to see himself as a sinner. Self-judgment is itself the fullest measure of humility, and as part of that judgment the Christian who makes spiritual progress turns increasingly to hatred of the flesh.[70] Ironically, when a person seeks to flee from God's judgment, he receives it, but when he humbly receives it, the God who has fled and left the person to himself draws near to him.[71]

We have seen that in the *Dictata* we do not find an entirely consistent, unambiguous theology. Both humility and faith occupy central positions in Luther's exegesis.[72] The following passage from Psalm 84 is indicative, however, of the direction of Luther's thought: "Indeed, faith, which is given by God's grace to the ungodly and by which they are justified, is the substance, foundation, fountain, source, chief, and the firstborn of all spiritual graces, gifts, virtues, merits and works. . . . Faith is the prerequisite before everything."[73] In this statement Luther dem-

---

ihnen weichen" (p. 95). For a fine study of Luther's developing understanding of the will, see Harry J. McSorley, *Luther: Right or Wrong? An Ecumenical-Theological Study of Luther's Major Work, "The Bondage of the Will"* (New York: Newman Press; Minneapolis: Augsburg Publishing House, 1969).

[70]*WA* 3, 465, 13–16 (Ps. 71:4); *LW* 10, 406; *WA* 3, 439, 16–23 (Ps. 68:29); *LW* 10, 382. On *iudicium* and *iustitia,* Bizer writes: "Iudicium und Iustitia sind tropologisch als Demut zu verstehen, und diese kann als fides Christi verstehen werden, weil auch Christus hat sich gedemütigt" (*Fides ex auditu,* p. 22). Bizer argues for the importance of both faith and humility for Luther in the *Dictata.* Steinmetz writes: "The principal meaning of *iudicium* in the *Dictata super Psalterium* is self-accusation or confession of sin, that humiliation of the self in which the sinner confesses his poverty and utter nothingness in the presence of God and conforms his trembling judgment to the severe mercy of the judgment of God. *Iudicium* is, quite frankly, humility, the admission that one is a sinner, unworthy of the least benefits of divine generosity and unable to reconstitute one's broken relationship with God" (*Luther and Staupitz,* pp. 81–82).

[71]*WA* 4, 377, 18–19 (Ps. 118:151); *LW* 11, 514. See the discussion of *iudicium* by Brandenburg, *Gericht und Evangelium,* pp. 33–42.

[72]Bizer discusses the importance of *humilitas* as the new righteousness worked by God in man (*Fides ex auditu,* pp. 15–22, esp. p. 22).

[73]*WA* 3, 649, 17–20 and 22–23 (Ps. 83:7); *LW* 11, 146.

onstrates that he perceives faith to be God's gift to the ungodly, and as essential for their justification. He only briefly articulates in the *Dictata* what will be fundamental to his exegetical understanding in the *Lectures on Romans*. Thus, although he writes that faith is the source of all other virtues, he does not develop the implications of this affirmation. In the *Dictata* attention is centered on both humility and faith. Luther stresses the need for humility in the fight against self-righteousness and security, the false attitude of resting where one now is. In brief, "Today no battle is so necessary as the one against peace, security, boredom, and lukewarmness."[74]

We can note some unresolved questions and apparent inconsistencies in Luther's interpretation of conversion in the *Dictata*. Luther offers contradictory positions regarding whether or not a person can prepare for his conversion to faith, or whether humility provides the disposition for conversion. It is very difficult to ascertain whether certain passages in the *Dictata* refer to the individual before his conversion to faith or rather describe the sorrowful conversion to God of the penitent Christian. In some cases Luther appears to see humility as a necessary prologue to conversion to faith; in other cases, affirming a more radical view of the individual as sinner, he disclaims such a possibility. At some points he even equates conversion with this acquisition of humility and self-knowledge.

Although there is no systematic treatment of conversion in the *Dictata*, it is a key concept in Luther's developing theology. Indeed, the very contradictions in his understanding of the concept are indicative of the theological problems he is seeking to resolve: Can man prepare for his own conversion through a disposition of humility and expectation, or is he so blinded by his sinfulness that self-preparation is impossible? What is the relation between conversion to faith and the beginning of Christian life and the Christian's conversion through penitence? In the *Dictata* there are no consistent answers to these questions. Yet in his exegesis of Psalm 84 Luther offers a framework for his con-

---

[74]*WA* 3, 417, 11–12 (Ps. 68:2); *LW* 10, 352.

cept of conversion. God's conversion in the incarnation opens up to man the possibility of a new life; conversion through faith and love places him on the path of spiritual pilgrimage; conversion through clear vision offers him the promise of a future vision of God *facie ad faciem*. In addition, Luther affirms that conversion to God is only through Christ, but sinful man can recognize the divinity hidden in humanity only when God Himself reveals it to him. Luther writes of the psalmist: "Consequently he is now speaking also about spiritual conversion and wrath. This is, therefore, supremely necessary, because this cannot be done by human strength, only by divine strength. This is true because God is hidden in the flesh, so that no man can recognize Him unless he has been enlightened by God's spiritual grace."[75] Although this emphasis on divine, not human, preparation is not consistently developed in the *Dictata,* it is the direction in which Luther's theology is moving. The following passage makes emphatically clear that he sees conversion to be of crucial importance to the Christian life: "Therefore it is extremely necessary for us now to be converted, lest we offend against the truth which meets us in marvelous ways, so that we could not turn to it anywhere unless God is gracious to us and turns [*convertat*] our face toward recognizing it by turning away His wrath from us, so that we do not turn our back to it and are thus turned away from it."[76]

The study of Luther's *Dictata* then, suggests that he is indeed a *viator* on the way to a clear evangelical understanding of conversion, justification, and sanctification. He has not yet however, reached his final theological formulation. "For these two impinge on each other: If we are converted to the truth, God's wrath is turned away from us. But if we turn ourselves away from the truth, God's wrath is turned [*convertitur*] toward us. Therefore be converted if you want to turn away the wrath. But as I have said, this is impossible for us on our own, unless we

[75]*WA* 4, 6, 39–7, 3 (Ps. 84:5); *LW* 11, 156.
[76]*WA* 4, 7, 22–26 (Ps. 84:5); *LW* 11, 157.

seek to be converted by God."[77] On the one hand, he emphasizes the divine initiative for conversion, but on the other, he still
asserts that man must make the first move toward God. His
Lectures on Romans marks a new and critical stage in his theological development and his understanding of conversion. To that
commentary we now turn.

[77]*WA* 4, 7, 26–30 (Ps. 84:5); *LW* 11, 157. The unresolved question continues
to be how man is able to "ask" God that he be converted. If man is fully a sinner
entrapped in *amor sui*, how does he come to recognize his need? Although
Luther's positions are inconsistent at times, the judgment of Carl Stange on the
Dictata is too harsh: "Vergegenwärtigt man sich den Gesamteindruck, den die
erste Psalmenvorlesung Luthers macht, so kann von einem Durchbruch seiner
reformatorischen Theologie nicht die Rede sein: es ist reine Scholastik, was uns
in der Psalmenvorlesung begegnet; inhaltlich kann man ihr keinen besondern
Wert zusprechen. Die Allegorie ist oft grotesk, die Exegese willkürlich und
schwankend, der Kreis der Probleme eng, die Gedanken monoton,—man kann
wohl sagen: im ganzen ist die Lectüre ermüdend" (*Die Anfänge der Theologie
Luthers*, Studien der Luther-Akademie, n.s. vol. 5 [Berlin: Alfred Töpelmann,
1957], p. 61). Although Luther continues to use scholastic concepts and terminology, his theology is no longer "*reine Scholastik.*" On this passage, see Lennart
Pinomaa, *Der Zorn Gottes in der Theologie Luthers: Ein Beitrag zur Frage nach der
Einheit des Gottesbildes bei Luther* (Helsinki, 1938).

[3]

Lectures on Romans
(1515–1516)

In the summer of 1532 Luther proclaimed to those eager to hear about his early days: "When I was a monk, I was a master of allegories. I allegorized everything. But after I went through the letter to the Romans, I came to the knowledge of another Christ."[1] In this context, as well as in his 1545 Preface, Luther emphasized the importance of Paul's words in forming his theology and determining the course of his reform.

As Jacob Heikennen writes: "Paul's Romans occupies a unique position in the history of western Christendom: at the decisive turning points, from Augustine to Barth, Paul's voice is heard anew."[2] Such indeed is the case with Luther's interpretation of Romans, which itself marks a theological milestone. As we shall see, it also marks a milestone in Luther's understanding of conversion as he gradually resolves some of the problems that clouded his interpretation in the *Dictata*.

[1]Otto Scheel, ed., *Dokumente zu Luthers Entwicklung [bis 1519]*, 2d rev. ed., Sammlung ausgewählter kirchen- und dogmengeschichtlicher Quellenschriften, n.s., vol. 2 (Tübingen: J. C. B. Mohr [Paul Siebeck], 1929), p. 98, no. 251.

[2]Jacob W. Heikinnen, "Luther's Lectures on the Romans (1515–1516)," *Interpretation: A Journal of Bible and Theology* 7 (April 1953), 178. For a fine introduction to Luther's commentary, see Wilhelm Pauck, ed., *Luther: Lectures on Romans*, Library of Christian Classics, vol. 15 (Philadelphia: Westminster Press, 1961).

Although there are significant differences between the theology articulated in the *Lectures on Romans* and that in the *Dictata,* ambiguities exist in much the same areas in both. For this reason, the discussion in this chapter will be structured in the same way as that of the preceding one: first, the question of the individual's preparation for conversion; second, the nature of conversion itself; and third, the character of Christian life after conversion.

The term *conversio* is not frequently mentioned in the commentary. In the *Dictata,* it occurred often in the biblical text, and Luther had ample opportunity to interpret it in his exegesis. This is not the case in Paul's epistle. Still, at several points in his lectures Luther does refer explicitly to *conversio* or *convertere.*[3] More important, throughout his lectures he is concerned in a very fundamental way with the concept of conversion, with conversion as the change or transformation from unbelief to faith in Christ and from unrighteousness to righteousness *coram Deo.* This transformation he links to both baptism and penitence. It cannot be overemphasized that throughout his commentary Luther speaks of the individual in transition—from unjustified to justified, sinner to saved, old man in Adam to new man in Christ, present despair to future hope.[4] For Luther change is a constant in Christian life. Change may even include the losing of one's faith. Thus one is not converted to faith once and for all; one may in fact experience conversion to faith more than once. The Christian's conversion to God in repentance for his sins may now have the added depth of being a return from unfaith to faith.[5]

Luther interprets conversion in two principal ways: as the

---

[3]The following are the more important instances; all references are from *WA* 56: 11, 4 (gloss to 1:18); 204, 17 (2:15); 266, 2–4 (3:28); 277, 16–18 (4:7); 278, 13–14 (4:7); 379, 10–12 (8:26); 422, 9 (10:14).

[4]*WA* 56, 272, 3–273, 2 (4:7); 340, 24–29 (7:14); 360, 28–361, 3 (8:3), among many others.

[5]*WA* 56, 257, 28–33 (3:21); *Luther's Works,* vol. 25: *Lectures on Romans,* ed. Hilton C. Oswald, chaps. 1 and 2 trans. Walter G. Tillmanns, chaps. 3–16 trans. Jacob A. O. Preus (St. Louis: Concordia, 1972) (hereafter cited as *LW* 25), p. 244. See also Ritschl, *Dogmengeschichte des Protestantismus,* vol. 2: *Orthodoxie und Synkretismus,* pt. 1: *Theologie der deutschen Reformation,* p. 171.

decisive event that begins Christian pilgrimage and as the repeatable event that occurs after the Christian has fallen away
from God through sin. Both aspects of his definition occur in
the scholion to 3:27. In this passage Christ also serves as the
center around which his interpretation of conversion is con-
structed. He writes: "For who has ever sought, or would have
sought, the incarnate Word, if He had not revealed Himself?
Therefore He was found when He was not looked for. But
having been found, He now wills to be sought and found over
and over again. He is found when we are converted to Him from
our sins, but He is sought when we continue in this conversion."[6]
The initial conversion from sins is the decisive event that establishes the course of an individual's life. The ongoing perseverance in conversion consists of living one's life in conformity
with the turning from sins that one has experienced. This text
does not specify, however, precisely what comprises perseverance in conversion. Defined most generally, it is constituted
by the constant battle against sin. It is not a state but an ongoing
struggle and movement. Luther continues to articulate the
theme of constant striving and progress that he espoused in the
Dictata.

In a second text Luther speaks more explicitly of conversion
as a repeatable event: "I call 'first grace' not that which is poured
into us at the beginning of conversion, as in the case of Baptism,
contrition, or remorse, but rather all that grace which follows
and is new, which we call a degree and increase of grace."[7] By
linking conversion both to baptism and to contrition or remorse,
Luther indicates that it is a repeatable event. It is equated not

---

[6]*WA* 56, 265, 31–266, 4 (3:27); *LW* 25, 253. Copyright © 1972 Concordia
Publishing House. Used by permission.

[7]*WA* 56, 379, 10–12 (8:26); *LW* 25, 368. On this passage Hans Hübner writes:
"Luther fasst die prima gratia dynamischer, als es vor ihm Gabriel Biel tat, der
diese Gnade als die rechtfertigende Gnade in den Sakramenten der Taufe und
der Busse begreift. . . . Es durfte kein Zweifel bestehen, dass diese Erklärung
der prima gratia sich ausdrücklich gegen Biel richtet. Luther will dadurch das
jeweilige Neu-werden der Heiligung im Menschen zum Ausdruck bringen"
(*Rechtfertigung und Heiligung in Luthers Römerbriefvorlesung: Ein systematischer Ent-
werf*, Glaube und Lehre, vol. 7 [Witten: Luther-Verlag, 1965], p. 138). See also
Oswald Bayer, *Promissio: Geschichte der reformatorischen Wende in Luthers Theologie*,
Forschungen zur Kirchen- und Dogmengeschichte, vol. 24 (Göttingen: Vandenhoeck & Ruprecht, 1971), p. 34n, and Kroeger, *Rechtfertigung und Gesetz*, p. 94.

only with entrance into the Christian life, but with a person's genuine sorrow for the sins he has committed and his repeated recognition and affirmation of himself as a sinner. In his discussion of *prima gratia* Luther decisively differs from the nominalist Biel by refusing to term *prima gratia* that grace which is given at the beginning of baptism or contrition. For Luther it comes later, as the increase and augmentation of grace, and as the successor to operating grace. He also emphasizes that a person cannot by his own efforts attain to *prima gratia,* but must instead be passive and wait, assuming the role of the Bride of Christ.[8] Luther's description of the waiting soul clearly reflects mystical terminology. Prayer and action may precede *prima gratia,* but at the moment of its reception the soul must be quiet and wait. To use a traditional image, Martha must become like Mary.

The dual dimensions of conversion as both unrepeatable entrance into the Christian life and repeatable return to that life after having wandered away from it in sin are illustrated by a passage in Luther's exegesis of 6:10. In that text he discusses the meaning of baptism: "Hence also we are baptized only once, by which we gain the life of Christ, even though we often fall and rise again. For the life of Christ can be recovered again and again, but a person can enter upon it only once, just as a man who has never been rich can begin to get rich only once, although he can again and again lose and regain his wealth."[9] A

---

[8]WA 56, 379, 1–9; *LW* 25, 368.

[9]WA 56, 327, 20–24 (6:10); *LW* 25, 315. On Luther's understanding of baptism, see the comprehensive study by Jetter, *Taufe beim jungen Luther.* With reference to this passage, he writes: "Für diese Auffassung steht also die Taufe als Eintritt in den neuen ordo beherrschend über der Gegenwart und der Zukunft des christlichen Lebens. Damit ist aber ein starker Bruch mit der Taufauffassung der letzten tausend Jahre vollzogen. Denn dort war sie, wenn man es einmal so summarisch gegeneinanderstellen darf, im wesentlichen als Regulativ der Vergangenheit begriffen. Diese Auffassung ist darum gegen das novatianische Missverständnis der Einmaligkeit der Taufvergebung nie wirklich gesichert gewesen. Luther versteht die *Einmaligkeit* der Taufe neu: sie meint nicht den einmaligen Vorgang, sondern seine einmalige Qualität. War sie bis dahin letzten Endes rituell verstanden worden, so begreift Luther sie jetzt eschatologisch: der neue ordo, den uns die Taufe eröffnet, in dem die Strahlen der Gnade vor Christus her das Leben im Glauben durchströmen, ist in Zeit und Ewigkeit unser eines, einziges Heil. Die vita spiritualis, als solche mit allen Zeichen des Noch-nicht behaftet, ist doch—gerade als solche—vita aeterna, die Taufe daher der Anfang des ewigen Lebens" (p. 317).

person is converted in baptism only once, but he may be converted in penitence again and again. This perception of conversion is closely related to Luther's understanding of the Christian as *semper penitens,* always penitent.[10]

These passages give us some insight into the meaning of conversion in the *Lectures on Romans* and suggest that it is a concept with which Luther is fundamentally engaged in his exegesis. For him, conversion, as we have seen, is equated with both baptism and contrition. Extrapolating from this concept, we can speak of the converted individual as being a faithful Christian and of conversion itself as leading to righteousness before God.[11] The complex and ambiguous relationship between faith and righteousness in the lectures complicates the task of defining the nature and results of conversion.[12] Conversion in baptism is to both faith and righteousness. For the person who has lost his faith, conversion in contrition is a return to faith and righteousness. Even after conversion, the Christian remains *egrotus in re, sanus in spe,* sick in fact but healthy in hope.[13] In a corollary to 3:21 Luther expresses this thought very clearly: "For God has not yet justified us, that is, He has not made us perfectly right-

---

[10]*WA* 56, 442, 18–22 (12:2); *LW* 25, 434.

[11]Ritschl convincingly argues that Luther does not simply equate conversion and justification: "Luther nämlich hat die Bekehrung und die Rechtfertigung noch gar nicht einfach mit einander identificirt. Sondern dieser Begriff deckt bei dem lediglich transscendentalen Charakter, der ihm eigen ist, wenn er im engern Sinne als göttliche Imputation verstanden wird, nicht allein die *conversio impii,* sondern auch die Gnadenverleihung durch die Taufe, ferner jede christliche Busse und jede im Glauben überwundene Anfechtung und Versuchung, so aber auch die ganze Person des Gläubigen selbst einschliesslich seiner unvollkommenen und mit unvermeidlicher Sündhaftigkeit befleckten guten Werke. Denn vermöge der göttlichen Rechtfertigung oder Anrechnung ist der Gläubige als solcher eben gerecht vor Gott trotz der Sünde, die bis zu seinem Tode in ihm bleibt" (*Dogmengeschichte des Protestantismus,* vol. 2: *Orthodoxie und Synkretismus,* pt. 1: *Theologie der deutschen Reformation,* p. 174).

[12]In some instances Luther appears to equate faith and righteousness, in others he sees righteousness as resulting from faith and humility. See *WA* 56, 227, 18–228, 2 (3:4); *LW* 25, 212 and *WA* 56, 284, 9–14 (4:7); *LW* 25, 271. Despite ambiguities, it is clear that Luther does not conceive of righteousness as a state in which one may securely rest after conversion. Conversion in penitence continues to occur precisely because the individual remains a sinner, although Luther claims that by grace such a person is also righteous.

[13]*WA* 56, 347, 8–14 (7:25); *LW* 25, 336.

eous or declared our righteousness perfect, but He has made a beginning in order that He might make us perfect. . . . This is pointed out in the story of the man half dead who was brought to the inn. After his wounds had been bandaged, he was not yet cured, but he was on the way to being made whole."[14] Thus, although conversion leads to righteousness, it is only the beginning, not the end, of man's pilgrimage. Luther strongly criticizes those who interpret Christian life in terms of security and who rest in their supposed righteousness. By doing so they prove how far they are from true righteousness and how desperately they stand in need of conversion.

Even after baptism a person may reject grace because of the *concupiscentia* that remains within him. In this way he can lose his faith and become an unbeliever, moving from righteousness to unrighteousness. In his exegesis of 1:23 Luther writes that a person may give up the true God for his own image of God.[15] Yet Luther insists that this very renunciation by man is itself linked to the will of God.[16] Behind Luther's understanding of man's ability to resist and to reject grace and thereby salvation are the larger issues of free will and of election and predestination.[17] Following Paul, he affirms that on the one hand God has consigned men to disobedience, and on the other hand, they have chosen to harden their hearts.[18] The relationship between God's election and man's own responsibility for continuing on the path of disobedience is a complicated one and Luther avoided discussing it, believing that it might lead to doubt and fearful

---

[14]WA 56, 258, 19–22 (3:21); *LW* 25, 245.

[15]WA 56, 178, 10–17 (1:23); *LW* 25, 158–159. This passage also demonstrates Luther's pastoral concern with the abuses he sees before him. At various points in the commentary he particularly criticizes *singularitas*, following one's own opinion as the guide for proper action.

[16]WA 56, 180, 7–14 (1:24); *LW* 25, 160–161. On the relation among sin, damnation, and election, see *WA* 56, 385, 32–386, 5 (8:28); *LW* 25, 376. Also see the discussion of predestination in the lectures in Rost, *Prädestinationsgedanke in der Theologie Martin Luthers*, pp. 105–112 and 133–152.

[17]Walter Grundmann emphasizes the importance of the free will problem for Luther in these lectures in his study *Der Römerbrief des Apostels Paulus und seine Auslegung durch Martin Luther* (Weimar: Hermann Böhlaus Nachfolger, 1964), p. 68. See also McSorley, *Luther: Right or Wrong?*, pp. 225–240.

[18]WA 56, 207, 11–14 (2:27); *LW* 25, 192.

wonderings on the part of his listeners. Nonetheless, predestination and election do provide the essential context for Luther's understanding of conversion.[19]

Related to this discussion of divine election and human responsibility is Luther's definition of the work of the apostle, a work that through humiliation may bring some people to conversion. As he writes in 2:27: "I answer that the whole task of the apostle and of his Lord is to humiliate the proud and to bring them to a realization of this condition, to teach them that they need grace, to destroy their own righteousness so that in humility they will seek Christ and confess that they are sinners and thus receive grace and be saved."[20] This is a complex passage, with its twofold emphasis on the work of the apostle and Christ and on man's coming to humility and recognition of himself as a sinner. There is at least a suggestion that this attainment of humility preceding the reception of grace involves to some degree man's own effort or at least his openness to God. As in the *Dictata*, in some instances the precise role of humility is ambiguous.[21]

[19]See Hans Vorster, *Der Freiheits-Verständnis bei Thomas von Aquin und Martin Luther*, Kirche und Konfession, vol. 8 (Göttingen: Vandenhoeck & Ruprecht, 1965), pp. 246–399; Seils, *Gedanke vom Zusammenwirken Gottes*, pp. 86–130.

[20]*WA* 56, 207, 7–11 (2:27); *LW* 25, 191–192.

[21]While there is general agreement among scholars that *humilitas* is not achieved by human striving, but is, like *fides*, a gift of God and also is nonmeritorious, there is little agreement concerning the relation between the two and their relation to justification. According to Leif Grane, "Er [Luther] meint nicht zwei aufeinanderfolgende Stadien, sondern zwei Seiten derselben Sache, wenn er sagt: 'Darum sind *humilitas* und *fides* notwendig'" (*Modus Loquendi Theologicus: Luthers Kampf um die Erneuerung der Theologie [1515–1518]*, Acta Theologica Danica, vol. 12 [Leiden: E. J. Brill, 1975], p. 73). In contrast Bizer writes: "Der Begriff der formalen Gerechtigkeit ist nicht überwunden; die Demut *ist* eine formale Gerechtigkeit, und es ist die Demut, nicht einfach der Glaube, die hier den Menschen rechtfertigt. An allen entscheidenden Stellen der Vorlesung erscheint die Demut als das, was vom Menschen gefordert wird, und sie ist nicht der Glaube, sondern sie folgt aus dem Glauben. . ." (*Fides ex auditu*, p. 51). Grundmann argues that Luther sees humility as a divine gift but has not yet clearly related it to grace: "Die Demut ist aber zugleich das Verlangen nach der Gnade. Demut und Gnade aber sind auf der Stufe der Römerbriefvorlesung von Luther noch nicht in einen inneren Einklang und Zusammenhang gebracht. Die Demut ist ebenso wie die Gnade nicht Werk des Menschen, sondern sie ist Gabe und Wirkung Gottes, denn sie kommt aus dem Hören und glaubenden Annehmen des Wortes" (*Römerbrief des Apostels Paulus*, p. 97). Lohse offers the moderate assessment: "Es ist umstritten, ob in der Römerbriefvorlesung noch eine sog. 'humilitas-Theologie' begegnet. Gegen den Versuch, hier bereits die volle refor-

Rudolf Damerau has questioned whether humility constitutes a disposition for righteousness. He suggests: "Luther's formulation in its deepest realization—in perfection—seems to understand humility as a disposition for the justification of the humble person by God. Against that, however, is the fact that Luther's concept of humility at this time is entirely stripped and emptied of any hope of merit and any trust in one's own efforts to influence God's grace."[22] Thus Damerau holds that "naked" humility alone can experience God's grace, and it alone is the true and right attitude of a Christian before God.[23] Damerau also stresses the difficulties in defining the precise relation between humility and grace in Luther's commentary.[24]

At the beginning of his scholia, in his exegesis of 1:1, Luther describes humility as a way of life essential for attaining right-

matorische Auffassung von der iustitia Dei und der iustificatio hominis ausgesprochen zu finden, hat insbesondere E. Bizer die Ansicht vertreten, dass die Demut des Menschen noch die Bedingung für den Empfang des Heils sei. In der Tat finden sich manche Passagen, welche die reformatorische Auffassung noch nicht zu enthalten scheinen. Andererseits begegnen in der Römerbriefvorlesung so wichtige Begriffe wie imputare, reputare (im Sinne von: für gerecht halten oder erklären). . . . Auch wenn sich immer wieder Stellen finden, die vielleicht noch nicht reformatorisch zu deuten sind, so ist die zunehmende Ausformung der reformatorischen Theologie sowie ihre Anwendung auf zahlreiche Einzelfragen kaum zu bestreiten" (*Martin Luther*, p. 156). None of these scholars discusses *humilitas* in relation to *conversio*.

[22]Damerau, *Demut in der Theologie Luthers*, pp. 122–123.

[23]Ibid., p. 124. Damerau further notes: "An einer anderen Textstelle spricht Luther davon, dass der Demütige erkenne, dass sein Willen schlecht und er selbst ein Nichts vor Gott sei; er wirke und handle dieser Erkenntnis gemäss. Diese geschilderte seelische Grundhaltung erkennt Luther als eine Vorbereitung auf die Gnade der Rechtfertigung an, denn in diesem seelischen Stand sei der Demütige schon auf irgendeine Art und Weise gerecht. So hat die traditionelle Anerkennung einer Gnadendisposition—sie ist hier durch die Demut hervorgerufen—bei Luther einen neuen Inhalt gewonnen" (p. 123). Although *humilitas* thus precedes justifying grace or the grace that makes one righteous before God, it is not clear whether *humilitas* itself is produced by preparatory grace.

[24]Damerau affirms that Luther's interpretation of *humilitas* as awareness of one's nothingness before God effects seemingly synergistic comments at the beginning of his commentary: "Wenn auch die Aussage Luthers zu Beginn seiner Vorlesung noch auf der meritorisch-synergistischen Vorstellungswelt der Scholastik zu stehen scheint, so hat doch die Demut die wahrheitsgetreue Erkenntnis eigener Nichtigkeit vor Gott zum Inhalt" (ibid., p. 123). The most difficult problem to resolve is whether man is able to contribute to bringing himself to humility.

eousness before God. He writes: "Therefore we must in all these things keep ourselves so humble as if we still had nothing of our own. We must wait for the naked mercy of God, who will reckon us righteous and wise. This God will do if we have been humble and have not anticipated God by justifying ourselves and by thinking that we are something."[25] The preceding text clearly establishes that Luther is describing the person who is a faithful Christian, who has been converted and appears to be persevering in that conversion.[26] Although converted, the Christian must constantly guard against justifying himself, against seeking righteousness by works. If he does do so, he must once again convert to God in penitence.

Luther also describes the individual before faith and consequently before conversion: "But the 'unformed faith' is no faith at all but rather the object of faith. I do not believe that a person can believe with an 'unformed faith.' But this he can do well: He can see what must be believed and thus remain in suspense."[27] Luther's intention in this passage is to oppose Nicholas of Lyra's interpretation of "from faith to faith" as progression from unformed to formed faith or from beginning to perfect faith.[28] He also implicitly affirms that a person cannot bring himself to faith

[25]WA 56, 159, 12–16; LW 25, 137. With respect to Luther's entire exegesis of Rom. 1–3, Grane writes: "Was Paulus in Röm 1–3 sagt, gilt nicht nur in dem Sinn *allen*, als es sowohl den Römern (den Heiden) als auch den Juden gilt, sondern es gilt allen im Sinne von 'uns allen'" (*Modus Loquendi Theologicus*, p. 67).

[26]WA 56, 159, 4–12 (1:1); LW 25, 137.

[27]WA 56, 172, 21–173, 2 (1:17); LW 25, 152.

[28]Jared Wicks writes of this passage: "On the words 'from faith to faith' in Romans 1, 17, Luther first rejects Lyra's idea that this is an indication of the distinction between unformed and formed faith. Nobody, argues Luther, can be just and 'alive' (as Rom. 1,17 has it) through unformed faith. Neither is the distinction between the faith of the old law and that of the new; these are not different 'faiths,' but, rather, different degrees of clarity in the one justifying faith. The phrase indicates that the justice we have from God is always 'from faith' in this life. We do make progress, but always in faith—'always believing more and more—never passing over to seeing face to face.' Thus faith is here part of the substance of our life of constant advance and progress' (*Man Yearning for Grace: Luther's Early Spiritual Teaching* [Washington and Cleveland: Corpus Books, 1968], p. 107). While Wicks's point about progress in faith is accurate and in keeping with Luther's exegesis, he does not note that Luther also links "unformed faith" to "object of faith," and suggests that the passage may be interpreted as moving from what one knows to believe (but is unable by one's own efforts to accomplish) to true belief or faith.

or, as may equally well be said, accomplish his own conversion. Yet a person can prepare for faith to the extent that he can perceive what is to be believed and then assume a position of suspense or waiting. Preparation appears to be minimal; the emphasis falls on the fact that faith comes from God alone. In this passage, however, there is something of the same ambiguity as in the *Dictata*. Luther is describing the individual before he receives faith. Such a person is not yet converted. Yet he is still able to attain to some knowledge *of* faith. The result is that he knows what he is missing, knows he cannot obtain it by himself, and waits for God to act. This interpretation suggests that man before conversion is still able to prevent himself from falling into a worse state through arrogant self-justification.[29] What remains

[29]In the context of our discussion of the individual's power or ability before conversion, it is useful to refer again to Luther's concept of the *synteresis*. There are three references to the term, in conjunction with his exegesis of 1:19–20, 3:10, and 4:7. In the first passage, Luther affirms that the *synteresis* is the source for man's knowledge of God; it is not itself open to error, but the practical consequences that can be drawn from it are (*WA* 56, 177, 14–18; see his entire discussion from 176, 15–177, 33; *LW* 25, 156–158). This reference to the *synteresis* is a positive one. In the second passage he decisively limits the power of the *synteresis* (*WA* 56, 237, 2–8; *LW* 25, 222) and then proceeds to dispute Seneca's statement that he would do the good even if the gods did not reward him and men did not notice. As Baylor succinctly describes his argument: "Luther was referring here to the *synteresis* of the will rather than of the reason—he spoke of a part of man 'affected toward good' (*ad bonum affecta*). He suggested that, in virtue of it, man without grace does in some respects seek the good. But the presence of the *synteresis* in all men did not prevent Luther from disputing Seneca's claim that he would strive for good even if God remained ignorant of his sins. So the positive value attached to the *synteresis* is severely qualified by its being located within a natural man who 'is always inclined to evil' (*semper ad malum inclinatus*) (*Action and Person*, pp. 174–175). This limitation on the *synteresis* becomes even more explicit in the final passage in which Luther mentions it, 4:7, where he argues against the scholastic idea that man is able to love God by virtue of his own powers (*WA* 56, 275, 17–23; *LW* 25, 262). Luther maintains that the *synteresis* is at the most "a tiny movement" that lacks the power to bring a person to do that which is really important, namely, to love God. For everything that counts, grace is essential. Thus, although Luther does not deny the existence of the *synteresis*, he places it within sinful man and denies that it can lead man out of sin. Ozment writes: "Here it is clear that Luther considers an *exaggerated* view of the powers of the *synteresis* to underlie the claim that man can love God above all things. For Luther's opponents, man's natural *ability* grounds salutary *activity* before God. Only as it is clear that man possesses no soteriological resources for initiating his saving relationship with God is it possible to overcome the conclusions drawn in the *facere quod in se est*" (*Homo Spiritualis*, p. 193). See also pp. 189–195 and Baylor, *Action and Person*, pp. 173–177. Baylor argues (pp. 175–176)

unclear from this passage is the extent to which grace is operative in helping the individual to reach this point.

A passage from Luther's exegesis of 3:7 offers another example of the notion that the individual can prepare for conversion by acknowledging his need for help. The passage also demonstrates how closely related are the themes of rejection of grace and preparation for conversion. He writes:

> This is like the case of the doctor (as Persius tells us) who wishes to heal his patient, but finds that he is a man who denies that he is sick, calling the doctor a fool and an even sicker person than himself for presuming to cure a healthy man. And because of the man's resistance the doctor cannot get around to recommending his skill and his medicine. For he could do so only if the sick man would admit his illness and permit him to cure him by saying, "I certainly am sick in order that you may be praised, that is, be a man of health and be spoken of as such, that is, when you have healed me."
>
> Thus, these ungodly and arrogant men, although they are sick before God, seem most healthy to themselves. Therefore they not only reject God as their physician, but they even regard Him as a fool and a liar and even sicker than themselves for presuming to heal such wonderfully healthy men and treating them as if they were sick.[30]

If these people had previously experienced conversion in the sacrament of baptism, it is quite clear that they have now rejected that conversion. They are *incurvati in se,* turned in upon

---

that Luther misunderstands the position of both the *via antiqua* and Biel on the *synteresis,* since they did not place it in the will. The importance of Luther's references to *synteresis* for our study of his understanding of conversion is that they show he is moving to a clearer conception of man as total sinner. The *synteresis* still exists, but it is of virtually no power in directing a person toward salvation. Thus not only does conversion occur as God's work alone but the possibilities for man's passive preparation for conversion are decisively restricted. As Ozment has rightly noted, the limitation of the *synteresis* has profound consequences for the *facere quod in se est.* In WA 56, 500, 15–504, 7 (14:1); LW 25, 494–498, Luther launches a furious attack on *facere quod in se est* and the various false attitudes to which it leads.

[30]*WA* 56, 217, 8–19 (3:7); *LW* 25, 202–203.

themselves, seeking their righteousness not in God but in themselves. Luther describes them as ungodly and their attitude demonstrates that they are without faith in Christ. Yet these same sinful people would have been healed by God if they had admitted their need. Confessing that one is ill and in need of God's grace appears to be a precondition of conversion and justification. It is important to stress that in no way is this preparation itself the cause of conversion, but that the person who does *not* admit his need makes God a liar and demonstrates his own unreceptiveness. From this passage it is unclear to what extent this preparation involves a person's own efforts or is directed by that grace which illuminates him to a realization of his true position before God.

With these passages in mind, we may now turn to those that appear to negate the possibility of preparing for conversion. In a section of the corollary to 3:5, Luther emphasizes the same theme as in the *Dictata,* namely, that man is able to recognize himself as a sinner and a liar only by God's grace.[31] Only through grace can he attain humility and reach out to God in need. If humility or recognition of need is still seen as constituting the prologue to conversion, it is nevertheless quite clear that it is a preparation worked entirely by God. As Luther writes:

> And thus God through His own coming forth causes us to enter into ourselves, and through this understanding of Him He gives to us also an understanding of ourselves. For unless God had first come forth and sought to be truthful in us, we could not have entered into ourselves and be made liars and unrighteous men. For man of himself could not know that he is such a person before God, unless God Himself had revealed it to him. . . . Therefore, we have to yield to this His revelation, His words, and believe and thus declare them righteous and true and thereby also confess that we ourselves are sinners according to them (a fact we did not know before).[32]

This statement presupposes a concept of man as so subject to sin

[31]*WA* 56, 229, 20–32 (3:5); *LW* 25, 213–214.
[32]*WA* 56, 229, 20–25 and 29–32 (3:5); *LW* 25, 213–214.

that he cannot possibly achieve a true perception of himself. It is only through the action of God that man comes to see himself as a sinner and to recognize his need for conversion. In a sense, such a person is indeed already converted—preparation and conversion are blended into one. How does this passage relate to that in Luther's exegesis of 3:7, in which the patient is held responsible for not recognizing his illness? The answer lies in Luther's affirmation that man is most definitely capable of rejecting grace, thereby preventing conversion and remaining in his sinful and unregenerate state. Further, the answer lies in the mystery of God's election and predestination, the discussion of which Luther indicates is only for those who are already strong in faith.[33] In this passage from 3:5 room is left open for man's response to grace, his yielding to the revelation he has received, but the accent falls on God's action and on the fact that He alone can bring man to humility.

Luther also interprets the Law as God's means of bringing man to humility and thereby preparing him for conversion. In 3:20 he writes that it is the Law that gives man the knowledge of his sins: "Behold, thus it has come to pass that through the Law there is knowledge of the sin which is in us, that is, of our evil will which inclines toward the evil and abhors the good. How useful this knowledge is! For he who recognizes it, cries to God and in humility begs that this will may be lifted up and healed. But he who does not recognize it does not ask, and he who does not ask does not receive, and thus he is not justified because he is ignorant of his own sin."[34] The Law serves the invaluable function of bringing man from self-righteous arrogance to percep-

---

[33]WA 56, 400, 1–12 (9:16); LW 25, 389–390. This passage also demonstrates the strongly pastoral emphasis in Luther's theology. The discussion of predestination and election among those who are not yet strong in faith can lead only to despair. Luther's superior in the order, Johannes von Staupitz, was of decisive importance in focusing Luther's attention on the wounds of Christ when he was distressed by these theological problems. See his Lectures on Genesis, WA 43, 461, 11–16. For the influence of Staupitz on Luther, see Wolf, Staupitz und Luther; Oberman, "'Tuus sum, salvum me fac,'" and most recently Steinmetz, Luther and Staupitz.

[34]WA 56, 254, 9–14 (3:20); LW 25, 240.

tion of himself as a liar and sinner. The Law thus serves as God's instrument in leading man to the Gospel.[35]

Luther's discussion of the relation between Law and Gospel is very complex, and we shall touch on only a few aspects of that discussion as it relates to his understanding of conversion. Luther affirms that the Law conveys knowledge to man.[36] First, by contemplating the precepts of the Law, man learns what he is to do; second, the Law demonstrates to man how sinful he is, since he cannot fulfill its commands—thus the Law provides the occasion for sin.[37] While the former function is positive and legitimately belongs to the Law, the latter is negative, not through the fault of the Law but because of man himself.[38] When man, governed by the *concupiscentia* within him, gains knowledge of the divine commandments, he chooses to follow his own will, not God's. Thus he seeks his pleasure and his salvation in the things of the world. Through this inclination manifested in repeated acts of turning against God, the Law becomes the instrument of man's damnation. In spite of his positive assessment of the Law in itself, Luther can still write the following: "For the Law shows nothing but our sin, makes us guilty, and thus produces an anguished conscience; but the Gospel supplies a longed for remedy to people in anguish of this kind. Therefore the Law is evil, and the Gospel good; the Law announces wrath, but the Gospel peace. . . . The Law oppresses the conscience with sins, but the Gospel frees the conscience and brings peace through faith in Christ."[39] We do not go astray here when we see Luther to be speaking with the voice of personal experience, as someone who has experienced the agony of an anguished conscience. For him, the Law itself is not evil but simply

---

[35]See Kjell Ove Nilsson, *Simul: Das Miteinander von Göttlichem und Menschlichem in Luthers Theologie*, Forschungen zur Kirchen- und Dogmengeschichte, vol. 17 (Göttingen: Vandenhoeck & Ruprecht, 1966), esp. pp. 166–167.

[36]*WA* 56, 254, 15–17 (3:20); *LW* 25, 240–241.

[37]*WA* 56, 253, 22–28 (3:20); *LW* 25, 240.

[38]*WA* 56, 360, 15–17 (8:3); *LW* 25, 349.

[39]*WA* 56, 424, 8–11 and 16–17 (10:15); *LW* 25, 416. See also *WA* 56, 360, 24–361, 3 (8:3); *LW* 25, 350 where Luther again terms the Law good, but speaks against those who trust in it.

inadequate insofar as it cannot bring about the fulfillment of that which it requires; only the Gospel can accomplish that demand. A person may be able to comply with the Law in his actions, but he is not able to do so with all his heart, and hence his actions are not truly good.

Luther affirms that those who perform the works of the Law without trusting in them and as preparation for righteousness do well.[40] However, those who perform these works in the hope that they will attain salvation through the Law make a mockery of the Gospel. Throughout his commentary Luther emphasizes that the path to righteousness is through Christ. Thus, seen most positively, the Law brings a person to the awareness of his sins and leads him to despair of his own abilities.[41]

The following passage from 11:8 posits again that it is God who gives man self-knowledge: "For when a man knows himself, he does so only when God gives him light; and without God he does not know himself and therefore is not displeased with himself."[42] Self-knowledge and hence humility are a divine gift. Yet this affirmation is not new; Luther expressed it in almost identical terms in the *Dictata*. Man does have the ability to reject the awareness he receives through grace, but all preparation for conversion and righteousness is God's gift. Although there remains some unclarity and ambiguity regarding Luther's understanding of preparation for conversion, especially with relation to humility, we find in these lectures a much stronger emphasis on man's total inability to prepare himself for conversion and on God's total responsibility for that preparation.

Now that we have considered the intricate problem of preparation for conversion, let us turn to Luther's definition of conversion itself. As we have seen, he links conversion to both baptism and contrition. In his joining of conversion and contrition

---

[40]WA 56, 254, 19–255, 3 (3:20); LW 25, 241. On the *opera praeparatoria*, see Kroeger, *Rechtfertigung und Gesetz*, pp. 113–117; Grane, *Contra Gabrielem*, p. 333, and *Modus Loquendi Theologicus*, p. 74. Also Mogens Lindhardt, "Magna pars iustitiae, velle esse iustum: Eine augustinische Sentens und Luthers Römerbrief-vorlesung," *Studia Theologica* 27 (1973), 130.

[41]WA 56, 253, 28–31 (3:20); LW 25, 240.

[42]WA 56, 431, 26–28 (11:8); LW 25, 424.

and in his affirmation that man should persevere in his conversion there are elements of the monastic *conversio morum*. For Luther, conversion is first of all God's work, not man's. If he remains somewhat ambivalent on the issue of preparation for conversion, there is no ambiguity whatsoever regarding the responsibility for man's conversion to faith. Spiritual birth in baptism occurs through the promise God has given to man in the incarnation. After baptism, when a person who has turned toward sin turns away from those sins in contrition, it is because God has given him the grace to do so. Interpreted in a negative sense, however, conversion may be seen as very much man's own work. In this interpretation of conversion Luther follows in the footsteps of Augustine. For example, in the scholion to 4:7 Luther writes: "Here it seems to apply to the same thing that a person is iniquitous (*iniquus*) because of a turning away [*aversionem*] and a sinner (*peccator*) because of a turning toward [*conversionem*]; in the first case, away from the good, in the second, toward the evil; defiled in the first instance because of an omission and in the second because of a commission. . . ."[43] I suggest that Luther in fact tends to see conversion as genuinely natural man's own action only when it is toward the lesser instead of the higher good. For conversion to be toward the higher good and thereby toward salvation, it must be directed by God's grace. Closely related to the description of aversion and conversion as sinful acts is the Augustinian view of man as *curvatus*, turned toward the lesser good. Luther transforms this concept into *incurvatus in se ipsum*, man turned in upon himself.[44] Man is absorbed in self-love and self-righteousness. Whether he is converted to the worship of idols or to seeking his salvation in the created world, man shows himself to be a sinner by having turned away from God and toward the desires of his own selfish

---

[43] *WA* 56, 277, 15–18 (4:7); *LW* 25, 264–265.

[44] *WA* 56, 304, 25–29 (5:4); *LW* 25, 291. Rupp notes: "It is a distinction between Luther and Augustine that while Augustine speaks of the sinner as bent, or crooked (curvatus), and so bowed down to the earth, and to earthly good things, Luther regards this curvature as a perversion to egoism" (*Righteousness of God*, p. 165).

heart. This attitude is manifested in the arrogant striving for *securitas*, the very opposite of a life of humility.[45]

Luther also discusses God's manner of converting sinful man. He affirms that God does not convert man by terror but by a view of His goodness. The results are that "he who is converted by love is completely burned up against himself and is far more angry with himself than anyone else can be with him, and he is totally displeased with himself."[46] Man reaches true self-knowledge only through conversion. Only when he is converted does man reach the fullness of anger against himself as a sinner. To the person who is truly converted through love, Luther contrasts the individual who is converted through terror and fear and thus hates his conversion. Indeed, as Luther concludes, such a man is in fact not converted so long as he remains in this fear and hatred. He is not yet a new creation in Christ. God's conversion of sinful man is patterned after His action in Christ: "God gave His only-begotten Son for His enemies, so that He might make us burn with the warmest love toward Him and that He might bring about in us the greatest possible hatred for ourselves."[47] We saw in the *Dictata* that it is God's act in the incarnation that makes conversion possible. We find in the *Lectures on Romans* that it is God's loving work in Christ that provides the paradigm for his conversion of sinful man. Luther's entire understanding of conversion is Christ-centered and is grounded in the dual events of the incarnation and crucifixion. The incarnation is the greatest conversion of all time and makes possible human conversion to faith and righteousness. The crucifixion exemplifies God's loving way of initiating human conversion and evoking true love of Himself and hatred of the self.

For Luther the issue of the means or method of converting a sinner has important practical implications within his own immediate context. Undoubtedly influenced by the Reuchlin af-

[45]*WA* 56, 281, 4–9, 22–24 (4:7); *LW* 25, 268, 269; Grane, *Modus Loquendi Theologicus*, p. 81.
[46]*WA* 56, 474, 10–16 (12:20); *LW* 25, 466.
[47]*WA* 56, 474, 23–25 (12:20); *LW* 25, 466.

fair, he argues against the forcible conversion of the Jews.[48] Attacking the Cologne theologians and others who have heaped insults upon the Jews, Luther proclaims that these men should instead show compassion and ponder the judgment that they themselves may one day face. He adds: "They wish to convert the Jews by force and curses, but God will resist them."[49] In no way do their efforts at conversion follow the model of Christ's humbling of Himself or reflect the divine love He showed for man. This love should be the example for man when he seeks to act as an instrument of God in the conversion of others. Indeed, Luther stresses that the conversion of the sinful takes place through the Word. It is the living Word, not man, that does the converting—an idea that comes to occupy a crucial position in Luther's reform program. In his exegesis of 10:14 he writes: "For when God sends forth His Word, 'then there is power afoot' [*so geht's mit Gewalt*], so that it converts not only friends and those who applaud it, but enemies and those who resist it."[50] In this context the notion of force does come into play, but it is of a

[48]Luther to Spalatin, August 5, 1514 (*WA Br* 1, 27–29), indicates his support for Reuchlin against the Cologne theologians. Luther also wrote to Reuchlin himself on December 14, 1518, comparing him to Christ as one who has been ground down into dust but then built up by God into a great mountain (*WA Br* 1, 268, 20–269, 25).

[49]*WA* 56, 436, 13–23 (11:22); *LW* 25, 428–429. See also Lewis W. Spitz, *The Religious Renaissance of the German Humanists* (Cambridge: Harvard University Press, 1963), pp. 76–77.

[50]*WA* 56, 422, 7–9 (10:14); *LW* 25, 413–414. Luther's insistence that the Word converts even those who resist it indicates that preparation for conversion has no role; indeed, here, unlike other passages in the commentary, Luther appears to discount human ability to resist conversion. In this discussion, however, Luther is primarily concerned with distinguishing the power of the Word sent by God through called preachers with the ineffectiveness of the "Word" preached by those who are not called. The relationship between the Word and conversion is important in Luther's developing theology. The Word can be understood only when it is heard and received in faith, but faith in turn comes from the Word. The Word is both the object of faith and the one conveying it, but Luther does not systematically develop the relation between these two modes in his exegesis of 10:16 (*WA* 56, 426, 18–31; *LW* 25, 418). Gerhard Ebeling gives an excellent description of the relation among incarnation, *Inverbation*, and inspiration in the context of the evangelium in *Evangelische Evangelienauslegung: Eine Untersuchung zu Luthers Hermeneutik* (Darmstadt: Wissenschaftliche Buchgesellschaft, 1969), pp. 359–369.

very different character from human force. The power of the Word is such that it may indeed destroy the old man in Adam; but unlike human force, which destroys without building up, the Word also brings forth a new creation in Christ. In the conversion enacted by God, love and power are in dynamic tension.

In his exegesis of 3:4 Luther discusses the power of the Word in connection with *mutatio,* change or transformation. We found in our analysis of the *Dictata* that Luther at times wrote of *mutatio* in much the same way as he did of *conversio.* This parallel usage also occurs in the following passage: "For He justifies, overcomes, in His Word when He makes us to be like His Word, that is, righteous, true, wise, etc. And He thus changes us into His Word, but not His Word into us. And He makes us such when we believe His Word is such, that is, righteous and true. For then there is a similar form of the Word and the believer, that is, truth and righteousness. Therefore when He is justified, He justifies, and when He justifies, he is justified."[51] Luther's discussion may rightly be judged circular, since faith itself is a gift of God through the Word.[52] Thus God justifies man for that which He Himself has given him. He changes man into the very Word through whom he was given faith and righteousness. This change or transformation is but another expression for conver-

---

[51]*WA* 56, 227, 2–8 (3:4); *LW* 25, 211.

[52]*WA* 56, 227, 18–228, 2 (3:4); *LW* 25, 212. This passage and the one cited above have been the subjects of much debate, especially regarding the role of humility. According to Bizer, "Die Demut erscheint ihm [Luther] als die Voraussetzung der Anerkennung der Verheissung. . . . Man kann hier Fortschritte im einzelnen konstatieren. Der Begriff der Iustificatio passiva ist beachtenswert. Er bringt eine starke Betonung des Wortes in der Rechtfertigung mit sich. Wenn er sagt, dass das Wort dem Menschen seine forma mitteile und ihn wahr mache, so wird es einigermassen verständlich, dass Gott auf die Demut so grossen Wert legt. So wird es freilich auch verständlich, dass diese in der Tat eine Art der Gerechtigkeit 'ist'. Aber einen grundsätzlichen Fortschritt über das bisher Gesagte hinaus vermag ich nicht zu erkennen" (*Fides ex auditu,* p. 57). Bizer thus emphasizes the importance of humility in Luther's conception of righteousness and the reception of the promise. For a rebuttal to Bizer, see Bornkamm, "Zur Frage der Iustitia Dei beim jungen Luther," *ARG* 52 (1961), 15–29; 53 (1962), 1–59. Damerau, to some extent paralleling Bizer, writes: "Die aktive und die passive Gerechtigkeit: Gott schenkt die Gerechtigkeit dem Demütigen" (*Demut in der Theologie Luthers,* p. 180). Both Bizer and Damerau argue that Luther understands humility as itself God's gift.

sion, God's turning man to Himself through the power of the Word.[53]

As we have now seen, the concept of conversion figures prominently both explicitly and implicitly throughout Luther's exegesis of Romans. By focusing our attention on this concept, we gain a highly useful vantage point from which to survey his complex discussion of justification, the transition from a life lived in fear of the wrath of God to one lived in hope and trust. Christian life after conversion to faith is one that is gradually being transformed into the righteousness and truth of the Word itself. For Luther, Christian life involves constant struggle—and thereby conversion as contrition. Already in the *Dictata* he had characterized Christian life as movement and progress rather than as a stable condition. In Romans he affirms more explicitly that Christian life is not always movement forward and growth in grace. Indeed, the Christian constantly sins, and he may even reach the point of losing his faith, of averting himself from God. Along with the Augustine of the *Retractiones*, Luther passionately protests against those who interpret Romans 7 as referring to Paul before his conversion and thereby denying that ongoing battle with sin constitutes the Christian life.[54] This life is a struggle between the *homo carnalis* and the *homo spiritualis*. Conversion in baptism is "into" the death of the old man in Adam and the birth of the new man in Christ. Regarding baptism, Luther professes: "For they are baptized 'into death,' that is, toward death, which is to say, they have begun to live in such a way that they are pursuing this kind of death and reach out toward this their goal. For although they are baptized unto eternal life and the kingdom of heaven, yet they do not all at once possess this goal fully, but they have begun to act in such a way that they may attain to it—for Baptism was established to direct us toward

[53]On the idea of *mutatio*, see also WA 56, 335, 2–336, 17 (7:1); *LW* 25, 323–324. On this passage, see Grane, *Modus Loquendi Theologicus*, p. 96.
[54]*WA* 56, 339, 5–18 (7:7); *LW* 25, 327. Also WA 56, 349, 23–30 (7:17); *LW* 25, 338, and Grane, *Modus Loquendi Theologicus*, p. 33; "Augustins 'Expositio quarandum propositionum ex epistola ad Romanos' in Luthers Römerbriefvorlesung," *Zeitschrift für Theologie und Kirche* 69, no. 3 (September 1972), 305.

death and through this death to life. . . ."[55] Conversion in baptism thus places one in the midst of the fight to persevere in conversion, to become like the Word instead of acting out of the *concupiscentia* still within one. This point merits somewhat more attention.

Like Augustine, Luther affirms that baptism serves to wash away the guilt of original sin so that it is no longer imputed as such.[56] Original sin is not removed, but continues to exist. Indeed, Luther perceives it not merely as a tendency to sin but as actual sin, *concupiscentia* or *lex membrorum*.[57] Even after man receives forgiveness for the particular sin he has committed, he remains nonetheless a sinner. It is only by God's grace that he is imputed to be righteous.[58] In his exegesis of 4:7 Luther cites the

[55]WA 56, 324, 17–22 (6:4); LW 25, 312. Luther's scholion to 6:10 emphasizes the transition wrought by baptism (WA 56, 327, 20–24; LW 25, 315). Jetter writes: "Wir können wohl aus diesem Leben im Glauben wieder herausfallen, die neue Richtung verlieren; aber wir können dann kein anderes Leben als das schon begonnene wieder beginnen, keinen andern als den in der Taufe ein für allemal begründeten neuen ordo wieder, immer wieder von neuem, aufsuchen" (*Taufe beim jungen Luther*, pp. 317–318).
[56]WA 56, 284, 20–285, 1 (4:7); LW 25, 272.
[57]WA 56, 287, 6–14 (4:7); LW 25, 274. On this point, Rupp notes: "The weakness of the human will, however, is a symptom of the radical evil wrought by sin in the human personality. The human solidarity in the sin of Adam does not remove individual responsibility, for each human being has joined himself by his own deeds to the mass of sin. . . . Concupiscence here is. . . much more than the temptation to fleshly lusts: it is the orientation of the whole human person in its egoism, its self-seeking and its rebellion against God" (*Righteousness of God*, pp. 164–165). Rupp rightly emphasizes that Luther understands original sin as truly one's own. For Luther's and Augustine's interpretations of baptism in Romans, see Jetter, *Taufe beim jungen Luther*, pp. 1–32 and 255–330, esp. pp. 309–330. He points to a difference between the two which relates to Luther's exegesis of 8:26, where both baptism and contrition are linked to conversion: "Und zum andern: auch über die Taufe selbst denkt Luther anders als Augustin. Sie ist ihm wohl die *eine* Taufe des einen Glaubens, des einen Herrn, des einen Geistes und einen Gottes in der einen Kirche, die doch verschiedene Geistesgaben hat; aber sie ist ihm nicht im selben Mass das eine einzige Gnadenmittel gegen die Erbsünde. Sie wird oft in einem Atemzug mit der Busse genannt, die dasselbe ausrichte: auch durch Busse kann man in den Geist wiedergeboren werden; auch durch sie wird die Erbsünde bedeckt und der Glaube, ja dieselbe Gnade, die das principium conversionis schaffende Gnade, empfangen wie in der Taufe" (p. 321). Thus the conversion that occurs through penitence receives a place of special importance as the Christian struggles to fight against the "old man." Jetter's discussion relates directly to what we have found to be the important twofold nature of conversion for Luther as both conversion in baptism to faith and conversion as repeated event in penance.
[58]WA 56, 269, 1–4 (4:7); LW 25, 257.

Psalm verse: "Blessed is the man . . . whose offense . . . is lifted and whose sins are covered," and then he responds, "that is, the very tinder of sin itself, through the nonimputation of God because of the humility and the cry of faith for it."[59] In this passage humility plays a significant role in the attainment of righteousness. It remains a problematical concept in the lectures, although Luther appears most often to perceive it as being a divine gift. This development in his theology parallels his decreasing emphasis on the *synteresis*. Nonetheless, according to this statement in 4:7, faith and humility work together to prepare the way for God's act of nonimputation.[60]

It is clear that for Luther in the *Lectures on Romans* humility is one aspect of persevering in conversion. It leads the Christian both to confess his own unworthiness for grace and righteousness and to acknowledge Christ as his Saviour.[61] With the recog-

---

[59]*WA* 56, 284, 9–10, 12–14 (4:7); *LW* 25, 271. To the charge that such phrases as *propter fidem, propter confessionem,* and *propter humilitatem* indicate that Luther still retains aspects of works righteousness in his theology, Karl Holl replies: "Gott, der mit den Gaben des Glaubens, der Demut, der Reue, den Grundstein im Menschen gelegt hat, nimmt sie schon für das ganze Gebäude, das er errichten wird, und darum kann er über das noch Schadhafte hinwegsehen" (*Gesammelte Aufsätze*, I: *Luther*, p. 127). I agree with Holl that Luther's phraseology should not be mistaken as remnants of works righteousness, but I find the relationship between faith and humility to be more complex than he suggests. I am indebted to the editor of *LW* 25, p. 271, for this particular reference to Holl.

[60]See Bizer, *Fides ex auditu*, p. 51. Jared Wicks believes that Luther clearly articulates in the lectures that one is justified by faith alone: "On the precise question of what is that living faith in which one is justified, Luther's theology is as yet flexible and free. That one is justified by faith exclusively—on this there is no hesitation; but what kind of faith this is—here Luther has in 1516 not yet reached a fixed and final position that could be enunciated in a single thesis, though the themes of humility and utter self-abnegation dominate in the cluster of themes grouped under *fides*" (*Man Yearning for Grace*, p. 111). The problem is more complex than Wicks suggests. As we have seen, Luther sometimes speaks of faith alone, sometimes of faith and humility together. Bizer has accurately described the difficult problem; see *Fides ex auditu*, pp. 24–25.

[61]Gerhard Müller notes what we found to be present already in the *Dictata*, as well as in the *Lectures on Romans*, namely, that conversion to God means conversion to Christ: "Die nacheinander kommenden Stufen: contritio—oder nur: attritio—cordis, confessio oris and satisfactio operis mussten vor der Lebendigkeit Gottes ins Wanken geraten. Denn ihr Grundgedanke, dass vom Menschen her etwas Gutes notwendig sei, bevor Gott ganz gnädig werde, war von Luther aufgegeben worden. Statt dessen war Gott in Christus dem Menschen nahegerückt. Zu Gott sich bekehren, heisst nun für Luther, sich zu Christus bekehren. Durch ihn kann der Mensch geistlich bestimmt sein und muss er sich nicht mehr an der Welt orientieren. Nur in Christus wurde Gott nicht mehr

nition of his sins and of himself as a sinner, humility serves to bring man to the conversion that occurs in contrition or remorse. In the *Lectures on Romans*, as well as in the *Dictata*, humility continues to be an important concept in Luther's theology and to be closely related to both faith and righteousness.[62]

We may now consider some more general observations regarding Luther's view of Christian life or the life of perseverance in conversion. As has been frequently noted, for Luther such a life is constant movement, not a static state. He writes that "the whole life of the new people, the faithful people, the spiritual people, is nothing else but prayer, seeking, and begging by the sighing of the heart, the voice of their works, and the labor of their bodies, always seeking and striving to be made righteous, even to the hour of death, never standing still, never possessing, never in any work putting an end to the achievement of righteousness, but always awaiting it as something which still dwells beyond them, and always as people who still live and exist in their sins."[63]

Luther is also well aware of the doubt and despair into which a repentant Christian may fall when he is accused by his heart of his sins.[64] Such a person might even consider himself to be among the damned if he were to concentrate solely on his sin. Luther conveys in this context much the same kind of reas-

---

verniedlicht. Gottes Majestät und Ehre werden im Leiden und Kreuz seines Sohnes erst recht deutlich" ("Die Einheit der Theologie des jungen Luther," in *Reformatio und Confessio: Festschrift für D. Wilhelm Maurer,* ed. Friedrich Wilhelm Kantzenbach and Gerhard Müller [Berlin and Hamburg: Lutherisches Verlaghaus, 1965], p. 41). See also WA 56, 298–300 (5:2); LW 25, 286–288. With respect to Luther's theology in the *Dictata* and *Lectures on Romans,* Müller writes: "Das Reden des jungen Luther von der Demut des Menschen, von seiner Demütigung, hat noch nicht ganz den Werkcharacter verloren, der vom jungen Mönch gefordert worden war" (p. 49).

[62]As Wicks observes (*Man Yearning for Grace,* p. 111), it is difficult to define precisely what Luther understands by faith in this commentary. Generally, it is both trust in Christ and belief that He was crucified and resurrected for oneself, and it includes the affirmation of all those words of God connected with this belief. This understanding is expressed perhaps most clearly in WA 56, 251–254 (3:20, 3:22); LW 25, 237–241. For an excellent description of the various aspects of the word faith in the Romans commentary, see Wicks, *Man Yearning for Grace,* pp. 106–111.

[63]WA 56, 264, 16–21 (3:27); LW 25, 251–252.

[64]WA 56, 204, 8–29 (2:15); LW 25, 188.

surance to the despairing Christian as he did in the *Dictata* when he argued that God often allows the devil to tempt the faithful and impede their progress in grace. This temptation, however, is a sign not that all is lost but rather that God is lovingly testing his flock and seeking to bring them to a new degree of virtue. In 2:15 Luther writes that Christ acts as the defender of the Christian who is accused by his conscience: "For if the heart of a believer in Christ accuses him and reprimands him and witnesses against him that he has done evil, he will immediately turn away from evil and take his refuge [*convertit*] in Christ and say, 'Christ has done enough for me. He is just. He is my defense. He has died for me. He has made His righteousness my righteousness, and my sin His sin. If He has made my sin to be His sin, then I do not have it, and I am free. If He has made His righteousness my righteousness, then I am righteous now with the same righteousness as He.' "[65] By proclaiming Christ as his only righteousness, the Christian avoids falling into the sin of either despair or self-righteousness. Conversion in this context consists of the dual confession of one's own unworthiness and of Christ as one's Saviour. Luther characterizes such confession as the principal work of the Christian.[66]

---

[65]*WA* 56, 204, 15–21 (2:15); *LW* 25, 188. Describing the relation between Christ and the Christian, Müller writes: "Während auf diese Art und Weise jedwede Selbstsicherheit vermieden wird, hat Luther andererseits den Menschen durch den Glauben eng mit Gott zusammengebracht. Weil er durch jenen 'fröhlichen Wechsel' Christi Gerechtigkeit an Stelle seiner Sünde sein eigen nennen darf . . . wird er selber 'im Glauben' zu Gottes Werk, wie auch Christus Gottes Werk ist" ("Einheit der Theologie des jungen Luther," pp. 45–46). For a discussion of *"der fröhliche Wechsel"* in relation to justification, see Friedrich Wilhelm Kantzenbach, "Christusgemeinschaft und Rechtfertigung: Luthers Gedanke vom fröhlichen Wechsel als Frage an unsere Rechtfertigungsbotschaft," in *Luther: Zeitschrift der Luther-Gesellschaft* 35 (1964), 34–45. Baylor notes Luther's use of the term *cor* in place of *conscientia:* "For the young Luther frequently did speak about the conscience as though it were correlative to the 'heart' (*cor*), the 'spirit' (*spiritus*), or even the 'soul' (*anima*) of man" (*Action and Person*, p. 206). On this passage, see Grundmann, *Römerbrief des Apostels Paulus*, p. 91. With respect to this passage and humility, see Grane *Modus Loquendi Theologicus*, p. 71. See also Dorothea Demmer, *Luther Interpres: Der theologische Neuansatz in seiner Römerbriefexegese unter besonderer Berücksichtigung Augustins*, Untersuchungen zur Kirchengeschichte, vol. 4 (Witten: Luther-Verlag, 1968), pp. 211–213.

[66]*WA* 56, 419, 19–26 (10:10); *LW* 25, 411. Already in the *Dictata*, Luther linked confession to the new life; here, however, he describes such confession more explicitly as a work of faith.

Luther also describes the Christian in terms of the robbed and beaten man left dying by the roadside who is ministered to by the Good Samaritan and brought to the inn to recover his health.[67] The man is not yet healed, although he is on the way to full recovery. In the same way Christians still suffer from the wound of *concupiscentia* and must struggle to recover, but through Christ they also live in the hope and promise of sanctification.[68]

Luther affirms that with each new increase in grace, a change or transformation of mind is required. This change is necessitated by the fact that God does not give His grace according to man's standards but according to His own.[69] Thus, although the Christian may find it difficult to believe, the very struggles and temptations that he incurs may be due to God's grace. Christian life is never characterized by *securitas* but by *pax,* not as the world knows it, but as does the Christian who places all his trust in Christ.[70]

In his exegesis of 12:2 Luther takes the five Aristotelian stages in nature and applies them to the spiritual life of the Christian. He speaks of new birth, which we may rightly also call the conversion of baptism, and of repentance, which we may describe as perseverance in conversion. This passage elucidates several aspects of Luther's perception of the Christian life:

> For just as there are five stages in the case of the things of nature: nonbeing, becoming, being, action, being acted upon, that is, privation, matter, form, operation, passion, according to Aristotle, so also with the Spirit: nonbeing is a thing without a name and a man in his sins; becoming is justification; being is righteousness; action is doing and living righteously; being acted upon is to be made perfect and complete. And these five stages in some way are always in motion in man. And whatever is found in the nature of man—

[67]WA 56, 272, 11–21 (4:7); LW 25, 260.

[68]WA 56, 350, 1–17 (7:17); LW 25, 338–339. The passage testifies to the fact that Luther sees Christian life as a continuous war against the devil and one's sins.

[69]WA 56, 446, 11–16 and 31–447, 1 (12:2); LW 25, 438–439.

[70]WA 56, 424, 27–425, 5 (10:15); LW 25, 416. See also WA 56, 510, 11–511, 20 (14:17); LW 25, 504–505.

except for the first stage of nonbeing and the last form of existence, for between these two, nonbeing and being acted upon, there are three stages which are always in movement, namely, becoming, being, and acting—through his new birth he moves from sin to righteousness, and thus from nonbeing through becoming to being. And when this has happened, he lives righteously. But from this new being, which is really a nonbeing, man proceeds and passes to another new being by being acted upon, that is, through becoming new, he proceeds to become better, and from this again into something new. Thus it is most correct to say that man is always in privation, always in becoming or in potentiality, in matter, and always in action. Aristotle philosophizes about such matters, and he does it well, but people do not understand him well. Man is always in nonbeing, in becoming, in being, always in privation, in potentiality, in action, always in sin, in justification, in righteousness, that is, he is always a sinner, always a penitent, always righteous. For the fact that he repents makes a righteous man out of an unrighteous one. Thus repentance is the medium between unrighteousness and righteousness. And thus a man is in sin as the *terminus a quo* and righteousness as the *terminus ad quem*. Therefore if we always are repentant, we are always sinners, and yet thereby we are righteous and we are justified; we are in part sinners and in part righteous, that is, we are nothing but penitents.[71]

The new birth of conversion moves man from nonbeing to being. From other texts we have seen that it is through this new birth that man receives faith and the nonimputation of original sin. Yet, as the above text so explicitly states, this new birth or conversion is only the beginning of the process of Christian life, the beginning of the struggle, which is constantly punctuated by the conversion of contrition as man moves from sin through penitence to righteousness.

This passage illustrates the progress Luther has made since the *Dictata* in his perception of the nature of Christian life and the relation between God and man. Let us note some further differences in Luther's theology in the two commentaries. First,

[71]*WA* 56, 441, 23–442, 22 (12:2); *LW* 25, 434.

already in the *Dictata* Luther voiced his opposition to the belief that a person can in any way earn righteousness before God. This opposition becomes stronger and indeed thematic throughout the *Lectures on Romans*.[72] As one scholar describes it: "Here is a principal structural idea of Luther's exegesis—two radically opposed ways of life: the one lived out of one's achievements; the other lived out of God's gift to us in Christ. This shows us immediately one tendency or purpose of Luther's work—to convert and humble a man, to show him the need of a radically new estimate of himself."[73] Wicks rightly analyzes Luther's purpose in the lectures as that of converting his listeners, bringing them to an awareness of the falseness of an attitude of self-reliance and works righteousness. Rightly also he joins conversion with humility, for the two remain explicitly and implicitly linked in Luther's exegesis and theology. To this point we shall return. Second, although some ambiguity remains, Luther claims more consistently in the *Lectures on Romans* than in the *Dictata* that preparation for conversion is God's work in man. In the earlier commentary it was unclear how much one must do by one's own efforts, at least by attaining an attitude of humility as passive receptiveness to God, to "seek" conversion. Third, he now characterizes Christian progress much more explicitly and consistently not as steady advance but as constant struggle, a movement back and forth, inching toward the goal of freedom from *concupiscentia* and perfect righteousness, a goal reached only in eternal life.[74]

In the *Lectures on Romans* Luther as theologian and exegete is

---

[72]My own conclusions regarding both Luther's progress and his continuing struggle regarding the relation between humility and conversion are in large part paralleled by those of Martin Brecht, *Martin Luther: Sein Weg zur Reformation, 1483–1521* (Stuttgart: Calwer, 1981). See his excellent discussion of Luther's reformatory breakthrough, pp. 215–230. Regarding Luther's protest against reliance on self and works and his continuing emphasis on humility, in both the *Dictata* and *Lectures on Romans*, he writes: "Zwar weiss Luther, dass es allein die göttliche Barmherzigkeit ist, die nicht die Sünde, sondern vielmehr die Gerechtigkeit zurechnet, aber sie tut dies allein bei den Gedemütigten. An dieser Voraussetzung laboriert er ständig" (p. 222).

[73]Wicks, *Man Yearning for Grace*, p. 97.

[74]WA 56, 258, 8–14 (3:21); LW 25, 245.

very much concerned with the question of how one perseveres in conversion. As he writes in his exegesis of 7:17:

> For we are not called to ease, but to a struggle against our passions, which would not be without guilt (for they really are sins and truly damnable) if the mercy of God did not refrain from imputing them to us. But only to those who manfully struggle and fight against their faults, invoking the grace of God, does God not impute sin. Therefore he who comes to confession should not think that he is laying down his burden so that he may lead a quiet life, but he should know that by putting down his burden he fights as a soldier of God and thus takes on another burden for God in opposition to the devil and to his own personal faults.[75]

Granted that salvation through works is impossible, the Christian must still keep his post at the battle front if God is not to impute his sins.

How much responsibility does the Christian then bear for maintaining his life in humility so that he may receive God's gift of righteousness? Luther's differing statements on the relation among faith, righteousness, and humility indicate that he is still attempting to formulate an answer to this question. His struggle to reach clarity marks his exegesis throughout his lectures. As we shall see when we turn in a later chapter to his tower experience, it is also central to his personal quest to understand his relationship to God and what he must do to be regarded by Him as righteous. From the *Lectures on Romans* we do know that he has arrived at a profound description of the Christian on the road to righteousness. Such a person is *semper peccator, semper iustus*, simultaneously justified and a sinner. Between these two poles of the Christian life, Luther places the phrase *semper penitens*, always penitent. It means always converting to God from one's sins; always persevering in conversion. With this phrase he makes unequivocally clear that conversion is at the very heart of Christian life and of his own theology. Yet a key problem re-

[75]WA 56, 350, 8–15 (7:17); *LW* 25, 339.

garding conversion remains unresolved. To what extent is the Christian through humility responsible for persevering in conversion? For Luther's efforts to solve this problem we must forge ahead to the years 1517–1519 and to the *Lectures on Hebrews* and the *Lectures on Galatians*.

[4]

Lectures on Hebrews (1517–1518)
and *Lectures on Galatians* (1519)

Only a short time after completing his *Lectures on Romans*, Luther turned his attention to another of Paul's letters, the Epistle to the Galatians. He began his lectures in late October 1516 and completed them in March of the following year. Unfortunately, Luther's own notes have not survived and his series of lectures have come down to us only through a student notebook.[1] More fortunately, he decided to return to Galatians two years later, and in early September 1519 his revised lectures were printed. It is to these revised lectures from Luther's own hand that we turn our attention. Between the time of his original lectures and his revision of them, however, Luther also completed a series of lectures, begun in April 1517 and completed in March 1518, on the Epistle to the Hebrews.[2] Once again, as with the original Galatians lectures, we lack Luther's own text with the glosses and scholia. In this instance, he did not revise his lectures for publication, and so, of necessity, we must depend on the student notes.[3]

[1]See *WA* 57, II.
[2]Bayer argues for a dating of winter semester 1517–1518 and summer semester 1518. For his arguments, see *Promissio*, pp. 203–206; for a negative reaction to his proposed dating, see Grane, *Modus Loquendi Theologicus*, pp. 152–153.
[3]For a discussion of the student notes, see Hagen, *Theology of Testament*, pp. 6–7.

It would be difficult to exaggerate the importance of this period in Luther's life. In the midst of his *Lectures on Hebrews,* on October 31, 1517, Luther proposed his *Ninety-five Theses* for university debate. Although no one appeared for the occasion, the theses came to have a wider distribution and impact than Luther could ever have imagined, and thrust the little-known monk and professor of Bible into the forefront of German life. As we study his *Lectures on Hebrews* we shall see that he reaches new clarity on both faith and the role of Christ. These lectures elucidate many of the subjects that were intimately connected with conversion in the *Dictata* and the *Lectures on Romans.* Above all, he reaches a fuller understanding of the meaning of perseverance in conversion.

In these lectures it is difficult to separate Luther's statements concerning faith from those he makes about Christ and the Word. He quite literally perceives faith to be the glue between the Word and the heart of man.[4] The way to God and the knowledge of Him are through Christ.[5] Luther's Christocentric emphasis, already evident in the *Dictata,* has now become his absolute and guiding principle. For example, he writes: "For it is exceedingly godless temerity that, where God has humiliated Himself in order to become recognizable, man seeks for himself

---

[4]He writes in his exegesis of Heb. 4:2: "For these three—faith, the Word, and the heart—become one. Faith is the glue or the bond. The Word is on one side; the heart is on the other side. But through faith they become one spirit, just as man and wife become 'one flesh' (Gen. 2:24). Therefore it is true that the heart is combined with the Word through faith and that the Word is combined with the heart through the same faith" (*WA* 57, III, 156, 20–157, 4; *Luther's Works,* vol. 29: *Lectures on Titus, Philemon, and Hebrews,* ed. Jaroslav Pelikan; *Lectures on Hebrews,* ed. Jarsolav Pelikan, trans. Walter A. Hansen (St. Louis: Concordia, 1968, p.160) (hereafter cites as *LW* 29). Of these lectures, Rupp notes: "Faith is a master word, and it is now linked much more closely with another growing theme, that of the Word of God." (*Righteousness of God,* p. 203). Concerning faith, he adds that "Luther has more to say [about it] than in any commentary thus far" (p. 210). Schwarz, comparing Luther and Bernard, adds: "Die fides bewirkt in der Relation zum Wort die adhaesio, den raptus und die coniunctio. Während Bernard zwar auch von der Vereinigung des Herzens mit dem—allerdings im hohen Grade hypostasierten—Wort spricht, aber die vereinigende, vermählende Kraft in der Liebe sieht, bezeichnet Luther ausdrücklich die fides verbi als das Band der Vermählung zwischen dem Herzen und Gott oder dem Wort" (*Fides, Spes und Caritas,* pp. 308–310).

[5]*WA* 57, III, 99, 1–4 (1:2); *LW* 29, 111.

another way by following the counsels of his own natural capacity."[6] In these lectures Luther develops fully the implications for the individual of God's conversion in the incarnation, what he described in the *Dictata* as the greatest conversion. Throughout these lectures he stresses the importance of Christ's humbling of Himself. It is that action that makes possible man's transformation through faith. Indeed, in these lectures faith receives a much stronger emphasis at the expense of humility. It is through faith that a person "becomes like the Word of God, but the Word is the Son of God. In this way, however, it comes about that everyone who believes in God is a child of God."[7]

As I have said, throughout these lectures, Luther stresses both faith and grace. He does cite Peter Lombard, who maintained that all of man's wishing and asking is the gift of God's prevenient grace, not our eliciting will, but he places this traditional formulation in the service of a Christ-centered theology.[8] To extrapolate, it is not man's will or even an attitude of humility that brings about his asking for or seeking of grace. His very wishing, what we have seen to be Luther's transformed concept of humility, is itself the result of prevenient grace. There is now absolutely no question for Luther of any preparation for conversion, not even in the sense of a self-generated attitude of waiting; grace alone is the preparation.

For the Christian the Word produces all good works. Luther writes that "first His very purification . . . also produces penitence in us, just as His righteousness produces our righteousness."[9] Man's conversion to God in penitence is not his own act but the action of the Word working within him. In the *Lectures on Romans* we found that Luther was still struggling with the meaning of perseverance in conversion and with the problem of hu-

---

[6]*WA* 57, III, 99, 8–10 (1:2); *LW* 29, 111. Copyright © 1968 Concordia Publishing House. Used by permission. Perhaps Luther is thinking of the *synteresis* when he suggests that man by his own counsel is directed toward God, but in the wrong way, since he wishes to ascend to God without first going by way of the humanity of Christ. The term *synteresis* does not occur in the lectures.

[7]*WA* 57, III, 151, 14–16 (3:13); *LW* 29, 155.

[8]*WA* 57, III, 116, 1–3 (2:4); *LW* 29, 125.

[9]*WA* 57, III, 101, 21–22 (1:3); *LW* 29, 112.

mility as the necessary attitude that the Christian must manifest through his own efforts. In the *Lectures on Hebrews* we discover that he now sees perseverance in conversion as also God's work through man in faith, itself God's gift. Thus even humility is not the product of human effort but stems from Christ.[10] It is faith in the Word that purifies man and makes him to be like the Word.[11] Luther insists that even the testimony the Christian receives from his own conscience is not from himself.[12] At the

[10]*WA* 57, III, 114, 7–10 (2:3); *LW* 29, 123. On 2:3 and its importance, see Bizer, *Fides ex auditu*, pp. 76–77. Brecht perceptively describes Luther's stronger emphasis on Christ in these lectures and his deemphasis of humility: "Die Vorlesung lässt erkennen, dass er gegenüber der Römerbriefvorlesung erheblich weitergekommen war. Der Text des Hebräerbriefes legte es nahe, dass die Lehre von Christus und seiner Erlösung stärker als bisher in Luthers Gesichtsfeld trat und nicht mehr nur das demütige Verhalten des Menschen. Die starre Blickrichtung änderte sich. Zwar gilt Christus auch hier noch als das Vorbild des gegenüber Gott Gehorsam, aber er ist doch weit mehr. Er wird verstanden als das Geheimnis (sacramentum), durch das Gott unsere Busse und Gerechtigkeit erst schafft, als der, der uns in die Sphäre Gottes hinüberträgt und uns mit dem Wort des Evangelium leitet. Von Gott her kommt durch Christus der Impuls zur völligen Existenzwende. Er stellt die Gleichförmigkeit mit Christus her und nicht der Mensch selbst. Nicht die Werke des Gesetzes machen den Menschen rein, sondern der Glaube, der sich auf Christus verlässt. Christus ist jetzt der, der für uns das Ungeheuer des Todes mit seinem Sterben überwindet und von der Todesfurcht befreit und damit die Kraft des Glaubens manifestiert" (*Martin Luther*, p. 217).

[11]*WA* 57, III, 147, 15–148, 3 (3:12); *LW* 29, 152. See Schwarz, *Fides, Spes und Caritas*, pp. 303–305.

[12]*WA* 57, III, 169, 20–23 (5:1); *LW* 29, 171–172. This passage appears also to displace the *synteresis* as that which witnesses against man. On this scholion, see Bayer, *Promissio*, pp. 205–212, esp. p. 207. Bizer argues that in 5:1 Luther is still formulating his definition of faith: "Luther scheint die Vorlesung noch im Banne der alten Anschauung begonnen zu haben. Dann hat er bei Hebr. 5.1 das Problem der persönlichen Gewissheit aufgeworfen und dabei Ansätze zu einer neuen Auffassung des Sakraments gefunden, indem er es als den Ort versteht, an dem der Mensch Gewissheit empfängt; er empfängt sie im Glauben, obwohl der Begriff des Glaubens dabei noch nicht klar scheint, sofern der Glaube die Reinheit des Herzens und die Voraussetzung zum Empfang des Sakraments bedeutet. Luther scheint hier noch an die fides formata zu denken" (*Fides ex auditu*, p. 91). Hagen rejects Bizer's assertion that in 5:1 Luther is still thinking in terms of *fides formata* (*Theology of Testament*, pp. 82–83). On the importance of this passage, see also Kroeger, *Rechtfertigung und Gesetz*, p. 166. It is evident that Luther emphasizes faith far more in the lectures than in his previous commentaries. Perseverance in conversion now definitely means adhering to Christ through faith, itself His gift. Humility has been displaced as a requirement for this perseverance; faith is now the sole necessity, although humility may rightly be seen as the expression of that faith.

same time he continues to emphasize the Christian's responsibility for maintaining his life in faith.

Throughout his lectures Luther is concerned with correcting false ideas about the nature of Christian life. He strongly opposes the belief that man obtains grace as a result of confession and the reception of priestly absolution, as if these were meritorious works.[13] The Christian receives grace not "because he is absolved or baptized or receives Communion or is anointed, but because he believes that he attains grace by being absolved, baptized, receiving Communion, and being anointed in this way."[14] In conjunction with this affirmation, Luther strongly criticizes those theologians who hold that the Christian will receive the benefits of the sacrament if he puts no obstacle in the way.[15] On the contrary, one must not only place no obstacle in the way of the sacrament, but also approach it with a pure heart. This purity is possible only through faith in Christ. This faith is especially directed toward the fact of His redemptive suffering and death.

Luther emphasizes repeatedly in his lectures the importance of the individual Christian's faith. It is not enough for a Christian to believe that Christ was sent by God to act on behalf of sinful men, but he must also affirm in faith that he is one of those men.[16] Faith thus comes to include confidence regarding one's personal salvation. Luther opposes the interpretation of Ecclesiastes 9:1 ("how the righteous and the wise and their deeds are in the hand of God; whether it is love or hate man does not know" [RSV]) which applies it to the present state of the Chris-

---

[13]*WA* 57, III, 169, 23–170, 10 (5:1); *LW* 29, 172.

[14]*WA* 57, III, 169, 23–170, 1 (5:1); *LW* 29, 172. See Bizer, *Fides ex auditu*, pp. 80–81.

[15]See Helmut Feld, *Martin Luthers und Wendelin Steinbachs Vorlesungen über den Hebräerbrief: Eine Studie zur Geschichte der neutstamentlichen Exegese und Theologie*, Veröffentlichungen des Institutes für europäische Geschichte Mainz, vol. 62 (Wiesbaden: Franz Steiner, 1971), for an interpretation of Luther's rejection of the nominalist position and Steinbach's affirmation of it.

[16]*WA* 57, III, 169, 10–11 (5:1); *LW* 29, 171. See Bayer, *Promissio*, p. 207, and Bizer, *Fides ex auditu*, p. 80.

tian.[17] This interpretation can lead only to despair, whereas the Christian should recognize that he stands through faith alone, and that through faith he is conformed to Christ.[18] The passage in Ecclesiastes refers to "perseverance and future circumstances, which are certain for no one, as the apostle says. . . ."[19] Vain speculation about the future is to be avoided. The Christian attitude toward the future is one of trust in God.

Although Luther thoroughly grounds Christian life in faith, his doing so does not mean that he no longer sees perseverance in conversion as a struggle. Faith works and triumphs in man, but at the same time it is not easy for man to cling to Christ in faith. Faith is given to man, but it also becomes man's own possession, which he may reject. Luther stresses the importance of Christ as both the *sacramentum* and *exemplum* for Christian life.[20] As *sacramentum* He suffered and died in order to free man from sin. As *exemplum* He acts as guide for the Christian in turning away from sin and toward God.[21] Luther explains: "But the apostle challenges us with a twofold exhortation to enter this new life. For it is an arduous and exceedingly hard thing, especially for those who are inexperienced, to put everything, even life, on Christ. Therefore he sets forth the example of Christ, our Leader, who fights in the forefront. Although under no compulsion, yet for the purpose of buoying up our confidence He crossed over first of all, and He smooths the exceed-

[17]*WA* 57, III, 216, 2–9 (9:24); *LW* 29, 217–218. See also Bayer, *Promissio*, pp. 215–216, and Gyllenkrok, *Rechtfertigung und Heiligung*, p. 72. It is worth noting that Luther's superior and friend Johannes von Staupitz did not follow the tradition of using Eccles. 9:1 to inspire self-doubt and self-criticism in Christians. He affirmed that the passage should lead one to a present trust in God rather than into a frightened questioning of one's position before Him. Oberman presents this research on Staupitz's theology in " 'Tuus sum, salvum me fac,' " p. 373. See also Bizer, *Fides ex auditu*, p. 90.

[18]*WA* 57, III, 124, 9–11 (2:10); *LW* 29, 131–132.

[19]*WA* 57, III, 216, 7–8 (9:24); *LW* 29, 217–218.

[20]*WA* 57, III, 223, 1–4; 24–224, 4 (10:19); *LW* 29, 225–226.

[21]On this passage, Bizer writes: "Danach aber erfolgt allerdings eine fühlbare Verstärkung dessen, was er im Römerbrief über die protectio und das adiutorium Christi gesagt hat. . . . Die im Römerbrief nur eben angedeuteten Gedanken von Christus als dem Helfer und Beschützer werden deutlicher. Christus als der Helfer, als der Fährmann, als Person, die zu dem Menschen hinzutritt, wird deutlicher" (*Fides ex auditu*, p. 79).

ingly rough road."[22] Indeed, Christ acts not only as *exemplum* but as helper, holding out His hand to those who follow Him.[23] In a powerful image Luther affirms that the person who has faith will in fact be carried over on Christ's shoulders from this world to the next.[24] What thought could be more comforting to a frightened and apprehensive Christian? Yet Luther does not deny that even with Christ as his *exemplum* and helper man can lose his faith. The person who refuses suffering, who forgets the Word, or who congratulates himself on his righteousness has fallen away and is in a spiritual sense dead.[25] Particularly dangerous is the false notion that a person can follow the *exemplum* without first affirming Him as *sacramentum*.[26] To attempt to do this is to displace Christ as the *sacramentum* with one's own works. Christ is the Testator, in whom God's testament and covenant are fulfilled. Primarily as *sacramentum* but also as *exemplum*, Christ suffered the alien work (*opus alienum*) of God in order to bring forth His appropriate work (*opus proprium*).[27] More specifically, the devil "worked death in Christ, but Christ completely swallowed up death in Himself through the immortality of His divinity and rose again in glory,"[28] The Christian thus follows Christ as the *exemplum* and benefits from Him as the *sacramentum:* "For just as Christ, by reason of His union with immortal divinity, overcame death by dying, so the Christian, by reason of his union with the immortal Christ—which comes about through faith in Him—also overcomes death by dying. And in this way God destroys the devil through the devil himself and accomplishes His own work by means of an alien work."[29]

In his exegesis of 9:24 Luther affirms that the sacrifice of Christ as Testator occurred once and for all time, while the remembrance of that sacrifice and the spiritual sacrifice of the

[22]*WA* 57, III, 223, 24–224, 3 (10:19); *LW* 29, 225–226.
[23]See Wicks, *Man Yearning for Grace*, p. 201.
[24]*WA* 57, III, 224, 13–15 (10:19); *LW* 29, 226.
[25]*WA* 57, III, 148, 12–15 (3:12); *LW* 29, 153.
[26]*WA* 57, III, 114, 15–19 (2:3); *LW* 29, 124.
[27]*WA* 57, III, 128, 13–19 (2:14); *LW* 29, 135.
[28]*WA* 57, III, 128, 17–19 (2:14); *LW* 29, 135.
[29]*WA* 57, III, 129, 21–25 (2:14); *LW* 29, 136.

church itself as it suffers, dies, and is reborn with its Lord occurs daily.[30] While continuing to affirm the real presence of Christ in the eucharist, Luther displaces attention from what occurs during the sacrament to the need for faith *before* one approaches the altar.[31] Although Luther does not systematically develop in this passage his understanding of the relation between the sacrament and the preaching of the Word, he does stress the importance of hearing the Gospel, since it is through this hearing that faith is gained.[32] In a passage that both emphasizes the importance of the Word and condemns any effort to gain righteousness through works, Luther writes: "For if you ask a Christian what the work is by which he becomes worthy of the name 'Christian,' he will be able to give absolutely no other answer than that it is the hearing of the Word of God, that is, faith. Therefore the ears alone are the organs of the Christian man, for he is justified and declared to be a Christian, not because of the works of any member but because of faith."[33] This statement does not imply that Luther sees the sacraments as unimportant but that he sees their efficacy to depend on faith. For him, in contrast to medieval exegetes, faith as substance is far more than

[30]*WA* 57, III, 217, 29–218, 1; 5–9 (9:24); *LW* 29, 219–220. On this passage, see Bizer, *Fides ex auditu*, pp. 90–91. Hagen points to the centrality of the concept of testament in Luther's exposition of the Epistle. He emphasizes the significance of Luther's departure from medieval exegesis in his concept of the sacrament of the altar as testament rather than sacrifice (*Theology of Testament*, pp. 111–113.

[31]See Iserloh's discussion of Luther's understanding of the sacrament in these lectures on pp. 32–33 of Hubert Jedin, ed., *History of the Church*, vol. 5: *Reformation and Counter Reformation*, ed. Erwin Iserloh, Joseph Glazik, and Hubert Jedin, trans. Anselm Biggs and Peter W. Becker (New York: Seabury Press, 1980).

[32]For a fine discussion of Word and sacrament in Luther's theology, see Ebeling, *Evangelische Evangelienauslegung*, pp. 369–375.

[33]*WA* 57, III, 222, 5–9 (10:5); *LW* 29, 224. Feld interprets Luther's emphasis on hearing the Word in faith in this way: "Das Organ des Glaubens beim Menschen ist das Herz. Allein der Glaube schafft ein reines Herz. Im Glauben geschieht eine Vereinigung und Vermischung von Wort Gottes und Menschenherz. In diesem Zusammenhange bedient sich Luther einer stark mystisch gefärbten Sprache. Seine in den entscheidenden Punkten echt biblische Mystik unterscheidet sich von der mittelalterlichen und katholischen Mystik durch die starke Abwertung der Rolle des Menschen" (*Martin Luthers und Wendelin Steinbachs Vorlesungen*, p. 233). See further Bizer, *Fides ex auditu*, pp. 92–93.

a foundation for the obtaining of other virtues.[34] As he writes in his interpretation of 3:14: "In Greek the bread is called 'super-substantial,' that is, the bread that transfers us into a new substance and creature in the Spirit. . . . And even though this interpretation of 'substance' does not seem appropriate in the commendation of faith below in ch. 11:1—for there 'of things hoped for' modifies substance—yet even in this passage it cannot seem inappropriate. Therefore let us unite both into one; for through faith Christ is called our 'substance,' that is, riches, and through the same faith we simultaneously become His 'substance,' that is, a new creature."[35] It is important to note that Luther speaks carefully in terms of transference or exchange of substance rather than of conversion in the eucharistic sense as transformation of substance. The difference is a subtle one, but it establishes that although man becomes a new creature through faith, he also remains human, and thus open to the ongoing possibility of sin. Luther's formulation reflects his awareness that the person in faith is *simul iustus et peccator*.[36] What is most evident from Luther's exegesis is his perception of

[34]See Hagen, *Theology of Testament*, pp. 79–80.

[35]*WA* 57, III, 153, 2–4; 5–10 (3:14); *LW* 29, 156–157. On the importance of these lectures for Luther's understanding of the eucharist and the centrality of the concept of testament, see Erich Vogelsang, *Die Bedeutung der neuveröffentlichten Hebräerbrief-Vorlesung Luthers von 1517/18* (Tübingen: J. C. B. Mohr [Paul Siebeck], 1930), pp. 20–21. Brecht presents a unified description of the most significant ideas in these lectures in *Martin Luther*, p. 217. He concludes: "In Ansätzen zeichnet sich hier bereits eine neue Sakramentslehre von enormer Tragweite ab. Der Glaube glaubt die Vergebung durch das Blut Christi, anders ist sie, wie die himmlischen Güter überhaupt, nicht zu erhalten. Insofern kann der Glaube eigenartig als die Substanz des Menschen, seine Basis und sein Vermögen bezeichnet werden. Die Fortschritte in Luthers Theologie waren fast immer auch Frucht intensiver exegetischer Arbeit. Die Hebräerbriefvorlesung, die erstaunlicherweise kaum aktuelle Anspielungen enthält, dürfte die Voraussetzung für die reformatorische Entdeckung geschaffen haben."

[36]It is interesting that in what appears to be a most appropriate context Luther does not mention the word *conversio*. Although an argument regarding lack of usage of a term can be only speculative, it is worthwhile to note that Luther does not refer to conversion when doing so would be especially appropriate. He may avoid using the word because its traditional eucharistic associations would serve to direct attention to the transformation that occurs within the sacrament rather than to the transference that takes place through faith between Christ and man, which is essential if the sacrament is to benefit an individual.

faith as not simply the foundation for acquiring other virtues but the possession of Christ in the present.[37]

Although he definitely regards faith as a present possession and as that very living in Christ which itself constitutes salvation, Luther also differentiates between what the Christian has now and what he will receive. As he writes in his exegesis of 3:14, "faith begins this, or faith is its beginning; for through faith we begin to possess what we shall possess perfectly in sight. Thus below in ch. 11:1: 'Now faith is the substance of things hoped for,' that is, the possession of future things."[38]These passages from Luther's exegesis of 3:14 remind us of his discussion of the three instances of conversion described in Psalm 84 in the *Dictata*. Luther has now developed and refined his fundamental perception of the Christocentric nature of conversion. Whereas in the *Dictata* he spoke of man's conversion as one in which Christ is united with a person through faith *and* love, in the *Lectures on Hebrews* he describes man as becoming a new creature, indeed becoming Christ's "substance," through faith. In the *Dictata* this second instance of conversion was described as man's own, as the individual's conversion to God, made possible through Christ's conversion to man in the incarnation. In the *Lectures on Hebrews* this conversion too is seen as Christ's action, His giving man both faith and Himself. Yet this conversion is man's own, indeed his own possession. It is the beginning of what one day he will possess perfectly in sight, the conversion through clear vision described in Luther's *Dictata* exegesis. Thus faith gives possession but not yet full possession. Were man to possess all things fully now, there would be no distinction between this life and the future one. This affirmation would also deny the possibility—which Luther well knows exists—that man may turn away from the Word in sin and even reject his faith.

[37]Hagen writes: "In stark contrast then to medieval exegetes who define faith as the beginning of a process of adding love and hope to faith, faith as 'possession' means for Luther that salvation is complete and full to one who has faith. Faith is the first, last, and only step towards salvation. What for medieval theology was future and belonged only to the realm of hope and love, Luther regards a reality in the present. Faith is not of one's own doing or of one's own nature, yet it is really one's own 'possession'" (*Theology of Testament*, pp. 81–82).
[38]*WA* 57, III, 152, 10–13 (3:14); *LW* 29, 156.

In this commentary, as in the previous ones, Luther affirms that the Christian sins and repents. He knows that man can fall from faith and adds that "we are cleansed from this pollution only when we return to the Word."[39] As in the *Lectures on Romans*, he asserts that there can be only one beginning to Christian life, but that a person may fall and rise again, even as did Peter.[40] Luther distinguishes in his exegesis between those who have fallen from faith into unbelief and those who not only have fallen but seek their salvation elsewhere, direct their faith toward someone else. While the former may be restored through penitence—Peter himself provides an example—restoration is impossible for the latter.

In no way does the possession of faith imply *securitas*.[41] Perseverance in conversion remains a battle in which the Christian must not only follow Christ as *exemplum* but above all believe in Him as *sacramentum*. In his exegesis of 11:8 Luther epitomizes his understanding of this present life of persevering in conversion as both struggle in faith and victory in Christ: "And this is the glory of faith, namely, not to know where you are going, what you are doing, what you are suffering, and, after taking everything captive—perception and understanding, strength and will—to follow the bare voice of God and to be led and driven rather than to drive."[42]

Certainly in those spring days of 1518, as Luther completed his *Lectures on Hebrews*, he must have had a deep sense of being driven in an unknown direction. His *Ninety-five Theses*, intended for university debate, had elicited a response throughout Germany that he had in no way expected. Archbishop Albrecht of

[39]*WA* 57, III, 149, 2–13 (3:13); *LW* 29, 154.
[40]*WA* 57, III, 182, 5–18 (6:6); *LW* 29, 182.
[41]See Brosché, *Luther on Predestination,* p. 188.
[42]*WA* 57, III, 236, 1–3 (11:8); *LW* 29, 238. Contrasting the trust of faith with the false *securitas* of works, Grane writes: "Auf der einen Seite könnte man sagen: das Vertrauen auf Werke schaffte *securitas*. Unter dem Gesichtspunkt, von dem her Luther die Dinge ansah, könnte man aber ebenso gut sagen, dass die Theologen, die so grosses Gewicht auf die Werke legten, die Menschen jeder Gewissheit beraubten. Seine Lösung auf diese Frage, dass nicht Reue und Beichte, sondern der Glaube an die Verheissungen Gottes rechtfertige, lag ganz auf der Linie seiner Auffassung der Schriftauslegung" (*Modus Loquendi Theologicus,* p. 160).

Mainz had already sent the matter on to Rome for study and possible action, and the Dominicans had wasted no time in bringing charges against a rival Augustinian, proposing them in late January 1518.

When Luther turned to the revision of his *Lectures on Galatians* approximately a year later, in the spring of 1519, his future must have seemed even more precarious. Yet Luther never allowed uncertainty or the threat of danger to impede his work. His 1519 *Lectures on Galatians* offer us important insight into his theology during the early years of the Reformation.

In these lectures Luther has a great deal to say about the life of the *nova creatura* in Christ. As in his *Lectures on Hebrews,* he places great emphasis on the hearing of the Word in faith. Our discussion of his Galatians commentary will thus center on both his understanding of faith and his related concept of authority. With regard to the question of authority, we look toward the future and the complicated problem of determining how and by whom reformation should be conducted. With regard to his concept of faith, we find Luther to be speaking with more clarity and certainty about a subject that was already of major concern to him in the *Dictata.*

It is significant that in passages such as 1:13–18, where Paul speaks of both his calling and his conversion, Luther focuses explicitly on the idea of calling or of Paul's authority in preaching the Gospel. One might well argue that Luther is simply following the main theme of Paul's own argument, which is directed toward establishing his authority as an apostle; however, it is interesting that Luther lets pass a perfect opportunity to discuss the conversion from old life by the Law to new life by the Gospel. He is not primarily interested in the question of Paul's authority in and of itself but in the content of the Gospel he is preaching, which establishes and legitimizes his authority.[43] The parallel between Paul's situation—as Luther sees it—and Luther's own is important. Luther's authority as a preacher of

---

[43]Karin Bornkamm, *Luthers Auslegungen des Galaterbriefs von 1519 und 1531: Ein Vergleich,* Arbeiten zur Kirchengeschichte, vol. 35 (Berlin: Walter de Gruyter, 1963), pp. 20–21.

the Gospel, like Paul's, has been challenged, and like Paul, he can defend himself only by defending the validity of what he is preaching.

Luther closely links the concept of vocation with the content of the Word itself. He writes: "Nobody produces fruit by means of the Word unless he is called to teach without wishing for it. For One is our Teacher, Jesus Christ (Matt. 23:10). He alone, through His called servants, teaches and produces fruit. But the man who teaches without being called does so to his own harm and that of his hearers, because Christ is not with him."[44] Luther's self-understanding and sense of being called to public activity against his own desires are reflected in this passage. In these lectures Luther even affirms that the actions of a person who is called to a particular task are in fact the actions of Christ within him.[45] At the same time that he can speak of man as an instrument of God, Luther also asserts that the Christian remains *simul iustus et peccator*.[46] Indeed, this concept of the dual aspects of Christian life is developed far more systematically in the *Lectures on Galatians* than in the previous commentaries. Luther's earlier understanding is articulated now with new clarity and precision as he resolves the contradiction posed by I John 1:8 and 5:18: "The same man sins, and at the same time he does not sin. It is here that those two statements of the apostle John are brought into harmony. The first is found in 1 John 1:8: 'If we say we have no sin, we deceive ourselves'; the second occurs in 1 John 3:9 and 5:18: 'No one born of God commits sin.' All the saints, therefore, have sin and are sinners; yet no one of them sins. They are righteous in accordance with the fact that grace has worked healing in them; they are sinners in accor-

---

[44]WA 2, 454, 40–455, 4 (1:2); *Luther's Works*, vol. 27: *Lectures on Galatians, 1535, Chapters 5–6, and 1519, Chapters 1–6*, ed. Jaroslav Pelikan; *Lectures on Galatians, 1519*, trans. Richard Jungkuntz (St. Louis: Concordia, 1964), p. 167 (hereafter cited as *LW* 27). Copyright © 1964 Concordia Publishing House. Used by permission.

[45]WA 2, 564, 22–34 (5:4); *LW* 27, 332.

[46]See Luther's exegesis of 2:19 in WA 2, 498–499; *LW* 27, 233, and Bornkamm's discussion in *Luther's Auslegungen*, pp. 76–84. She details his description of the Christian as *simul iustus et peccator* and *partim iustus, partim peccator*.

dance with the fact that they still must be healed."[47] In this passage Luther conveys his perception of the relation between justification and sanctification. For the Christian both despair at the recognition of his sin and security in the fact of his imputed sinlessness are foreclosed. Christian life as process continues to involve both the conversion of repentance and the gradual healing, sanctification, worked by God.

This life as *simul iustus et peccator* is possible only through faith. Man's efforts to fulfill the Law in an attempt to earn righteousness *coram Deo* are doomed to failure. In terms of both action and intent, man is unable to follow the commandments of the Law. As Luther stresses in his *Lectures on Hebrews,* it is faith alone that sets one free from the impurity of one's heart.[48] With Paul, Luther insists that "faith in Christ is all that is necessary for our righteousness."[49] These lectures, however, unlike the *Dictata* and *Lectures on Romans,* contain no suggestion that righteousness is gained through faith and humility. Nor does Luther refer to humility when he writes of man's initial reception of faith: "It is our function passively to receive God and His working within us. . . . Thus our knowing is a being known by God, who has also worked this very knowing within us. (For Paul is speaking of faith.) Therefore God has known us first."[50] The thrust of Luther's statement is to dispel any thought of preparation for faith. God precedes man in everything, including the preparation of man's heart to receive faith.

Luther also closely follows Paul in describing the consequences of righteousness through faith. As we have seen many times throughout the commentaries, righteousness does not mean that man is free to do whatever he pleases. In gratitude for the righteousness he has received and in the freedom from having to earn merit before God, he can act as a Christ to his neighbor—thus fulfilling the true intent of the Law.[51] In the same way

---

[47]WA 2, 592, 15–21 (5:22); *LW* 27, 372.
[48]WA 2, 469, 7–8 (1:13, 14); *LW* 27, 188.
[49]WA 2, 485, 22–23 (2:11–13); *LW* 27, 213.
[50]WA 2, 539, 5–10 (4:9); *LW* 27, 294.
[51]WA 2, 576, 4–6 (5:14); *LW* 27, 349. In comparing this work with the *Lectures on Romans,* Grane writes: "Der Ton ist unbefangener, der Kampf gegen die Eigengerechtigkeit ist weniger engagiert, weil die Gerechtigkeit aus dem

that Paul inveighed against those who sought to lead the Galatians into a new slavery by their assertions that righteousness depends on the observance of certain laws, Luther protests against the tyranny of laws and of a tradition that prevents trust in Christ alone for one's salvation. He protests: "For how many souls are strangled and perish every day on account of this one tradition which forbids wives to all priests without any distinction! It is horrible to contemplate the offenses as well as the perils caused by this one law. Similar to this are the many others, which are simply the handmaids of sin, death, and hell, to say nothing meanwhile of the loss of sincere godliness, which has gradually died away under the tyranny of these laws."[52] Luther is not advocating that all priests should race to the marriage altar, but that the prohibition against priestly marriages should not be regarded as a divine law, which one must obey in order to earn righteousness. For Luther, as for Paul, the true purpose of the Law is to drive men to Christ, who alone is able to make them righteous.[53] This Law, given by God to man, is not to be confused with those human traditions and customs to which man has falsely ascribed the authority of divine Law.

Following Paul, throughout his *Lectures on Galatians* Luther is dedicated to teaching that salvation is dependent on faith, which in turn is gained through the hearing of the Word. The Word is the power of God that acts upon man to transform him into a new creature, and where the Word is not preached, and thus not heard, there can be no salvation. Luther is thus concerned with correcting those who teach that there are alternative routes to salvation. Indulgences provide only one example of a new and dangerous legalism that pretends to offer the possibility of righteousness. In reaction to this legalism, Luther argues that the proclamation of the Word must be reinstated as the center of Christian life and the source of faith and righteousness. As he

---

Glauben selbstverständlicher ist. An Stelle der ewigen Betonung der *humilitas* tritt die *libertas* in den Vordergrund" (*Modus Loquendi Theologicus*, p. 120). Grane is referring to the lectures of 1516–1517, but what he says applies also to the 1519 Commentary.

[52] *WA* 2, 616, 28–34 (6:18); *LW* 27, 408.
[53] *WA* 2, 528, 1–3 (3:23); *LW* 27, 277.

says: "For only that work is good which proceeds from a good and pure heart. A good heart, however, is born only out of grace. Grace does not come from works; it comes from faith in Christ. Thus Abraham's circumcision would have amounted to nothing at all had he not first believed. After he had been accounted righteous on the basis of this faith, he did a good work by receiving circumcision."[54] The question of how Abraham came to faith is not considered; what is most crucial to Luther is that he did not seek to earn righteousness through works.

In characterizing Christian life, Luther also joins together the hearing of the Word and the reception of the Spirit.[55] Hearing the Word has both physical and spiritual aspects.[56] He explicitly affirms that "the Word of God is not heard even among adults and those who hear unless the Spirit promotes growth inwardly. Accordingly, it is a Word of power and grace when it infuses the Spirit at the same time that it strikes the ears."[57] In order to dismiss fully the notion of any human preparation for grace, Luther cites the infant who receives faith. Stressing the Spirit, he writes that "if it does not infuse the Spirit, then he who hears does not differ at all from one who is deaf. Consequently, when an infant is not confused by other things, it is easier for the very sound of the Word—the sound uttered through the ministry of the church—to be operative through the Spirit. Then there is greater susceptibility on the part of the child."[58] The Holy Spirit unites preparation for the Word with its reception.

As we have seen in even this brief discussion of his lectures, Luther concentrates his attention on proclaiming the primacy of

---

[54]WA 2, 563, 26–30 (5:3); LW 27, 330.

[55]Bornkamm, Luthers Auslegungen, p. 65; WA 2, 509, 3–4 (3:2–3); LW 27, 249; WA 2, 536, 33–35 (4:6); LW 27, 290–291.

[56]Bornkamm, Luthers Auslegungen, p. 59.

[57]WA 2, 508–509, 1–4 (3:2–3); LW 27, 249.

[58]WA 2, 509, 4–7 (3:2–3); LW 27, 249. In this context Luther also emphasizes his opposition to any reliance on meritum de congruo. As he writes: "The Word, I say, and only the Word, is the vehicle of God's grace. For what you call works of congruity either are evil or the grace that produces them must already have come. The verdict that the Spirit is received from the hearing of faith stands firm. All those who have received the Spirit have received it in this way" (WA 2, 509, 14–18 [3:2–3]; LW 27, 249).

faith for Christian life and on combating the works righteousness he sees around him. Although Luther repeatedly emphasizes that it is Christ who lives and works in the Christian, he also asserts that the Christian is not a puppet or a shell within which God operates. A person may still turn away from God, renounce the grace he has received, and become a sinner before God, although he may appear righteous to himself. As in the previous commentaries, Luther perceives of perseverance in conversion as a battle. He formulates this idea beautifully in his exegesis of 5:5: "It is the whole man who loves chastity, and the same whole man is titillated by the enticements of lust. There are two whole men, and there is only one whole man. Thus it comes about that a man fights against himself and is opposed to himself. He is willing, and he is unwilling. And this is the glory of the grace of God; it makes us enemies of ourselves."[59] Sanctification is a never ending process in this earthly life, for we are "sinners as long as we are in the flesh and . . . in every work we need the forgiving mercy of God."[60]

Moving from the lectures on Romans to those on Hebrews and Galatians, we find that faith has become increasingly the central concept in Luther's exegesis and theology. By 1519 perseverance in conversion means living and acting out of faith. Faith, in turn, is the possession of Christ in the present and His working within one to bring forth good works. The question of man's responsibility for maintaining himself in humility is answered by faith itself. Through faith, Christ both is the *exemplum* of humility for the Christian to follow and, even more important, gives him the grace to live in humility before God.

Throughout both lectures Luther prepares the way for the conversion of repentance by repeatedly stressing that righteousness and salvation are possible only through faith. In the *Lectures on Galatians* he speaks not only as exegete and theologian but as a reformer. His authority, like Paul's, rests on the Gospel that he preaches. Thus he proclaims: "These are the matters that

[59]*WA* 2, 586, 15–19 (5:17); *LW* 27, 364.
[60]*WA* 2, 587, 16–17 (5:18); *LW* 27, 365.

should have been treated among the people, and treated in the order in which they are presented by the apostle, namely, that those who despair of their own strength hear the Word of faith first; that those who hear, believe; that those who believe, invoke; that those who invoke, be heard; that those who have been heard, receive the spirit of love; that after receiving the spirit they walk in the spirit and do not perform the desires of the flesh but crucify them; and that those who have been crucified, arise with Christ and possess the kingdom of God."[61]

Luther's energy is now directed toward making clear the need for conversion, the return in penitence to trust in Christ for one's righteousness and the turning away from any effort to attain salvation through works. By so doing, Luther has brought to its full development the understanding he obtained in the course of his exegesis of the Psalms, namely, that the conversion that occurred in the incarnation alone makes possible both man's conversion and his life in faith, his perseverance in conversion. Let us now follow the course of this development in Luther's other writings, through September 1516.

[61]WA 2, 591, 32–37 (5:22); LW 27, 371–372.

[5]

Early Writings and Sermons
(1501–September 1516)

Before the indulgences controversy of 1517 and in the same years in which Luther was lecturing on the Psalms and the Epistle to the Romans, he was an exceedingly active man with a variety of responsibilities. He was frequently called upon to preach, first in the Augustinian cloister and later in the City Church.[1] At the meeting of the Augustinian chapter at Cologne in 1512 he was elected subprior of the Wittenberg monastery, and at the next meeting, in Gotha in 1515, he was named district vicar.[2] Occupied by these monastic duties, Luther complained,

---

[1]Some uncertainty remains regarding the circumstances and precise date of Luther's first sermon in the City Church, although there is general agreement that he began to preach there in 1514. See E. G. Schwiebert, *Luther and His Times: The Reformation from a New Perspective* (St. Louis: Concordia, 1950), p. 282, and Brecht, *Martin Luther*, who writes: "Die ersten sicher datierbaren Predigten sind aus dem Jahr 1514 erhalten. Damals scheint Luther auch den städtischen Predigtauftrag übernommen zu haben" (p. 150). Helmar Junghans offers a more detailed description of the circumstances: "Denn bald bittet ihn der Rat der Stadt Wittenberg, in der Pfarrkirche zu predigen. Er sträubt sich dagegen, übernimmt aber schliesslich diese Aufgabe, von der wir wissen, dass er sie mindestens seit 1514 wahrnimmt. Meist wird angenommen, Luther habe in Vertretung des Stadtpfarrers gepredigt, der dafür nicht geeignet gewesen sei. Da Luther aber 1522 behauptet, der Rat der Stadt habe ihn berufen, ist eher daran zu denken, dass Luther die Stelle eines Prädikanten innehat. Sie bringt ihm die Predigtverpflichtung in der Stadtkirche, so dass sie Luthers eigentliche Predigtkirche wird" (*Wittenberg als Lutherstadt* [Berlin: Union, 1979], pp. 79–80).

[2]Brecht, *Martin Luther*, p. 155.

like many an administrator before and after him, that he did nothing but write letters.[3]

The letters, sermons, and other works from these years provide us with important evidence about Luther's personal and theological development.[4] The disputation theses submitted by Bartholomäus Bernhardi of Feldkirch are generally regarded, and rightly so, as a reform writing. Luther himself did not write the theses, but Bernhardi attributed to him the theology presented in them. Luther also presided over the disputation, and in a letter to his friend Johann Lang he took pains to defend the ideas expressed in the theses and to substantiate the attack on the theology of Gabriel Biel.[5] Although Luther had previously proposed changes in the university curriculum and had criticized aspects of both ecclesiastical doctrine and practice, he had formulated no systematic statement of his reform ideas. The Bernhardi disputation embodies Luther's chief criticisms of nominalist theology, most especially the concept of merit. The theses mark the *terminus ad quem* of this chapter, and as a reform writing serve as the transition into the more familiar reform documents of 1517, the *Disputation against Scholastic Theology* of September 4 and the *Disputation on the Power and Efficacy of Indulgences,* more popularly known as the *Ninety-five Theses,* of October 31.

From the time of the Bernhardi theses Luther as a reformer articulated and defended publicly what he perceived to be the theology of Paul and the early church fathers. In his developing theology, however, the old and the new exist side by side. There are points in common between Luther's earliest writings (his

---

[3]*WA Br* 1, 72, 4–6; *Luther's Works,* vol. 48: *Letters I,* ed. and trans. Gottfried Krodel (Philadelphia: Fortress Press, 1963), p. 27 (hereafter cited as *LW* 48). Although this letter was written on October 26, 1516, his complaint certainly applies to times well before that date.

[4]Of the many treatments of Luther's early career as a professor, see Boehmer, *Junge Luther,* pp. 77–139; Robert Herndon Fife, *The Revolt of Martin Luther* (New York: Columbia University Press, 1957), pp. 179–244, and Brecht, *Martin Luther,* pp. 129–172. On Luther's early sermons, see Elmer C. Kiessling, *The Early Sermons of Luther and Their Relation to the Pre-Reformation Sermon* (Grand Rapids, Mich.: Zondervan, 1935).

[5]*WA Br* 1, 65–67.

attack on free will, for example) and his later letters and sermons. Still, there is a major difference between the young professor of the *Dictata,* struggling with the question of preparation for conversion, and the expositor of Hebrews and Galatians, emphasizing to his readers and listeners that faith constitutes perseverance in conversion. In the various writings considered in this and the following chapter we shall see that Luther was still concerned with many of the same questions and problems that had engaged him in the biblical commentaries. In these writings, too, conversion and issues connected with it are very much on Luther's mind.

Scholars continue to disagree about which sermon should be accepted as earliest and whether the first letter from Luther's hand should be dated 1501 or later. In individual instances, we shall note discrepancies in the dating of a particular letter or sermon, but we shall not attempt to settle disputes. With few exceptions, however, these writings fall between 1513 and autumn 1516, thus paralleling Luther's work on the *Dictata* and *Lectures on Romans.*

As in the early commentaries, the most difficult problem with regard to conversion in these writings centers on preparation. Several of his sermons offer differing responses to this problem.

In a sermon delivered on St. Stephen's Day, December 26, 1514, Luther discusses the role of the *synteresis.*[6] Already at this early point in his theological work there is a blend of old and new directions.[7] It is undeniable that Luther affirms that man

[6]WA 1, 30–37 (*Sermo de propria sapientia et voluntate,* on Matt. 23:24). For the dating of this sermon and others I have followed Kurt Aland, *Hilfsbuch zum Lutherstudium,* 3d rev. and expanded ed. (Witten: Luther-Verlag, 1970).

[7]Of this combination of old and new, Ozment writes: "Despite his positive conclusions about the *synteresis,* there remains in this sermon a very uneasy tension between the 'alien, covering' righteousness of Christ and man's innate *synteresis.* In one sense they are allies; in another, however, deadly enemies. Even the best in man can lead him to hell" ("Luther and the Late Middle Ages," p. 137). On Luther's early sermons to 1516, Kiessling writes: "It would be difficult to find a single adequate term to characterize them all, yet they all have certain features in common. For instance, they unmistakably betray their author. Only Luther could have poured out these intense, outspoken, colorful effusions. Another striking characteristic is their tone of high ethical seriousness. . . . But perhaps the most distinctive feature of all these sermons is the impress of scho-

has an innate tendency that directs him toward salvation, but he does not define precisely how much influence or power it has. On the one hand, Luther asserts that the *synteresis* is the remnant in man which is capable of being restored through grace. If God had not left this "seed" in man, he would have become a Sodom.[8] This "seed" is the part in man which naturally wills the good, and which in its dual aspects as *synteresis rationis et voluntatis* is conformed to the wisdom and will of God.[9] Through the *synteresis* a person can at the very least prepare himself in a significant way for conversion and thereafter can continue to aid in his own attainment of salvation. However, this positive assessment of the *synteresis* as the part of the reason and the will that can achieve conformity with God is counterbalanced by Luther's statement that the *total* will is deficient in loving the good and the *total* reason in knowing the right and true.[10] Two other statements diminish further the role of the *synteresis*. First, Luther maintains that man can be saved only through Christ.[11] Second, although all men want to be saved, not all recognize the way to be saved.[12] Thus the *synteresis* can lead man astray by allowing him to think he can attain salvation in his own way. The affirmation that man is saved only through Christ's action is not compatible with the suggestion that man by virtue of the *synteresis* can contribute to the attainment of righteousness. In this same sermon Luther also asserts that the Law gives knowledge of sin, but that this knowledge is unable to conquer sin. Instead, man must despair of himself and humbly appeal to Christ for help.[13] Luther does not discuss the precise relation between humility and

---

lasticism—in form and treatment, and often also in material. . . . We may therefore look upon the earliest sermons chiefly as examples of the scholastic heritage in Luther, the preacher" (*Early Sermons of Luther*, pp. 77–78).

[8]*WA* 1, 32, 1–6, 8–11 (Sermon on Matt. 23:24).

[9]On the basis of Luther's statements, Ozment concludes: "Human nature, therefore, because of the *synteresis*, remains capable of 'revivification,' if only no obstacle is placed to grace. Indeed, right or errant willing apparently not only initiates but determines salvation and reprobation" (*Homo Spiritualis*, p. 141).

[10]*WA*, 1, 36, 13–19 (Sermon on Matt. 23:24); Ozment, *Homo Spiritualis*, pp. 141–142.

[11]*WA* 1, 31, 3–8; see also 36, 6–11 (Sermon on Matt. 23:24).

[12]*WA* 1, 30, 31–31, 2 (Sermon on Matt. 23:24).

[13]*WA* 1, 35, 34–39 (Sermon on Matt. 23:24).

the *synteresis.* It is unclear whether humility results from the working of the *synteresis* or is in fact at the core of the realization that one cannot attain salvation through the *synteresis,* but only through Christ. The context suggests the latter, but either interpretation is possible. It is evident that Luther does not yet consistently perceive man as a total sinner, incapable of taking a step toward God. He still sees a remnant of goodness in man, whatever its power to direct him toward conversion and ultimate salvation may be.

As we saw, in the *Dictata* the issue of preparation for conversion was closely linked to the concept of humility. In Luther's exegesis of Psalm 84 he also emphasized God's conversion to man in the incarnation, Christ's humbling of Himself as He assumed human nature. In a sermon from December 25, 1514, Luther reiterates the importance of God's act.[14] The affinity between his remarks in this sermon and those in the *Dictata* is quite clear. He writes: "Nor is the Word thus made into flesh that He forsakes Himself and is changed into flesh but that He assumes flesh and unites flesh to Himself. By this union He is said not only to have flesh, but also to be flesh. In the same way we who are flesh are not made the Word so that we are substantially changed into the Word, but we through faith assume Him and unite Him to ourselves. Through this union we say not only that we have the Word, but also that we are the Word."[15] Luther is concerned to avoid any hint of the idea that by becoming man Christ gives up His divinity. He is equally concerned to avoid the misunderstanding that through faith man is converted into deity in such a way that human nature is lost and man becomes divine. As we noted, Gerson voiced such concern in his protest against eucharistic imagery. Luther draws a distinction both between divine and human nature and between the notions of "having" (*habere*) and "being" (*esse*). Christ not only takes on or has flesh, but he becomes or is flesh. Through union with him a person does not have the Word—as if he somehow had Christ in his

---

[14]*WA* 1, 20–29 (Sermon on John 1:1).
[15]*WA* 1, 28, 36–41 (Sermon on John 1:1).

power—but he is the Word, in the sense that the Word now works through him. Luther speaks in terms of union, not possession. In a subsequent passage in the sermon he describes what is necessary so that a person may be united with the Word. In order to receive the Word, a person must forsake everything and empty himself, denying himself totally.[16] Thus, although throughout this sermon Luther explicitly states that man is not united with the Word by virtue of his merits, he does suggest that a process of self-denial is a necessary prerequisite.

Luther makes repeated references to humility in the series of sermons preached in German on the Ten Commandments, *Decem praecepta Wittenbergensi populo*, from late June or early July 1516 to February 24, 1517, but available only in a 1518 Latin edition.[17] In a sermon preached on July 27, 1516, Luther emphasizes the importance of humility in conjunction with the fear of God.[18] In another sermon, Luther makes humility part of an important sequence of events: "He who does not fear, how shall he be humble? He who is not humbled, how shall he acquire grace? He who does not acquire grace, how will he be justified? He who is not justified, how shall he be saved?"[19] Humility plays a major role in the attainment of righteousness, whether it is seen as preparatory to faith and conversion or as an integral part of perseverance in conversion. Indeed, Luther criticizes the abuse of indulgences since they subvert a man from reaching humility. Indulgences can allow a person to remain a Pharisee without ever reaching the humility of the publican. In a sermon of August 15, 1516, in celebration of the Ascension of Mary, Luther stresses that preparation for salvation consists in the acceptance of God's work. He cites Mary, who was blessed not because of her good works but because she accepted the good

---

[16]*WA* 1, 29, 6–10 (Sermon on John 1:1).

[17]*WA* 1, 60–141, 398–521. Aland, *Hilfsbuch zum Lutherstudium*, p. 139, dates the sermons from June 29 on, following the *WA* dating. Brecht proposes the date of July 2 for the first sermon (*Martin Luther*, p. 150).

[18]*WA* 1, 63–65; see esp. 63, 24–26 (Sermon on Ps. 113:5–6).

[19]*WA* 1, 429, 38–430, 2 (*Decem praecepta Wittenbergensi praedicata populo*). According to *WA* 1, 430n, 1 this sermon may have been preached on August 10, 1516.

work of God.[20] Before men those people are praised who do much, but before God those are praised who accept much.[21] In this sermon the same theme occurs as in some passages of the *Dictata,* where Luther wrote that a person receives self-knowledge and grace as a gift.

In a sermon of August 3, 1516, Luther offers his fullest discussion of conversion in the writings from this period. Although the analogies that he uses to describe conversion are simple ones, it is not so simple to understand exactly what he intends them to convey about the nature of conversion.[22] He describes conversion as a process that can be foiled by man's attempt to take control. He writes that when God converts a person, He acts like a music teacher who is giving a pupil his first lessons. In order that the pupil may become familiar with the instrument, he lays out before him the rudiments so that his fingers may grow accustomed to it. Once the student masters these initial steps, however, he withdraws and boasts to all about his musical ability and his talent in playing the cithara.[23] He is completely unreceptive to admonitions that he should learn more. Luther says that this act resembles faith, which, when it finds itself unable to move, withdraws like the misguided music student. After citing two other analogies, he comments that they are all descriptive of the works of carnal man (*homo sensualis*), by which God prepares and instructs the individual. Man falsely thinks that these works suffice and is unable to be moved and directed toward other things. In this text Luther focuses less attention on God's converting activity than on the false impression that man derives from this activity. Although conversion initiates progress in faith, man can through his own efforts reject this beginning and thus reject his conversion. Luther's critique is directed

[20]*WA* 1, 77, 27–32 (Sermon on Luke 1:48–49).
[21]*WA* 1, 78, 20–24 (Sermon on Luke 1:48–49).
[22]*WA* 1, 72, 38–73, 12 (Sermon on Mark 7:37).
[23]It is not surprising that Luther chooses such an example to make his point about conversion, since he deeply loved music. He had played the lute since his student days and believed that music could soothe the soul and help to drive away the devil. On Luther's own music and songwriting, see H. G. Haile, *Luther: An Experiment in Biography* (Garden City, N.Y.: Doubleday, 1980), pp. 49–57.

against those who think that once they have received faith in conversion they are secure and need make no more progress. This parable of the boastful student parallels Luther's attacks on *securitas* in his commentaries from these years and his repeated stress, following Bernard of Clairvaux, that to stand still is to fall behind. It also demonstrates his deep and unresolved concern, as we found in the *Lectures on Romans,* with the question of what man is required to do to persevere in conversion.

Throughout the sermons of these years Luther stresses humility, but humility consists of passivity or expectation and self-abnegation rather than of active, meritorious effort. In the text we have just considered from the sermon on Mark 7:37, conversion is God's work, but man can misunderstand and misuse it. Although Luther emphasizes humility or openness for conversion, and affirms that even after conversion man can reject what he has received, he denies that man can merit grace or in any way deserve justification because of his accomplishments. As background for the Bernhardi theses, Luther's comments of 1515 or 1516 on the *Collectorium in quattuor libros sententiarum* of Gabriel Biel are worthy of note.[24] To a lengthy passage in which Biel bolsters his defense of the *facere quod in se est* by referring to several biblical passages, including Zech. 1:3 ("Return to me . . . and I will return to you" [RSV]), Luther responds that Biel and his followers wish that what they say were the case, but it is not. Not even *meritum de congruo* is preliminary to justifying grace.[25] Man without grace cannot be converted. Regardless of

[24]*Luthers Randbemerkungen zu Gabriel Biels Collectorium in quattuor libros sententiarum und zu dessen Sacri canonis missae expositio Lyon 1514,* Festgabe der Kommission zur Herausgabe der Werke Martin Luthers zur Feier des 450. Geburtstages Luthers, ed. Hermann Degering (Weimar: Hermann Böhlaus Nachfolger, 1933). Grane proposes that Luther wrote the marginal notes between January and October 1516 (*Contra Gabrielem,* p. 367).

[25]*Luthers Randbemerkungen.* Luther's comment refers to L3. D 27. Art. 3. Dub. 2. Q. prop. 2 of the *Collectorium,* p. 16. Grane writes the following regarding Luther's position: "Luther kann nicht sehen, dass diese Worte, dass man sich Gott zuwenden, ihn suchen soll usw. mit der Sache an sich etwas zu tun haben. Sie bedeuten nicht, dass es, abgesehen von der Gnade, in unserer Macht steht, die Dinge zu tun, von denen hier die Rede ist. Er weist auf Psalm 13, 2 (Vulgata) hin: *Non est intelligens, non est requirens deum* etc. Hieraus, meint Luther, kann man ersehen, dass es nicht Sache des Menschen ist, sich Gott zuzuwenden" (*Contra Gabrielem,* pp. 363–364). On Luther's marginal notes to the *Collectorium,* see the entire chap. 9, pp. 348–368.

the preparatory role that humility and the *synteresis* may play, conversion occurs only by grace and hence only by God's act. Man cannot convert to God by virtue of his own natural powers. Luther articulates this position throughout the writings of this period, particularly from late 1515 onward. For example, in a moving passage from a letter of April 8, 1516, to his fellow Augustinian Georg Spenlein, Luther questions:

> Now I should like to know whether your soul, tired of its own righteousness, is learning to be revived by and to trust in the righteousness of Christ. For in our age the temptation to presumption besets many, especially those who try with all their might to be just and good without knowing the righteousness of God, which is most bountifully and freely given us in Christ. They try to do good of themselves in order that they might stand before God clothed in their own virtues and merits. But this is impossible. While you were here, you were one who held this opinion, or rather, error. So was I, and I am still fighting against the error without having conquered it as yet.[26]

Luther acknowledges that the false notion of earning righteousness by works and merit has intruded even into that order that prided itself on following the anti-Pelagian teachings of Augustine. In his next comments to Spenlein he stresses that the crucified Christ is alone responsible for man's righteousness. He then adds the warning: "Beware of aspiring to such purity that you will not wish to be looked upon as a sinner, or to be one. For Christ dwells only in sinners. On this account he descended from heaven, where he dwelt among the righteous, to dwell among sinners. . . . For why was it necessary for him to die if we can obtain a good conscience by our works and afflictions? Accordingly you will find peace only in him and only when you despair of yourself and your own works."[27] As in the *Dictata*, Luther points to God's conversion, His humbling of Himself, which alone makes man's salvation possible.

In several sermons from this period Luther describes how

[26]*WA Br* 1, 35, 15–23; *LW* 48, 12. Copyright © 1963 by Fortress Press. Used by permission.
[27]*WA Br* 1, 35, 28–34; *LW* 48, 12–13.

man is brought to grace and righteousness. He asserts that a person receives grace and comes to faith through the Word. In a memorable phrase from a sermon preached at a synod meeting in Litzka, home of a Premonstratensian monastery, probably in 1512, Luther states: "quale verbum, talis et partus: qualis partus, talis populis."[28] As is the word, so is the birth; as is the birth, so are the people. While Luther's statements in the sermon are in large part aimed at improving morals, especially clerical ones, he also strongly affirms the power of the preached Word. Indeed, he denies that any improvement in morals can precede the preaching of the Word. Since all rests on the nature of the message that is preached, whether it is the Word or a human substitute, the pastors bear the responsibility for the sins of the people if they fail to preach the Word of truth. Although Luther both places the Word at the center of his sermon and rejects any

---

[28]*WA* 1, 12, 20 (Sermon on I John 5:4–5, 1512 or 1515?). Bizer dates the sermon in 1512 and discusses it with particular reference to faith (*Fides ex auditu*, pp. 59–60). He writes: "Der Glaube ist hier nicht 'Rechtfertigungsglaube' oder 'Verheissungsglaube', sondern als die 'Substanz' des Unsichtbaren Mittel zum Kampf gegen die 'Welt', d.h. um die Reinheit von den bösen Affekten, Mittel der Wiedergeburt und also zur Sündlosigkeit. Der Glaube ist der notwendige Anfang einer Bewegung, die sich erst im Sieg über die Affekte vollendet, und die Voraussetzung des Gebets um die göttliche Hilfe in diesem Kampf; sein Inhalt ist ganz allgemein 'das Unsichtbare' oder 'Christus'. Es wäre nicht schwer, zu jedem dieser Züge Parallelen aus zeitgenössischen katholischen Predigten beizubringen." As Bizer's comments suggest, the sermon has been a subject of debate regarding its "reformatory" elements. Recently it has been the subject of scholarly controversy between Oberman and Grane. Oberman proposes that this sermon itself is a *Programm* or *Manifest* ("Reformation: Epoche oder Episode," *ARG* 68 [1977], 107–108). He proposes that through this sermon Luther already shows himself as a reformer of the church, and he notes the continuity between this sermon and Luther's reformatory theological writings. Leif Grane, in contrast, finds that Oberman reads too much into the sermon: "Zwar habe Luther in den Jahren 1513 bis 1516 noch 'den genauen Inhalt des Schriftwortes' für sich klären müssen, aber 1512 sei schon der 'von allen geteilte entscheidende Grundsatz formuliert' usw. (S. 107). . . . Luther betont stark die Notwendigkeit der Predigt; die Kirche könne nur in *verbo Dei* existieren. Ist aber damit wirklich ein 'Grundsatz' gegeben, zu dem Luthers Arbeit in den frühen Vorlesungen bloss die Klärung des genauen Inhaltes des Schriftwortes hinzufugte? . . . Die Predigt als Zeugnis eines Reformvorhabens zu sehen, zu dem die in den frühen Vorlesungen gewonnene Erkenntnis nur als Folge zu verstehen wäre, hiesse mit den Texten ziemlich frei ungehen" ("Lutherforschung und Geistesgeschichte: Auseinandersetzung mit Heiko A. Oberman," *ARG* 68 [1977], 312). We do not find in this sermon any indication that Luther has resolved the problem of perseverance in conversion.

power of human merit or even human effort to bring about the new birth, he does not go so far as to say that faith and the hearing of the Word are identical. In other words, there is no resolution in this sermon of the more subtle aspects of human responsibility in preparing for conversion or the new birth. As he says at the conclusion of the sermon: "Everyone who calls on the name of God will be saved; but he alone calls, who believes; but he alone believes, who hears the Word of truth; but he alone hears the Word of truth, who hears the Gospel; he alone hears the Gospel, who hears the priest as a messenger of God."[29]

The ongoing necessity for preaching is at the very core of Luther's understanding of life in the Christian community. We have already seen some aspects of this life. A Christian may neither seek to attain righteousness through his works and thereby displace faith from the center of his life nor simply sit back and rest in *securitas*. In his sermon on Matthew 7:12 Luther maintains that whether one acts toward one's neighbor as one would have him act toward oneself is a criterion by which to judge whether or not one will be saved.[30] Luther does not imply that by so acting one merits salvation, but rather that the person who is justified will act in such a way out of love and gratitude and thereby testify to his status.[31] In this same sermon he decries the laxity in moral behavior that has been caused by scholastic theology's definition of love as response to extreme need. He demands: "Just see whether what you wish is that the other person be favorable toward you in his heart and is content to leave it at that, without doing anything for you in deed. If not, then it is not sufficient for you either. For the Lord did not say: Whatever you wish men would do to you, grant it to them in your heart; but rather '*do* so to them.'"[32] At the same time, Luther also acknowledges in his sermons that man cannot fully imple-

[29]WA 1, 17, 2–6.
[30]WA 4, 590–595; *Luther's Works*, vol. 51: *Sermons I*, ed. and trans. John W. Doberstein (Philadelphia: Fortress Press, 1959), pp. 5–13 (1514?) (hereafter cited as *LW* 51) (American ed. 1510? or 1512?).
[31]WA 4, 594, 8–19 (Sermon Matt. 7:12); *LW* 51, 12.
[32]WA 4, 594, 24–28 (Sermon on Matt. 7:12); *LW* 51, 13. Copyright © 1959 by Fortress Press. Used by permission.

ment the commandments of God and attain to perfect love of Him in this life.[33] In these early writings there is an awareness of the Christian as one who does not attain to perfection but who in humility struggles to make progress and to fulfill the will of God. However, the interpretation of progress in faith as decisive for righteousness before God could also issue in self-doubt and even despair. In his later theology Luther retains the concept of progress in faith while dissociating it from the imputation of righteousness, but he does not do so in the writings we are now considering. He does, however, lay the groundwork for this shift by stressing the crucified Christ as central to Christian life. In a fragment of a sermon dated November 11, 1515, he proclaims: "The veil signifies the preaching of the naked and crucified Christ, so that man will learn to hope (to have faith) in desperation and adversities."[34] Faith is a constant source of strength as man continues to struggle and persevere in conversion.

Faith is a dominant theme in the sermons of 1516 as Luther sets reliance on the crucified Christ against a false *securitas* stemming from one's own works. In a sermon given at the end of March on Samson's riddle in Judges 14:14, "Out of the eater came something to eat. Out of the strong came something sweet" (RSV), Luther offers a fascinating moral interpretation. He tells his listeners: "Morally the food issues from the eater, when the man is converted and dead to sin. The same man who formerly ate dung now serves to others the food of the Word of God. For the person who lives in sins eats carnal food and drinks iniquity like water, but when he has been slain, he is able to nourish others. So it is with Saint Paul, Saint Augustine and in Psalm 50."[35] The person who is converted is dead to sin because he no longer lives in Adam but in Christ. Although Luther does not discuss in this passage precisely what constitutes conversion, he does describe what its consequences are. Only when the carnal man is dead and replaced by the new man in Christ can he devote himself to offering to others the Word of forgiveness and

[33]WA 1, 40, 15–18 (Sermon on Sir. 15:1, December 27, 1514).
[34]WA 1, 53, 2–3 (*Fragm. serm. in Die Divi Martini habiti*, November 11, 1515).
[35]WA 1, 60, 8–12 (Sermon on Judg. 14:14).

to performing loving deeds. As Luther also says in his sermon on Luke 18:9–14, the proud person grants contingency to God and sufficiency to himself, and the humble person thinks exactly the opposite.[36]

In a sermon on Matthew 6:24, delivered on August 24, 1516, Luther preaches that man is made righteous by God's imputation, since righteousness consists not in works, but in faith, hope, and charity. He also proclaims that no one is able to achieve self-resignation and abnegation unless he believes and confides totally in God.[37] In other words, freedom from self-concern is possible only after a person is converted and comes to place his trust in God alone. He expresses this same thought in a letter to Spenlein of April 8, 1516: "Even so, if you seem to yourself to be better than they are, do not count it as booty, as if it were yours alone, but humble yourself, forget what you are and be as one of them in order that you may help them."[38] Christian life consists in persecution and suffering as the holiest of relics.[39] Such a life is a true following of the Cross. As in the *Dictata* and *Lectures on Romans,* Luther frequently reiterates that the battle against sin is constant. So he writes on September 25, 1516, to Prior Michael Dressel and a bickering cloister of Augustinians in Neustadt: "That way of miserable and useless living comes either from the weakness of your humility—because where there is true humility, there is peace—or it originates in my negligence. As a matter of fact, it must be both your fault and mine, because we do not weep aloud before the Lord who has created us and we do not pray that he make our way straight in his sight and lead us in his righteousness."[40] In the sermons and letters of 1516 Luther demonstrates an increased awareness of the difficulty that even the stalwart Christian has in attaining humility and continuing to practice it. This recognition parallels what we found in his *Lectures on Romans,* that is, his preoccupation with the problem of

[36]*WA* 1, 63, 30–64, 3 (Sermon on Luke 18:9–14, July 27, 1516); *LW* 51, 15.
[37]*WA* 1, 84, 17–22 (Sermon on Matt. 6:24, August 24, 1516).
[38]*WA Br* 1, 36, 43–45; *LW* 48, 13.
[39]*WA Br* 1, 37, 15–38, 25 (Luther to Georg Leisser, April 15, 1516).
[40]*WA Br* 1, 57, 8–12; *LW* 48, 20–21.

perseverance in conversion. It manifests itself also in the formulation in the Romans commentary that the Christian is *simul iustus et peccator* and *semper poenitens*.

We turn now to the final work we shall consider in this chapter, the *Quaestio de viribus et voluntate hominis sine gratia disputata* of September 25, 1516. The disputation offers a succinct summary of Luther's theological development to this point. The theses and their corollaries contain a firm affirmation of Christ as man's only hope for righteousness and salvation and a concomitant denial that man can in any way earn grace, even to the extent of the *meritum de congruo*.[41]

In the first conclusion or thesis, Luther's student Bernhardi proposes that man, whose rational soul is made in the image of God and thus is suited to (*aptus*) God's grace, by his own natural powers alone subjects whatever creature he uses to vanity; he seeks only his own and what is carnal. In the second corollary to the thesis he affirms that the old man is called carnal not only because he is directed by the concupiscence of the senses, but because (even if he is chaste, wise and just) he has not been reborn by God through the Spirit.[42] This corollary appears to suggest, then, that even before rebirth or conversion man can attain chastity, wisdom, and righteousness. In this instance, however, Bernhardi is less concerned with resolving the extent of man's natural abilities than with establishing that whatever man's attainments may be, they have no value for salvation if he has not been reborn or converted. No matter how "good" a person may appear or even actually be (although the first thesis undercuts this possibility), he remains the old, carnal man until he is reborn by God's action.

In the second thesis Bernhardi expands on the two biblical texts, Habakkuk 2:4 and Hebrews 11:6, added to the third corollary of the first thesis. Both passages affirm that the righteous person lives from faith, and that without faith it is impossible to please God. He now asserts that the person who is excluded

[41]*WA* 1, 145–151. On this disputation and its importance for Luther, see Grane, *Modus Loquendi Theologicus*, pp. 110–115.
[42]*WA* 1, 145, 10–146, 16.

from God's grace can in no way fulfill the divine commandments, nor can he prepare himself for grace, either *de congruo* or
de condigno; instead, he remains necessarily in sin. Thus
Bernhardi explicitly attacks the nominalist position that man by
doing what is within him *(facere quod in se est)* can prepare *de
congruo* for grace. Bernhardi cites a number of biblical texts to
substantiate his thesis.[43] They present two main ideas: first, that
the Law is given so that man will seek grace, and second, that
man comes to God only through God's act. Any conception that
man can merit grace is strictly prohibited. In his first corollary,
he proceeds to demolish the anthropological foundation that
supports the belief that a person can attain even partial or con-
gruent merit before grace. He asserts that without grace man's
will is enslaved, not free.[44] This position implicitly denies the
possibility of any active preparation for grace. In the second
corollary he proposes that when a person does what is within
him, he sins, since he is unable by himself to think or to will in
any other way. He adds that without faith operating in love, man
can do nothing other than sin.[45] In his third corollary to the
second thesis, Bernhardi states that while the righteousness of
the faithful is hidden in God, their sins are made manifest in
them. Thus it is true that only the righteous will be damned, and
the sinners and prostitutes will be saved.[46] As he writes, every
saint is conscious of being a sinner and truly unconscious of
being righteous; he is a sinner in fact and righteous in hope; a
sinner in reality but truly righteous by the imputation of merciful God. The prostitutes or those who impute sin to themselves
and are prostitutes and sinners in their own eyes, confessing
their impiety to God and praying for their forgiveness at the
right time, placing their hope in Him and not in themselves, will
be saved.[47] These statements of Bernhardi express the same

[43]*WA* 1, 147, 10–36.
[44]*WA* 1, 147, 38–39. See further McSorley, *Luther: Right or Wrong?*, pp.
239–240.
[45]*WA* 1, 148, 14–15, 18–20.
[46]*WA* 1, 148, 35–37.
[47]*WA* 1, 149, 8–14.

theology that we found in Luther's *Lectures on Romans.* In Bernhardi's disputation and in Luther's lectures there is a thematic rejection of the notion that man can somehow actively contribute to the achievement of salvation, and the affirmation that man is dependent on God for righteousness. At the same time, both professor and student emphasize the need for man constantly to recognize his sinfulness and to confess it before God. We encounter in Bernhardi, as in Luther, the problem of man's responsibility for persevering in conversion; in other words, the question of how responsible the Christian is for maintaining his life in faith and humility.

It is dramatically clear that Bernhardi's theses and their corollaries oppose the nominalist perception of man as capable of earning partial merit, *meritum de congruo,* by his own natural efforts. They offer a sharp critique of the statement that God does not deny His grace to the individual who does his best. Behind both theses is Luther's fundamental belief that the person who strives by his own will to put himself on the path to salvation undercuts the necessity of Christ's life and death. In order to do good works before God, one must be reborn through the Spirit. In order to live righteously before Him, one must live in faith.

In the third and final thesis Bernhardi directs his attack against the scholastic weakening of the commandment of love.[48] He affirms that a love that makes itself known only in situations of extreme need is in fact an inactive love and not real love. In contrast to this inactive love, Christian love is constantly zealous for the welfare of the neighbor. In both the first and second corollaries to this thesis, Bernhardi asserts the power of Christ and His absolute centrality to man's life and work. In the first corollary, he posits that Jesus Christ, our power, our righteousness, who searches our hearts and minds, is the only one who knows and judges our merits.[49] To extrapolate, a sense of se-

---

[48]*WA* 1, 149, 20–22.

[49]*WA* 1, 149, 33–34. In this context Bernhardi quotes Eccles. 9:1 and appears to apply it to the present circumstances of the Christian. As we noted in Chapter 4, in his interpretation of this passage in the *Lectures on Hebrews,* Luther relates it to the future, not the present, lest it cause a Christian to fall into despair.

curity and continuous despair and self-doubt are equally inappropriate. In his second corollary, Bernhardi affirms that since for the person who believes through Christ, everything is possible, it is superstitious to ascribe according to human will one kind of help from this saint, and one kind from another.[50] As Luther was to pronounce ever more emphatically in the sermons and writings of the coming years, this practice distracts man's attention from the naked and crucified Christ and bolsters his self-centered opinion that by his works—in this case, offerings, appeals, and promises made to a particular saint—he can achieve the end he desires.

The theses for scholarly debate proposed by the aspiring *Sententarius* Bernhardi von Feldkirch[51] were followed less than a year later by those explicitly written by Luther, the *Disputation against Scholastic Theology* and shortly thereafter the *Ninety-five Theses*. Although Luther complained in October 1516 about his many responsibilities, he was experiencing the last tranquil months of his life. Years later he must have looked back on his earlier complaint with wry humor.

It is difficult to draw any decisive conclusions from the varied writings through September 1516. Still, we can make some general comments about Luther's work in these years. First, although he referred to the *synteresis* in his December 1514 sermon, he restricted its power to direct man toward conversion and salvation. It later drops out of the vocabulary of his sermons, as well as that of the biblical commentaries, as we have seen. Second, the works of these years bespeak a growing emphasis on Christ as the source of man's faith and righteousness. Third, it is unclear from his sermons and letters, as it is from his lectures, what role humility plays both in preparing for the initial conversion to faith and in perseverance in conversion. Nonetheless, as in his exegetical works, humility does not appear as a

---

[50]*WA* 1, 150, 4–5.

[51]Of the Bernhardi theses, Grane writes: "Die Bedeutung der Disputationsthesen Bernhardis liegt vor allem darin, dass sie die Diskussion um Luthers Theologie in Wittenberg eröffneten. Wir müssen vermutlich damit rechnen, dass diese Diskussion den Winter hindurch lebhaft fortgesetzt wurde, obwohl wir darüber sehr wenig wissen" (*Modus Loquendi Theologicus*, pp. 114–115).

meritorious attitude or work but rather as a disposition or recognition that one cannot attain righteousness by one's own efforts. Certainly, along with faith, it occupies a fundamental place in Christian life. Fourth, as the example of the music master and his student demonstrates, Luther saw conversion as God's act alone. Yet he also affirmed that it is a beginning that man can subsequently abandon. Thus, although Luther rejected the notion of merit, as the Bernhardi theses resoundingly demonstrate, he had not resolved the difficult problem of human responsibility for conversion—for rejecting it or persevering in it. As we shall see, only in the following years, culminating in 1518, did Luther gradually achieve certainty that God Himself gives man the grace to persevere in conversion through the gift of faith, the very possession of Christ.

[6]

Reform Writings and Sermons
(October 1516–1519)

The Bernhardi theses of September 1516 launch the reformatory period of Luther's life and work. During the years 1516–1519 he increasingly took on the role of defending the Wittenberg theology against those who perceived it as both heretical and dangerous.[1] This initial phase of reform writings includes the *Disputation against Scholastic Theology*, the *Disputation on the Power and Efficacy of Indulgences,* the Heidelberg disputation, and the Leipzeg debate. While it is possible to consider these reform writings as a unit, it is also necessary to differentiate the works of one year from those of another in terms of the development of Luther's theology. With respect to conversion, points that remain ambiguous or unresolved in 1516 and 1517 are given a new clarity and definiteness in 1518 and 1519. Luther's literary output during these years was prodigious, and we shall limit ourselves to a consideration of those works that relate especially to his understanding of conversion.

A concern with the nature of penitence permeates many of

---

[1]Of the many treatments of Luther and the beginnings of the Wittenberg theology, see Karl Bauer, *Die Wittenberger Universitätstheologie und die Anfänge der deutschen Reformation* (Tübingen: J. C. B. Mohr [Paul Siebeck], 1928); Boehmer, *Junge Luther*, pp. 143–283; Heiko A. Oberman, "Wittenbergs Zweifrontenkrieg gegen Prierias und Eck: Hintergrund und Entscheidungen des Jahres 1518," *Zeitschrift für Kirchengeschichte* 80 (1969), 331–358.

the writings of late 1516. In large part, this concern manifests itself in an attack on the abuse of indulgences, which leads a person into a false sense of security.[2] Penitence is interior and is composed of true contrition, true confession, and true satisfaction. As Luther explicitly says, when repenting is truly pure, one is displeased with oneself in all that one does and effectually is converted to God and purely acknowledges one's guilt and confesses to God in one's heart.[3] Luther directs his critique against a notion of penitence as an outward act, an idea that he finds the indulgences have fostered. True repentance, as opposed to gallows penitence—sorrow for sin engendered by the fear of punishment—expresses itself in the search not for indulgences but for crosses.[4] While he affirms that God comes to people in need of grace and mercy, not to those who suppose that they are righteous, Luther does not explicate the extent of the individual's responsibility for realizing his need and thus standing before God in humility.[5]

This absence of clarity concerning humility is also evidenced in the *Lecture on the Book of Judges* (*Praelectio in librum Iudicum*), published in 1518 but written between 1516 and 1518.[6] In one passage Luther declares that no one is born from the spirit unless he has been humble, because humility prepares us to be born from the Spirit, since God is close to a contrite heart.[7] The

[2]WA 1, 98, 39–99, 2 (Sermon on Luke 19:8, October 31, 1516).

[3]WA 1, 99, 1–4 (Sermon on Luke 19:8).

[4]WA 1, 99, 7–12 (Sermon on Luke 19:8).

[5]WA 1, 97, 25–26 (Sermon on Luke 19:8).

[6]WA 4, 529–586. Bernhard Lohse discusses the complicated question of the authenticity of this writing in *Mönchtum und Reformation: Luthers Auseinandersetzung mit dem Mönchsideal des Mittelalters*, Forschungen zur Kirchen- und Dogmengeschichte, vol. 12 (Göttingen: Vandenhoeck & Ruprecht, 1963), pp. 317–325. He suggests: "Die Frage der Echtheit kann also nicht in dem einen oder anderen Sinn glatt beantwortet werden. Es ist vielmehr wahrscheinlich, dass entweder ein Freund oder Schüler Luthers hier in einer sehr weitgehenden Freiheit eine Vorlesung von Luther selbst überarbeitet hat, oder dass ein Freund oder Schüler Luthers unter Verwendung von zahlreichen Äusserungen Luthers eine eigene Vorlesung gehalten hat. Nur so lässt sich das Miteinander von zweifellos echten und zweifellos unechten Aussagen Luthers erklären" (p. 324). See also L. M. Blankenheim, "Die Richtervorlesung Luthers," *ARG* 51 (1960), 1–18, who argues for Luther's authorship.

[7]WA 4, 560, 27–29.

importance of humility for spiritual birth or conversion is clear; less clear is precisely how one comes to humility, the recognition of one's own need.

Three sermons, given within a week in December 1516 as part of a series of advent sermons, specifically discuss humility.[8] In a sermon on John 1:23 Luther declares that God gives his grace to the humble, and he outlines the route by which a person reaches humility. The understanding of the spiritual law that is the Gospel teaches people perfect knowledge of sin and of themselves, thus demonstrating that grace is necessary for all, and that whoever has this understanding is close to grace, because God gives His grace to the humble. The Law as letter (*lex literae*) makes people proud and puffs them up, but spiritually understood it humbles, preparing them for grace and directing them to Christ.[9] It appears that the attainment of humility is grounded in the hearing and understanding of the Gospel, but the question remains unanswered as to how sinful man can hear and understand the spiritual law and thus emerge from his arrogant love of self. Luther is really conflating here *evangelium* with the Law spiritually understood, a confusing usage that he later

[8]Sermons on John 1:23 (December 14), *WA* 1, 107–109; Luke 3:5 (December 21), *WA* 1, 109–111; Ps. 19:2 (Ps. 19:1) (December 21), *WA* 1, 111–115, *LW* 51, 17–23. See Kiessling, *Early Sermons of Luther*, pp. 78–108, and, more generally on his preaching, Weier, *Theologieverständnis Martin Luthers*. On this series of sermons, see Kroeger, *Rechtfertigung und Gesetz*, pp. 229–232. On Luther's preaching, Harold J. Grimm writes, "He brought his evangelical convictions out of the study and the lecture hall directly to the man in the street, clarifying complicated theological doctrines as he developed them. . . . Consequently his sermons were in many respects conversations with his hearers in which his human qualities were given free rein. . . . The dynamic qualities of the Reformation sermon lay primarily in the fact that it was intended to convey to others the *logos*, the living Word of God. . . . Allegories, fables, and quotations of church fathers and secular writers gradually disappeared and were replaced by the simple, direct exposition of the Bible" ("The Human Element in Luther's Sermons," *ARG* 49 [1958], 50–51). On this last point Ulrich Nembach writes: "Unter den 1978 erhaltenen Lutherpredigten findet Ebeling nur 165, die ohne einen *bestimmten* Bibeltext gehalten wurden (Ebeling, *Evangelische Evangelienauslegung*, Tabelle I, S. 456f.), von denen jedoch ein Teil sich auf Texte bezogen, und die sich alle, alle 165, in ihrem Gehalt biblisch verstanden" (*Predigt des Evangeliums: Luther als Prediger, Pädagoge und Rhetor* [Neukirchen-Vluyn: Neukirchener Verlag, 1972], pp. 39n–40n).

[9]*WA* 1, 108, 13–18 (Sermon on John 1:23).

abandons. In his following sermon, on Luke 3:5, Luther follows much the same line of thought.[10] In the sermon on Psalm 19:2 he presents another aspect of his perception of humility. He indicates that God Himself performs an alien work in bringing man to see himself as a sinner.[11] A person must first recognize himself as a sinner, unrighteous, a liar, sad, foolish, and lost, before he can be justified. As Luther forcefully affirms: "God's alien work, therefore, is the suffering of Christ and sufferings in Christ, the crucifixion of the old man and the mortification of Adam." This action precedes God's appropriate work, "the resurrection of Christ, justification in the Spirit, and the vivification of the new man."[12] The prototype for both works is Christ, who "died for our sins and was raised for our justification. Thus, conformity with the image of the Son of God . . . includes both of these works."[13] Luther phrases these same ideas somewhat differently in the same sermon when he writes that by an alien work of the Gospel God prepares a perfect people by manifesting to them their sins and making those who are self-righteous penitent.[14] Thus, although he writes more frequently of the alien work of the Law, Luther can also describe this alien work in connection with the Gospel, which through Christ makes manifest to man his sins. He links to the alien and appropriate works the baptisms of repentance and remission of sins:

> Therefore the gospel magnifies sin in that it so broadens the law that no man can be found just, that there is none who does not transgress the law. And as all sin and have sinned, so it is obvious that all must receive the baptism of repentance before the baptism of remission of sins. Accordingly, it is not only written concerning John that he preached a baptism of repentance, but "into" or "for the forgiveness of sins" is added. That is to say that through it men are prepared for grace, which effects the remission of sins. Sins are remitted only to those who are dissatisfied with themselves, and

[10]WA 1, 110, 31–36 (Sermon on Luke 3:5).
[11]WA 1, 112, 24–32 (Sermon on Ps. 19:2); LW 51, 19.
[12]WA 1, 112, 37–113, 1 (Sermon on Ps. 19:2); LW 51, 19.
[13]WA 1, 113, 1–3 (Sermon on Ps. 19:2); LW 51, 19.
[14]WA 1, 113, 16–19 (Sermon on Ps. 19:2); LW 51, 20.

this is what it means to repent. But only those are dissatisfied with themselves who know this. But only those know it who understand the law. But no one understands the law unless it be explained to him. This, however, the gospel does.[15]

The Gospel teaches man of his sinfulness, urges him to dissatisfaction with himself, and guides him to repentance. In this and the preceding passages there is a stronger emphasis both on the work of Christ and on the Gospel. Humility is in no way man's own achievement, even in the sense of an attitude of waiting and expectation. Yet one question remains: How is sinful man capable of hearing the Gospel so that he can attain the necessary understanding of the Law and the resulting dissatisfaction with himself which constitutes repentance? In 1516 Luther had not formulated the answer to this question, although he was well on the way to doing so. We have already followed his progress of resolution through the *Lectures on Hebrews* and the *Lectures on Galatians.*

The theme of the alien and appropriate works of God is related to an important passage concerning conversion from Luther's sermon of December 27, 1516. Luther writes that first grace (*prima gratia*) converts man to God, while second grace (*secunda gratia*) allows man to make progress in God.[16] To extrapolate, the first grace brings man from aversion to conversion and places him on the path of pilgrimage. Although still a sinner, he is at the same time justified. The second grace allows him to progress on his lifetime journey of pilgrimage toward the ultimate goal of sanctification. This discussion is an elaboration and refinement of Luther's description of the second conversion in his *Dictata* exegesis of Psalm 84:7. It now includes both justification and sanctification, the initial conversion to God in faith and the repeated return to God in the conversion of repentance as one realizes ever more poignantly the depth of one's sinfulness.

In the writings of 1517 Luther again attacks the concept of

[15]*WA* 1, 114, 26–35 (Sermon on Ps. 19:2); *LW* 51, 22.
[16]*WA*,1, 116, 36–39 (Sermon on Sir. 15:1–2).

facere quod in se est. In the *Disputation against Scholastic Theology* of September 4, he affirms that only God prepares man for grace. Luther writes: "The best and infallible preparation for grace and the sole disposition toward grace is the eternal election and predestination of God."[17] He links his condemnation of the nominalist perception of the way man obtains grace to a false understanding of conversion. In thesis 26 he voices his objection to the assertion that man can by his own nature perform an act of perfect friendship. He declares: "An act of friendship is not the most perfect means for accomplishing that which is in one [*faciendi quod est in se*]. Nor is it the most perfect means for obtaining the grace of God or turning toward [*convertendi*] and approaching God."[18] For Luther, the person before grace is totally sinful, and since he is incapable of escaping from the shackles of *amor sui*, such an act of love is impossible. Thus in the following thesis he concludes: "But it is an act of conversion already perfected, following grace both in time and by nature."[19] In thesis 28 he offers his judgment of those people who assert that man can convert to God by his natural powers. In brief, "if it is said of the Scripture passages, 'Return to me, . . . and I will return to you' (Zech. 1:3), 'Draw near to God and he will draw near to you' (Jas. 4:8), 'Seek and you will find' (Matt. 7:7), 'You will seek me and find me' (Jer. 29:13), and the like, that one is by nature, the other by grace, this is no different from asserting what the Pelagians have said."[20] These three theses offer a powerful rebuttal to the position of Gabriel Biel in his *Collectorium*, already criticized by Luther in his marginal notes.[21] They also present another formulation of what we have seen to be Luther's adamant belief that conversion is primarily

[17]*WA* 1, 225, 27–28; *Luther's Works*, vol. 31: *Career of the Reformer I*, ed. Harold J. Grimm (Philadelphia: Fortress Press, 1957), p. 11 (hereafter cited as *LW* 31). Copyright © 1957 by Fortress Press. Used by permission.

[18]*WA* 1, 225, 17–19; *LW* 31, 11. *Actus amiciciae* or *actus amoris amicitiae* implies more than friendship: an attitude and action of unselfish love for one's neighbor, in distinction to the selfish *amor concupiscentiae*. See Grane, *Contra Gabrielem*, p. 251.

[19]*WA* 1, 225, 20–21; *LW* 31, 11.

[20]*WA* 1, 225, 22–26; *LW* 31, 11.

[21]See Grane, *Contra Gabrielem*, pp. 371–377.

God's action, which alone makes possible man's conversion to God.[22] When Luther refers to a "conversion already perfected," he is describing a condition in which a person is able by grace to perform genuinely good works.

Luther had prepared the theses on behalf of his student Franz Günther from Nordhausen. It was Günther's task to defend the theses in a debate before the faculty on September 4 so that he might earn the degree of *baccalaureus biblicus*.[23] His professor, however, considered the theses to be much more than a matter for ordinary intramural discussion. He promptly sent a copy of the theses off to his friend Johann Lang in Erfurt, and via the former Wittenberg professor Christoph Scheurl he had a copy forwarded to Johannes Eck in Ingolstadt.[24] He was eager to debate with any who were willing, but no one came forward. Ironically, it was not this set of disputation theses but that of October 31 that would set off a debate of massive proportions throughout Germany and Western Europe.

[22]Brecht offers an assessment of this disputation which connects it to Luther's lectures of the time but does not see in it "the program of a new theology." As he writes, "Das neue Programm erscheint hier ebensowenig ausgeführt wie in den bisherigen Vorlesungen. Was Luther aufgedeckt hatte, war der Gegensatz zwischen Paulus mit seiner Kritik der menschlichen Möglichkeiten einerseits und Aristoteles mit seiner Behauptung der sittlichen Leistungfähigkeit des Menschen andererseits. Es war eine ganz und gar kritische, noch nicht konstruktive Theologie. Diese deutet sich höchstens in Ansätzen an. Die Thesenreihe repräsentierte damit genau das Interesse, das Luthers Theologie damals noch beherrschte" (*Martin Luther*, p. 171). The Catholic church historian Erwin Iserloh finds that in these theses Luther is, in part at least, still an Ockhamist: "With his stressing of prevenient grace, with his requiring of the grace of justification as the basis for *acceptatio divina*, and with his teaching that grace is not added as a condition to an already good natural activity but that it forms man's activity from the very beginning and leads to God, Luther contests what would have been censured by Thomism too and above all by Augustinianism. But at the same time Luther remains dominated by Ockhamism. And therefore he does not succeed, for example, in showing the relationship of the love of neighbor and of God and in seeing creation as an image of the divine nature" (Jedin, ed., *History of the Church*, vol. 5: *Reformation and Counter Reformation*, ed. Iserloh, Glazik, and Jedin, p. 41).

[23]Subsequently Günther became a preacher in Jüterbog, a small town north of Wittenberg, where he encountered opposition from the local Franciscans. He was succeeded in his post for a time by Thomas Müntzer, who in 1519 still appeared to be at one with the Wittenberg theology. Günther remained throughout his life a loyal Martinian.

[24]Brecht, *Martin Luther*, pp. 171–172.

In the *Disputation on the Power and Efficacy of Indulgences* or the *Ninety-five Theses* Luther directs his pen against a false conception of conversion or repentance as the doing of penance.[25] The popular understanding of the indulgences even included the belief that a person could be forgiven his sins and released from punishment without contrition. Against this dangerous misconception, Luther proposes in thesis 76: "We say on the contrary that papal indulgences cannot remove the very least of venial sins as far as guilt is concerned."[26] The indulgences have turned people away from a life under the Cross and have given them a false sense of security and peace. Exemplifying his own concern with the problem of man's responsibility for persevering in conversion, Luther proclaims in thesis 30: "No one is sure of the integrity of his own contrition, much less of having received plenary remission."[27] In his final two theses Luther urges that "Christians should be exhorted to be diligent in following Christ, their head, through penalties, death, and hell; and thus be confident of entering heaven through many tribulations rather than through the false security of peace (Acts 14:22)."[28]

In his *Sermon on Indulgence and Grace* Luther explicitly joins conversion with carrying the Cross of Christ. As he writes, "No one can show from Holy Scripture that divine righteousness desires or requires any suffering or satisfaction from the sinner other than his heartfelt and true repentance or conversion and the intention of carrying the Cross of Christ from then on and

---

[25]*WA* 1, 233–238; *LW* 31, 25–33. See also Kurt Aland, ed., *Martin Luther's 95 Theses with the Pertinent Documents from the History of the Reformation* (St. Louis: Concordia, 1967).

[26]*WA* 1, 237, 9–10; *LW* 31, 32.

[27]*WA* 1, 234, 35–36; *LW* 31, 28.

[28]*WA* 1, 238, 18–21; *LW* 31, 33. I agree with Brecht that the theses show Luther still to be in theological transition and continuing to center on humility. In my terms, he is attempting to resolve the meaning of perseverance in conversion and the question of human responsibility. Brecht offers the following analysis of the *Ninety-five Theses:* "Der Geist, aus dem sie geschrieben sind, ist noch nicht der spätere evangelisch-reformatorische, so sehr auch der gängigen kirchlichen Praxis und ihren problematischen Begründungen widersprochen wird. Dies geschieht noch alles vom Boden der Demutstheologie und -frömmigkeit aus. Die Busse lieben, wie Christus es forderte; darum ging es" (*Martin Luther*, p. 194).

practicing the works mentioned above (put upon him by no one). Thus He speaks through Ezekiel: 'If the sinner converts and does right, I will no longer reckon his sin.' "[29] Satisfaction is not limited to the sacrament of penance, nor can it be met through the use of indulgences. Instead, satisfaction must be composed of a genuine conversion, manifested thereafter in carrying the Cross.

In a passage from the *Sermons on the Seven Penitential Psalms,* composed at the beginning of 1517, Luther writes that Christian life does not consist in many works, but in crucifying and killing the old man. Whether a person's strivings are directed toward accumulating the riches of this world or toward attaining a semblance of holiness in the eyes of others, they should be destroyed.[30] One's life should become nothing but a hatred of the old man and a seeking for the life of the new man.[31] The old man labors under the fear of the judgment of God, but along with fear there is also hope regarding the mercy of God. Faith and hope are linked together in this life.[32] In this text the stress falls once more on the necessity of human perseverance in conversion. We do not find in this passage the emphasis on Christ as the one who gives the Christian the faith that is the very possession of Himself and that allows him to carry on in joy and trust. Luther writes: "In the same way as the judgment of God works fear, so fear brings forth the cry; the cry, however, receives grace. So the whole time that the old man lives, the fear, that is, his Cross and death, will not stop, and he will not forget the judgment of God. Whoever lives without the Cross and fear and God's judgment, does not live rightly."[33] We do not go astray in sensing behind these words Luther's own self-doubt and uncertainty about salvation. Unanswered once again is the extent of human responsibility for persevering in this life, but Luther's

---

[29] WA 1, 244, 15–21 (*Ein Sermon von Ablass und Gnade,* 1517?). The date of the sermon is uncertain; see further Aland, *Martin Luther's 95 Theses,* p. 105.

[30] WA 1, 162, 34–163, 1. See further Bayer, *Promissio,* pp. 144–158.

[31] WA 1, 163, 3–5.

[32] WA 1, 207, 26–31.

[33] WA 1, 207, 31–36.

words portray the life of a Christian as both demanding and fearful.

Humility is a major theme in the *Sermons on the Seven Penitential Psalms*. Some passages suggest human participation or responsibility for attaining humility before God while others suggest the opposite. For example, the stress on humility is obvious in this part of Luther's sermon on Psalm 32: "You comfort and raise up a man as soon as he undertakes to humble himself. As soon as he recognizes himself as as sinner and cries out to you, so soon is he righteous and pleasing before you."[34] In his sermon on Psalm 51, Luther speaks of human effort in another way: "I will no longer teach human righteousness and human ways as the arrogant do, but rather the way of grace and of your righteousness. For thereby sinners come to you and are truly converted."[35] Human effort helps to bring sinners to God and to conversion, but this action, although in one sense man's own, is his action as an instrument of God, and thus the action of God working through him. The Word mediated through preaching has the power to convert sinners. Luther describes this process more fully in his sermon on Psalm 102: "The stones of Zion are the elect of God who are themselves prepared for grace through the prophets, apostles and preachers. The preparation is sent through the Word of God. . . . Whoever truly hears will be humble and terrified and will fall at the feet of God and cry out his misery as this psalm does to this point. When that has happened, then it is time, and rightly so, for God to come, for He does not come except to the humble."[36] Although Luther affirms that preparation for God or, in other terms, for grace, is the work of the Word of God, he does not explicate the relation between grace and human preparation in bringing man to "truly hear" the Word.

Other passages from the *Sermons on the Seven Penitential Psalms* and other writings from 1517 offer more light on the problem of human preparation for grace. In his exegesis of the peniten-

[34]*WA* 1, 170, 13–16.
[35]*WA* 1, 192, 9–11.
[36]*WA* 1, 201, 10–12, 15–18.

tial Psalm 51:3, Luther asserts that *prima gratia* is the beginning of washing and purifying oneself.[37] Increasingly in the works of 1517 Luther emphasizes grace in connection with both a person's entry into the Christian life and his ongoing struggle to persevere in conversion. The life of a Christian consists in constant reliance on God and constant struggle. As Luther succinctly describes the situation: "The life of a holy person consists more in taking from God than in giving, more in desiring than in having, more in becoming pious than in being so. As St. Augustine says, faith acquires what the law requires."[38] As he also writes to Archbishop Albrecht of Mainz, in a letter that accompanied a copy of his *Ninety-five Theses:* "No man can be assured of his salvation by an episcopal function. He is not even assured of his salvation by the infusion of God's grace, because the Apostle (Paul) orders us to work out our salvation constantly 'in fear and trembling.' "[39] Christian life thus remains a struggle in which a person is always in need of grace. In a sermon of January 1517 Luther asserts that the "doctrine of faith teaches that man ought always inwardly to sigh for grace, knowing that his heart is not pure if the works are worldly, and that the will is not necessarily healthy because the habits are good."[40] The writings we have considered from 1516 and 1517 demonstrate both a profound realization that God and His grace initiate human conversion and that humility is the most necessary and appropriate way for the Christian to approach God. These two themes exist side by side in uneasy tension, leaving unresolved the question of human responsibility for perseverance in conversion.

It is in the writings of 1518, in the midst of confrontation and controversy, that Luther attains clarity on the meaning of perseverance in conversion. While at times Luther has proposed that it is God Himself that brings man to humility, in other instances he has suggested that humility is a nonmeritorious disposition that man is responsible for attaining. In 1518 this

[37]*WA* 1, 186, 21–22.
[38]*WA* 1, 212, 19–21.
[39]*WA Br* 1, 111, 27–29; *LW* 48, 46.
[40]*WA* 1, 118, 37–40 (Sermon on Luke 2:21, January 1, 1517).

ambiguity is resolved. In the Heidelberg disputation of April 1518, in which Luther defended the Wittenberg theology before a general meeting of the Augustinians, we can follow the shift in Luther's perception of humility.[41] In his proof attached to the fourth thesis, Luther refers, as he does in his *Lectures on Hebrews*, to the *opus alienum*, the alien work of God: "And that it is which Isa. 28(:21) calls the alien work of God that he may do his work (that is, he humbles us thoroughly, making us despair, so that he may exalt us in his mercy, giving us hope), just as Hab. 3(:2) states. . . . Such a man therefore is displeased with all his works; he sees no beauty, but only his ugliness."[42] Through his reference to the alien work of God, Luther lays the basis for negating the idea that humility as man's disposition precedes God's turn toward man in justification. Yet he has not entirely resolved the conflict between humility as man's responsibility and as God's work in man, as the following two statements demonstrate: "This ugliness, however, comes into being in us either when God punishes us or when we accuse ourselves. . . . In this way, consequently, the unattractive works which God does in us, that is, those which are humble and devout, are really eternal, for humility and fear of God are our entire merit."[43] Absent in this

[41]WA 1, 353–374; LW 31, 39–70. In his analysis of the Heidelberg disputation, Brecht finds that the early theses continue to present a theology of humility. He contends: "Bis zu diesem Punkt bietet die Heidelberger Disputation eigentlich nur noch einmal eine Zusammenfassung der kritischen Demutstheologie. Das Neue kann man allenfalls ahnen. Erst mit der vierten Thesengruppe (25–27), die das Verhältnis von Glauben und Werken behandelt, wird das anders: 'Nicht der ist gerecht, der viel wirkt, sondern der ohne Werke viel an Christus glaubt.' Die Gerechtigkeit konstituiert sich nicht aus dem Handeln wie bei Aristoteles; man kommt zu ihr nur durch den Glauben an Christus. Die Werke sind nur Folge des Glaubens, und sie sind eigentlich gar nicht die Werke des Glaubenden, sondern die Gottes, und insofern kann sich der Glaubenden ihrer gar nicht rühmen" (*Martin Luther*, p. 227). We find signs of transition as early as thesis 4, with Luther's affirmation that the alien work of God causes man's humility and despair.
[42]WA 1, 357, 6–10; LW 31, 44.
[43]WA 1, 357, 12–17; LW 31, 44. On the dialectic of the *opus alienum* and *opus proprium* in the proof of thesis 4, see Jos E. Vercruysse, "Gesetz und Liebe: Die Struktur der 'Heidelberger Disputation' Luthers (1518)," *Lutherjahrbuch* 48 (1981), 13. See also in the same volume Rune Söderlund, "Der meritum-Begriff der 'Heidelberger Disputation' im Verhältnis zum mittelalterlichen und zur späteren reformatorischen Theologie," pp. 44–53; Karl-Heinz zur Mühlen,

passage is the affirmation that faith, as the very possession of Christ, leads to humility and righteousness. Although Luther asserts man's inability to attain salvation through his works, he still bears a responsibility for seeking grace, as Luther states in his proof of the sixteenth thesis: "Now you ask, 'What then shall we do? Shall we go our way with indifference because we can do nothing but sin?' I would reply, By no means. But, having heard this, fall down and pray for grace and place your hope in Christ in whom is our salvation, life, and resurrection. For this reason we are so instructed—for this reason the law makes us aware of sin so that, having recognized our sin, we may seek and receive grace. Thus God 'gives grace to the humble' (1 Pet. 5:5), and 'whoever humbles himself will be exalted' (Matt. 23:12)."[44] This passage seems to suggest that while the Law makes man aware of sin, it is man's responsibility to "seek" grace, or, in other words, to await grace in humility. In his next words, however, Luther rejects this possibility and explicates the relation between grace and humility: "The law humbles, grace exalts. The law effects fear and wrath, grace effects hope and mercy. 'Through the law comes knowledge of sin' (Rom. 3:20), through knowledge of sin, however, comes humility, and through humility grace is acquired. Thus an action which is alien to God's nature results in a deed belonging to his very nature: he makes a person a sinner so that he may make him righteous."[45] While retaining his emphasis on humility, Luther places it within the context of God's alien work. Man does indeed acquire grace through humility, but God brings forth this humility through the alien work of the Law. In his last theses Luther presents his understanding of righteousness and life in Christ. In thesis 25 he writes that "he is not righteous who does much, but he who, without work, believes

"Luthers Kirtik am scholastischen Aristotelismus in der 25. These der 'Heidelberger Disputation' von 1518," pp. 54–79; and Edgar Thaidigsmann, "Kreuz und Wirklichkeit: Zur Aneignung der 'Heidelberger Disputation' Luthers," pp. 80–96, which discusses the analyses of Otto Ritschl, Bizer, Bayer, von Loewenich, and other scholars, stressing the final emergence of Luther's *theologia crucis*. See further Grane, *Modus Loquendi Theologicus*, pp. 146–151.
[44]*WA* 1, 360, 34–361, 1; *LW* 31, 50–51.
[45]*WA* 1, 361, 1–5; *LW* 31, 51.

much in Christ."[46] Lest this statement be interpreted as a new demand made on man, in his proof Luther asserts that "grace and faith are infused without our works. After they have been imparted the works follow." Thus, as Luther now proclaims, "man knows that works which he does by such faith are not his but God's. For this reason he does not seek to become justified or glorified through them, but seeks God. His justification by faith in Christ is sufficient to him. Christ is his wisdom, righteousness, etc., . . . that he himself may be Christ's action and instrument."[47] In his proof to thesis 27, Luther affirms: "Since Christ lives in us through faith so he arouses us to do good works through that living faith in his work. . . ."[48] We find articulated in these final theses from the Heidelberg disputation the same stress on Christ and faith that we found Luther developing in his *Lectures on Hebrews* and the 1519 *Lectures on Galatians*. His theology expresses a new joyfulness, a new spirit of freedom. Certainly perseverance in conversion remains a struggle, but it is now a struggle in which the Christian can confidently rely on Christ as both the substance of his faith and his only source of righteousness. Righteousness is not dependent on humility and faith, but on faith alone, which through God's action also leads man to humility. Man is able to hear the Gospel in faith and to respond to it because Christ is at work within him, bringing him to faith. The spirit of freedom and confidence that we find now in Luther's theology results from his having developed fully the perception already expressed in his *Dictata* exegesis of Psalm 84:7. It is God's conversion that alone makes possible man's conversion. Apart from God's conversion to man and his loving conversion of man to Himself, neither faith nor humility nor righteousness nor sanctification is possible for man.

Although Christ enables man to do good works, Luther also indicates that man's works under grace are very much his own, and the following of the Cross is very much his own struggle. Luther emphasizes so often that all the good that man does is

[46]*WA* 1, 354, 29–30; *LW* 31, 41.
[47]*WA* 1, 364, 8–9, 12–16; *LW* 31, 56.
[48]*WA* 1, 364, 30–31; *LW* 31, 56.

dependent on grace in order to make absolutely clear that man by himself and though his own efforts cannot earn merit or establish himself before God. Were the contrary the case, he would not be constantly in need of the forgiveness made available to him as a result of Christ's conversion in the incarnation and his subsequent suffering, death, and resurrection. Two passages, referring to differing aspects of Christian life, demonstrate Luther's persistent emphasis on God's work. First, in a sermon on John 9:1–38, Luther tells his congregation: "But those who say: Ah, but I have done as much as I possibly can; I have done enough, and I hope that God will give me grace— they set up an iron wall between themselves and the grace of God. But if you feel within yourself the urge to call upon God and pray and plead and knock, then grace is already there; then call upon it and thank God." He adds that those people turn the matter completely around who say that they will wait until grace comes: "Ah, you fool, when you feel what has been effected within you, then grace is already there; just go on and follow."[49] Grace may be at work in man even when he does not perceive it, since only by grace is he able to call out to God. Yet man can impede grace by believing that he can earn it through his own efforts. In his *Sermon on the Threefold Righteousness,* Luther indicates that man is purified by the works that God imposes or calls forth, not by those that man himself chooses to do. These works include sufferings, infirmities, want, disgrace, and death.[50] God accomplishes these works, and it is for man patiently to accept them. Christian life is characterized by God's action both in the alien work of suffering that He imposes on the Christian and in the appropriate work that gives man faith and strength.

In sum, Luther affirms that faith in the Word of God justifies, makes alive, dignifies, and prepares man for righteousness. A person is not righteous because of his own particular disposition, but one lives because of one's faith.[51] Luther launches an im-

[49]*WA* 1, 272, 26–31, 35–37 (Sermon on John 9:1–38, March 17, 1518); *LW* 51, 43.
[50]*WA* 2, 47, 11–13 (*Sermo de triplici iustitia,* 1518).
[51]*WA* 2, 14, 6–9 (*Acta Augustana,* 1518).

plicit attack against those people who equate righteousness with man's own experience or perception of "how he is doing." Righteousness depends on faith alone, and faith, in turn, includes man's acceptance and recognition of the forgiveness that he has received through the life and work of Christ.

Luther's emphasis on faith as alone necessary for justification leads him to protest vigorously against a false view of indulgences as themselves responsible for man's attaining merit before God. One is saved as a result of God's mercy, not because of one's merits.[52] With regard to contrition, as part of the sacrament of penance, Luther also professes that too much attention has been focused on man's having certain knowledge of his contrition, a practice that can lead to both doubt and self-absorption. At the same time, with regard to the debate between those theologians who argue that attrition, simple fear of punishment, is sufficient and those who claim that only contrition, genuine sorrow for offending God, deserves absolution, Luther sides with the contritionists.[53] For Luther, however, contrition must rest on faith.[54] Contrition based on faith provides the prelude and context for forgiveness in the sacrament of penance.[55]

By basing forgiveness on faith, Luther departs from the medieval obsession with attempting to determine whether or not one was fully contrite and had made a complete confession. In his view, all of these concerns had turned a consoling sacrament into one that inspired terror and scrupulosity—as he had himself experienced.[56] Luther's emphasis on faith also had implications for the role of the sacrament as a disciplinary instrument, making it primarily a sacrament of consolation.[57] As in his *Lec-*

[52]*WA* 2, 10, 35–36 (*Acta Augustana*).
[53]See the discussion by Tentler, *Sin and Confession*, esp. pp. 349–370. For a description of the theological development behind the sacrament of penance, see Bernhard Poschmann, *Penance and the Anointing of the Sick*, trans. and rev. Francis Courtney (Freiburg: Herder; London: Burns & Oates, 1964), pp. 155–193 and 210–232.
[54]*WA* 1, 632, 17–18 (*Pro veritate inquirenda et timoratis conscientiis consolandis conclusiones*, 1518).
[55]Tentler, *Sin and Confession*, p. 354.
[56]Scheel, ed., *Dokumente zu Luthers Entwicklung*, p. 104, no. 271.
[57]Tentler describes the change in the sacrament that Luther effects in this way: "Luther's salvation by faith not only asserts the necessity of trusting belief in the promise of forgiveness; it also rejects unequivocally all the requirements of

tures on Hebrews, Luther stresses that the sacrament itself does not justify or mediate forgiveness, but faith in the sacrament transforms it into a word of peace and consolation to the trusting sinner.[58]

Luther continues his exposition of the true meaning of the sacrament of penance in his sermons and writings of 1519. In his *Sermon on Penance* he insists that the Christian should not debate with himself about whether or not he has sufficient contrition.[59] Instead, he should flee to God for grace. Contrition is not a human act that must be measured for its goodness before being presented to God, but it is itself the result of grace. In addition to the usual division of the sacrament of penance into contrition, confession, and satisfaction, Luther proposes another schema that aptly characterizes his own understanding of the sacrament. He states that the sacrament consists of three elements: the Word of God, which is absolution; faith in the absolution; and peace, which is the forgiveness of sin and which follows after faith.[60]

Luther's stress on faith and on the direct forgiveness that flows from God to the sinner leads to a diminishing of the power of the priest. He retains his role as the person who has received the call to pronounce the words of absolution, which give the sinner peace and reassurance, and Luther has great respect for this role. It is only when the sinner hears these words that he truly knows himself to be forgiven. The priest, however, no longer retains his extensive disciplinary power as the one who

---

sacramental confession. In other words, Luther cut every traditional element of discipline out of the theory of justification and made it as purely a theory of consolation as he could. A logical consequence of this doctrine is the abolition of reservations, the jurisdiction of one's own priest, and the canon law meaning of excommunication. A compatible corollary is the rejection of the whole structure of satisfaction for sin—penances, indulgences, and purgatory itself" (*Sin and Confession,* p. 355).

[58]*WA* 1, 286, 16–18 (*Asterisci Lutheri adversus Obeliscos Eckii,* 1518). Luther also indicates that it is a serious error to go to confession and emerge from it with a self-satisfied feeling of purity, thinking oneself worthy of the eucharist (*WA* 1, 255, 24–28 [*Eine kurze Erklärung der zehn Gebote,* 1518]).

[59]*WA* 2, 718, 9–15 (*Ein Sermon von dem Sakrament der Busse,* 1519); *Luther's Works,* vol. 35: *Word and Sacrament I,* ed. E. Theodore Bachmann (Philadelphia: Muhlenberg Press, 1960), p. 15 (hereafter cited as *LW* 35).

[60]*WA* 2, 721, 8–11 (*Ein Sermon von dem Sakrament der Busse*); *LW* 35, 19.

must extract a complete confession from the sinner and assess the amount of his contrition before granting his forgiveness.[61] A load is lifted from the shoulders of the priest, but simultaneously his power over the lives of his parishoners is substantially reduced. Since forgiveness rests on faith, not on the power of the priest in his special office, it is not surprising to find Luther advocating that in times of need one Christian may absolve another of his sins.[62] With that statement he takes a significant step toward articulating the doctrine of the priesthood of all believers, formulated in his tract *To the Christian Nobility of the German Nation* of 1520.[63]

In 1519 Luther preached his sermon *Two Kinds of Righteousness*, in which he expounded further on his concept of righteousness and of life under the Cross. He indicates that Christian righteousness is twofold. The first righteousness is alien to a person and is poured in or infused.[64] This righteousness is the one by which Christ is righteous and by which He justifies through faith. It is given to a person at baptism and at all times of true repentance.[65] Further, it is based on faith and, to cite Luther's words, "it is the basis, the cause, the source of all our own actual righteousness."[66] It is the source for the second righteousness, which the Christian may look upon as his own. As Luther explains, "The second kind of righteousness is our proper righteousness, not because we alone work it, but because we work with that first and alien righteousness."[67] Most definitely a

---

[61]Tentler discusses the duties and privileges of the priest and notes the importance of his eliciting a full confession from the penitent (*Sin and Confession*, pp. 104–133).

[62]*WA* 2, 722, 16–21 (*Ein Sermon von dem Sakrament der Busse*); *LW* 35, 21.

[63]*WA* 6, 404–469 (*An den christlichen Adel deutscher Nation von des christlichen Standes Besserung*).

[64]*WA* 2, 145, 7–9 (*Sermo de duplici iustitia*); *LW* 31, 297. See Bornkamm, *Luthers Auslegungen des Galaterbriefs*, pp. 302–303; Gyllenkrok, *Rechtfertigung und Heiligung*, pp. 106–109; and Bizer, *Fides ex auditu*, pp. 127–130.

[65]*WA* 2, 145, 9–10, 14–15 (*Sermo de duplici iustitia*); *LW* 31, 297.

[66]*WA* 2, 146, 16–17 (*Sermo de duplici iustitia*); *LW* 31, 298. For a discussion of righteousness in this sermon, see Martin Brecht, "Der rechtfertigende Glaube an das Evangelium von Jesus Christus als Mitte von Luthers Theologie," *Zeitschrift für Kirchengeschichte* 89 (1978), 47–49.

[67]*WA* 2, 146, 36–37 (*Sermo de duplici iustitia*); *LW* 31, 299.

person does not achieve or merit this righteousness through his own efforts, but he attains it by cooperating with the first righteousness, given him by grace. This second righteousness is comprised of a life of good works in which the flesh is mortified and the desires are crucified.[68] Most fundamentally, this righteousness is comprised of love toward one's neighbor and of humility and filial fear toward God. It is in fact "the product of the righteousness of the first type, actually its fruit and consequence. . . ."[69] This second righteousness perfects the first because it is always at work, bringing about the death of Adam and the destruction of the body of sin. It is constituted by a hatred of the self and a love of the neighbor, by never seeking what is one's own but by giving to the other. According to Luther, it is in these things that the Christian finds his entire way of living in the world.[70] In other words, this is the life of perseverance in conversion.[71]

With his description of man's second and cooperative righteousness, Luther offers an important counterpart to his heavy emphasis on righteousness by grace through faith, which excludes man's efforts. This second righteousness is not a restatement of *facere quod in se est,* since it comes about only as the fruit of the primary righteousness infused by God. In so speaking Luther is expanding on the affirmation he made in his *Disputation against Scholastic Theology* of 1517: "We do not become righteous by doing righteous deeds but, having been made righteous,

[68]*WA* 2, 146, 38–147, 1 (*Sermo de duplici iustitia*); *LW* 31, 299.
[69]*WA* 2, 147, 2–3, 7–8 (*Sermo de duplici iustitia*); *LW* 31, 299–300.
[70]*WA* 2, 147, 12–15 (*Sermo de duplici iustitia*); *LW* 31, 300.
[71]Although Steinmetz refers explicitly to the *Sermo de poenitentia* of 1518, his comments apply equally appropriately to the *Sermo de duplici iustitia* and to Luther's understanding of conversion in 1518 and thereafter: "The repentance to which a Christian is called is a continuous and lifelong process. While conversion begins, as everything in history does, at some point in time, the process of conversion is not completed until every aspect of the human personality is driven out into the light of God's severe mercy, judged and renewed. Repentance proceeds layer by layer, relationship by relationship, here a little, there a little, until the whole personality and not merely one side of it has been recreated by God. Penance refers not only to the initial moment of faith, no matter how dramatic or revolutionary it may seem, but to the whole life of the believer and the network of relationships in which that life is entangled" (*Luther and Staupitz,* p. 120).

169

we do righteous deeds."[72] In this way he also offers a rebuttal to those people who would attempt to find in righteousness by faith an excuse for laziness and for failure to conform to the Cross. By emphasizing this second righteousness, Luther makes clear that man's transformation from old man to new is a process that lasts throughout this earthly life.

In his writings of 1518 and 1519 Luther explicitly and thematically describes conversion as God's work. For example, in his *Exposition of Psalm 109 (110)* of 1518, Luther writes: "These same children he calls the dew, in that no soul is converted and turned from Adam's sinful filiation into the kingdom of grace consisting of sonship in Christ by the work of man, but rather, only by the work of God from heaven, just like the dew."[73] Luther proclaims that it is the power of the Word that changes man. The Word comes to a person's heart and awakens it.[74] Unlike worldly lords, Christ does not rely on force to win man's obedience, but instead trusts fully in the power of the Word of God. Against sin, sinner, and the devil He strives only with words, and yet with His Word He has converted and brought under His power the entire world.[75]

Luther also continues to preach and to write about conversion as ongoing repentance. In his *Explanations to the Ninety-five Theses* he questions: "Do you not see that he imposes no penance except that of observing the commands of God, and that he therefore desires that penance be understood as nothing except conversion and the change to a new life?"[76] This conversion manifests itself in the following of the Cross and obedience to the commandments. Conversion includes satisfaction, not in the limited sense of performance of the third part of the sacrament of penance, but in a way that includes one's entire life. It does

---

[72]*WA* 1, 226, 8; *LW* 31, 12.

[73]*WA* 1, 701, 37–40 (*Auslegung des 109. [110.] Psalms*).

[74]*WA* 1, 695, 33–35 (*Auslegung des 109. [110.] Psalms*). See Philip Watson, *Let God Be God!: An Interpretation of the Theology of Martin Luther* (Philadelphia: Muhlenberg Press, 1949), esp. p. 151 on the Word.

[75]*WA* 1, 695, 1–5 (*Auslegung des 109. [110.] Psalms*).

[76]*WA* 1, 538, 11–14 (*Resolutiones disputationum de indulgentiarum virtute*, 1518); *LW* 31, 96.

not mean an effort to earn merit, but a new attitude of love and
trust that issues in works freely and joyfully done for the sake of
God and one's neighbor. Those people err who see satisfaction
as being composed of a single work or act. As Micah records,
God does not require works to make satisfaction for sin, but
"rather he requires justice, compassion, and fear. This, as I have
said, means a new life."[77] Perseverance in conversion, the following of this new life, is man's own responsibility, in the same
way that second righteousness is truly man's own, but man can
persevere in conversion only because he has first been converted
by God to faith, even as he can have righteousness only because
he has first been infused with an alien righteousness from God.
A life of persevering in conversion now means for Luther a life
of responsibility, but joyful, not fearful responsibility, for Christian life is grounded and rooted in faith, a gift that no person
can earn.

Luther spoke out against fear during what may have been the
most important event for him in 1519, his debate with Johannes
Eck in Leipzig. Part of their debate centered on the question of
penance. At one point, Eck approvingly cited the following gloss
from Cassiodorus: "The fear of judgment is the door of conversion to God."[78] Luther adamantly opposed Eck's belief that servile fear provides a way to conversion. Without grace, he proclaimed, fear not only does not provide a door for conversion,
but on the contrary, it works nothing but wrath.[79] Conversion as
God's act does include the alien work of bringing man to fear,
but it also includes the appropriate work of granting him forgiveness and faith. Man's "own" fear is merely another aspect of
amor sui and cannot lead him to conversion. In defending his
position, Luther referred to Paul's conversion. Paul would not
have been converted if his heart had not been inwardly converted by grace.[80] Indeed, Paul provides a superlative example of

[77]WA 1, 538, 33–35 (*Resolutiones disputationum de indulgentiarum virtute*); *LW*
31, 97.
[78]WA 2, 366, 17.
[79]WA 2, 370, 28–30.
[80]WA 2, 370, 22–24.

171

conversion as God's act, without any human preparation—in fact, in spite of human resistance.

In distinction to the dramatic conversion of Paul, Luther speaks often of baptism as the new birth. In a sermon of 1519, he indicates that in contrast to the eucharist, a person needs the sacrament of baptism only once.[81] Baptism is, as we have seen in his various biblical commentaries from the *Dictata* to the *Lectures on Galatians,* the entrance into a new life for Luther; but because this new life, this life of perseverance in conversion, is beset with many difficulties, the Christian needs the strength that is mediated to him through his faithful participation in the eucharist. When Luther writes that baptism is a blessed dying to sin and a resurrection in the grace of God, through which the old man is drowned and the new man arises, he has not forgotten that the struggle between the old man in Adam and the new man in Christ is a lifelong one.[82] Baptism is the conversion that sets man on the road of daily struggle until the moment of his death, a moment that Luther in his *Sermon Concerning Preparation for Dying* also calls one of new birth.[83]

In 1519, denounced by some as a Hussite and a heretic and proclaimed by others as a reformer and a hero, Luther was uncertain of his future before pope and emperor but quite certain of what is necessary to stand before God. In his writings of 1518 and 1519 Luther demonstrated that he was free of his problems concerning the meaning of perseverance in conversion. A Christian perseveres in conversion because God gives him the power through faith to do so. Conversion is first and foremost God's act. It includes both the alien work, in which He makes man aware of his sin and thereby brings him to humility, and the appropriate work, in which He forgives man, grants him faith, and justifies him. The prototype for both parts of God's action is His work in Christ: His crucifixion and death as the

---

[81]*WA* 2, 746, 6–8 (*Ein Sermon von dem hochwürdigen Sakrament des heiligen wahren Leichnams Christi und von den Brüderschaften,* 1519).

[82]*WA* 2, 727, 30–33; 728, 10–12 (*Ein Sermon von dem heiligen hochwürdigen Sakrament der Taufe,* 1519).

[83]*WA* 2, 685, 30–686, 2 (*Ein Sermon von der Bereitung zum Sterben,* 1519.)

alien work and His resurrection and glorification as the appropriate work. In 1516 Luther wrote that first grace converts man to God while second grace allows man to make progress in Him. In 1518 he clarified this statement when he pronounced that the first righteousness man receives is alien and infused. The second righteousness, which is the fruit of the first, is man's own righteousness, which displays itself through faith in both good works and love of neighbor and God. Perseverance in conversion is thus not a demand but a joyful responsibility, which one can fulfill because of the first righteousness given by God through faith. God Himself answers the question of how man is to persevere in conversion. He alone grants man that alien righteousness which makes his progress in God, the process of sanctification, a reality. All of man's perseverance in conversion, both his return to God in repentance and his good works, is rooted in grace and faith. Both grace and faith, as Luther affirmed in his Heidelberg disputation, are infused by God.

The issue of perseverance in conversion was far more than an academic matter for Luther. For him theological questioning and personal searching were conjoined. As he himself tells us, he agonized over his relationship with God, how he was to please Him, how he was to fulfill the command not only to follow the Law but to be righteous. We have followed Luther's path to his attainment of the perception that faith is God's gift and conversion is God's work, grounded in the incarnation. But Luther did not reach his insights only on paper; he reached them first in his own experience, in a struggle that was terminated only by God Himself. The moment of resolution of this struggle has for long been known to Luther scholars as the tower experience. Let us now see how Luther describes this experience and how his understanding of conversion illuminates that description.

[7]

Luther's Tower Experience

Luther's tower experience (*Turmerlebnis*), or evangelical break-through, was one of the most significant events in Western religious history. How that momentous "conversion" relates to his theological development and biblical understanding of conversion itself is a challenging and intriguing problem. The amount of material devoted both to the dating of this experience and to its precise content is awesome.[1] We shall limit ourselves to two basic questions: First, how does Luther's concept of conversion as articulated in his exegetical and other writings relate to the account he gives of this experience? Second, how does Luther's description of his theological breakthrough relate to the development of his theology as it has been outlined in the preceding chapters? These are two approaches to the same historical problem.

One may ask at the very outset whether or not Luther did in fact experience what he remembers he did and to what extent this event in the tower determined his understanding of evan-

[1]An excellent representation of the various scholarly positions regarding Luther's evangelical breakthrough is provided in the anthology edited by Bernhard Lohse, *Der Durchbruch der reformatorischen Erkenntnis bei Luther*. Both Lohse's *Vorwort* and the selection by Pesch, "Zur Frage nach Luthers reformatorischer Wende," give helpful overviews of the massive amount of literature concerning both the *Turmerlebnis* and the development of Luther's reform theology.

gelical faith.[2] In other words, does this event really constitute a conversion, and does it really stand at the base of Luther's mature theology? Some scholars have equated the tower experience with Luther's conversion and have interpreted it as his theological insight into the meaning of justification by faith. They have argued that Luther had attained his insight by April or May 1513—in other words, while working on the *Dictata*.[3] While some scholars have argued for a specific date on the basis of Luther's

[2]Luther is by no means unique in his experience of a conversion through Scripture. Augustine's reading of Rom. 13:13 was the culmination of his conversion, according to his account in the *Confessions*. In the fourteenth century Richard FitzRalph, the archbishop of Armagh and chancellor of Oxford, recorded an experience similar to that described by Augustine as he was led from philosophy to scriptural theology. Although he does not employ the word *conversio* in his description of the experience, he does most definitely describe it as a conversion, as an experience of profound illumination that led him to a new course of action. For a discussion of FitzRalph, see Pantin, *English Church*, pp. 132–133. FitzRalph's long autobiographical prayer recounting his experience is in the *Summa contra Armenos*, lib. 19, cap. 35, given in full in L. L. Hammerich, *The Beginning of the Strife between Richard Fitzralph and the Mendicants*, Det Kgl. danske Videnskabernes selskab. Historisk-filogiske meddelelser., vol. 26, 3 (Copenhagen: Levin & Munksgaard, Ejnar Munksgaard, 1938), pp. 18–22. Heiko Oberman also describes the nominalist Thomas Bradwardine as having experienced a conversion while struggling with the problem of grace: "This problem haunted him, and already before he started his theological study, which in all probability he intended to do earlier, the great change came. From then on, Romans 9:16 remains the central text of his theological work, and he never tired of quoting it. 'However, even before I became a theological student, the text mentioned came to me as a beam of grace and in a mental representation of the truth I thought I saw from afar how the grace of God precedes all good works in time and in nature; that is, the gracious will of God, who in both these media wills beforehand that he who does deserving works shall be saved. . . .' The most important fact is that afterwards he himself regarded the new insight into Romans 9:16 as the great conversion" (*Archbishop Thomas Bradwardine, A Fourteenth Century Augustinian: A Study of His Theology in Its Historical Context* [Utrecht: Kemink & Zoon, 1957], p. 15). Oberman also discusses the tradition of describing conversion in terms of Augustine's own account in "'Iustitia Christi' and 'Iustitia Dei': Luther and the Scholastic Doctrines of Justification," *HTR* 59 (1966), 9–10. Some of Luther's contemporaries, such as Zwingli and Vadian, related their conversions and roads to reformation to the immediate power of the Word rather than to Luther's influence or any other source.

[3]Heinrich Boehmer, *Road to Reformation: Martin Luther to the Year 1521*, trans. John W. Doberstein and Theodore G. Tappert (Philadelphia: Muhlenberg Press, 1946), pp. 109–117. Boehmer writes: "The inner struggle in his soul continued with scarcely diminished vehemence. It was not until April or May, 1513, that an almost sudden change took place" (p. 109). "But in April and May, 1513, Luther himself had no conception of these far-reaching consequences of his new 'insight.' He perceived at first only the liberating and reviving effect it had upon him. The oppression which had weighed so long upon his soul had suddenly vanished" (p. 117). See also Fife, *Revolt of Martin Luther*, pp. 197–202.

1545 account of his experience, others have sought to determine the date of his evangelical insight on the basis of when the concept of justification by faith first appeared in his writings.[4] Others, taking seriously Luther's own words that he did not arrive at this theology without much struggle, have been more hesitant to argue for a specific date.[5]

One polar position is that the tower experience must be dissociated from Luther's conversion. According to this approach, it is possible to delineate two experiences, one far earlier than the other. The first experience, the conversion that occurred in large part through the influence of Johannes von Staupitz and his Augustinian theology, was one of the forgiveness of sins and of faith in Jesus Christ.[6] The tower experience, as distinct from

[4]For example, Karl Holl wrote: "Als sicher erscheint mir, dass Luther die ihn erlösende Gewissheit in der Zeit zwischen seiner neuen Übersiedlung nach Wittenberg und dem Beginn der Psalmenvorlesung, also rund zwischen Sommer 1511 und Frühjahr 1513, gewonnen hat. Luthers Angabe, dass ihm auf dem Turm des Wittenberger Klosters die Erleuchtung zuteil geworden sei, muss wegen ihrer anschaulichen Bestimmtheit als eine in der Hauptsache zuverlässige Erinnerung gelten. . . . Ebenso scheint es mir unbestreitbar, dass der Durchbruch zur Rechtfertigungslehre bei Luther noch vor dem Beginn der Psalmenvorlesung erfolgt sein muss" (Gesammelte Aufsätze zur Kirchengeschichte, vol. 1: Luther, p. 193). Thus Holl argues that Luther was correct about the place of his insight, but the evidence of his theological writings indicates that the time is incorrect. Erich Vogelsang also argued on the basis of a textual study that Luther arrived at his insight during the course of his work on the Dictata (Anfänge von Luthers Christologie).

[5]For example, according to Gordon Rupp: "It is clear that, in all essentials, his theology was in existence before the opening of the Church struggle in 1517" (Luther's Progress to the Diet of Worms [New York: Harper & Row, 1964], p. 39).

[6]Saarnivaara, Luther Discovers the Gospel, pp. 19–49, esp. pp. 33–34. See also Steinmetz, Luther and Staupitz: "Most of the suggestions which have been made by historians about the relationship of Luther to Staupitz—that Staupitz is the mediator of a late medieval Augustinian school tradition to Luther (Oberman), or that Luther was a disciple of Staupitz in his earliest approach to the interpretation of the Bible (Bauer) or in his first articulation of his doctrine of justification (Bizer)—seem to me not to be justified by the documentary evidence. Luther's understanding of Word and faith, his reluctance to make election the center of his thought, and his tendency to subject traditional modes of thought to a radical critique set him apart from Staupitz, who, for all his theological originality, is content to follow a more traditional and well-marked path established by generations of conservative Augustinian theologians." Steinmetz also notes "the astonishing degree of independence from his teachers Luther exhibited from the very beginning. Luther is always more than the sum of the parts of his theological heritage" (p. 141).

this conversion, resolved the problem of how Luther could be justified by God.[7]

This interpretation is particularly interesting because it resolves two problems. First, it explains how Luther could describe his progress before the discovery of the true meaning of *iustitia Dei*, the righteousness of God, in these terms: "I had then already read and taught the sacred Scriptures most diligently privately and publicly for seven years, so that I knew them nearly all by memory. I had also acquired the beginning of the knowledge of Christ and faith in Him, i.e. not by works but by faith in Christ are we made righteous and saved."[8] Achieving the beginning of the knowledge of Christ and acquiring faith in Him and resolving theologically the problem of justification thus constitute two separate events. Second, this interpretation seems to solve the problem of the dating of the tower experience. Luther's own late dating of the event may now stand unchallenged, since it marks the end, and not the beginning, of theological discovery.[9] In terms of our study, it is the culminating realization that God Himself works both the preparation for conversion and conversion itself, in which He gives man the grace and faith that allow him to persevere in conversion. The tower experience as Luther describes it occurred in the time after the outbreak of the

---

[7]According to Saarnivaara, "Luther's experience in the tower was not his conversion. It was the final exegetico-religious discovery of the evangelical way of salvation. We say exegetico-religious, because it was not simply an exegetical discovery of the true teaching of Scripture on this point; neither was it a mere subjective personal experience. At the same time that it was the discovery of the true interpretation of Scripture, it was also an answer to a deep personal spiritual yearning, which resulted in the attainment of a deeper personal assurance of salvation or justification" (*Luther Discovers the Gospel*, p. 46).

[8]WA 54, 183, 25–29 (*Preface to the Complete Editon of Luther's Latin Writings*, 1545); *Luther's Works*, vol. 34: *Career of the Reformer IV*, ed. Lewis W. Spitz (Philadelphia: Muhlenberg Press, 1960), p. 334 (hereafter cited as *LW* 34). Copyright © 1960 by Muhlenberg Press. Used by permission.

[9]In Saarnivaara's words, "the 'tower experience' of Luther was not the beginning but the relative end of his development. Prior to that he knew, in the Augustinian sense, that man is justified and saved through faith in Christ and not by works. It was the discovery of the true meaning of Rom. 1:17 that opened to him the final evangelical insight into justification. . . . Justification is not a change in man, but the gracious declaration of God by which He pronounces righteous the sinner who is not righteous" (*Luther Discovers the Gospel*, p. 46).

indulgence controversy when the full implication of salvation by grace alone for all aspects of theology suddenly dawned on him.

A second position, which constitutes a refinement of the first, is that there were three phases in Luther's religious development. Melanchthon's biography of Luther supports the contention "that there was no single 'conversion' upon which all else depended, but a succession of crises and break-throughs."[10] The tower experience may be associated with any of these three phases: the first phase, in which Luther learned that God's righteousness is soteriological; the second, during the *Lectures on Romans,* when he attained the insight that God Himself produces the works of faith; and the third, when he discovered in 1518–1519 that "justification does not rest at all upon the works of men, not even works of faith worked by God, but that it rests solely upon the work of Christ; in terms of later teminology, it was the discovery that the passive righteousness of Christ is imputed to the believer by grace through faith."[11]

Third, a cogent argument has been made for a differentiation between the tower experience and Luther's reformatory transition or turn (*reformatorische Wende*). There is, according to this position, no reason to doubt the validity and factuality of Luther's account. In terms of Luther's own self-understanding, the tower experience may be designated as the reformatory breakthrough (*reformatorische Durchbruch*), but this event should be sharply differentiated from the reformatory turn in Luther's thought, which consisted of a series of stages that reached their culmination in 1518.[12]

Although many scholars have maintained that Luther's 1545

[10]Green, "Faith, Righteousness, and Justification: New Light on Their Development under Luther and Melanchthon," *Sixteenth Century Journal* 4 (1973), 84.
[11]Ibid., p. 86. Green does not argue that one of the three phases is synonymous with the tower experience, but instead writes: "If one is determined to identify the 'Tower Experience' with one of the three steps outlined above, it doesn't matter with which of these it is associated, so long as the genetic issues are kept clear." On this point he differs from Saarnivaara, who maintains that the tower experience has a definite content and may be assigned a specific date (*Luther Discovers the Gospel,* pp. 92–120, esp. p. 101).
[12]Pesch, "Zur Frage nach Luthers reformatorischer Wende," in *Durchbruch der reformatorischen Erkenntnis bei Luther,* ed. Lohse, pp. 498–501.

account must be evaluated on the basis of the understanding of *iustitia* presented in his early works—especially in his first two commentaries, the *Dictata* and the *Lectures on Romans*—recent scholarship has come increasingly to accept Luther's own dating and description of what was for him a decisive experience.[13] Luther's recollection of his experience is supported by the fact that the *Operationes in Psalmos*, begun in 1519 and finally completed during Luther's exile at the Wartburg, contains a passage that closely parallels his 1545 description:

> We must accustom ourselves to understand the 'righteousness of God,' which we shall later frequently encounter, according to the correct biblical [*canonica*] meaning, namely, that it is not the righteousness by which God himself is righteous and according to which he also condemns the godless, as it is usually understood to be. But, as St. Augustine writes in *De spiritu et litera,* it is that [righteousness] which He puts on man in that He justifies him: namely, the justifying mercy or grace itself, by which we are considered to be righteous by God. About this kind the Apostle writes in Romans 1[:17]: 'For in it the righteousness of God is revealed through faith for faith, as it is written, "He who through faith is righteous shall live." ' And Romans 3[:21]: 'But now the righteousness of God has been manifested apart from the law, although the law and the prophets bear witness to it.' But the righteousness of God is also called our righteousness, because by His grace it is given to us, just like that is called the work of God which He works in us, just like that word of God that He speaks in us, just like the virtues [*virtutes*, powers] of God that He works in us and many other such things.[14]

[13]This shift in scholarly opinion has been due in part to the work of Ernst Bizer, who argued that in Luther's early theological works he does not concentrate on the Word as the instrument of grace, nor does he emphasize *sola fide* as he does in his works during and after 1518 (*Fides ex auditu*).

[14]*WA* 5, 144, 1–11 (Ps. 5:9). With regard to Luther's exegesis, Ebeling writes: "Während er in seinen exegetischen Anfängen, nämlich in seiner ersten Psalmenvorlesung (1513–15), noch ganz in den Bahnen der mittelalterlichen Auslegungsweise befangen ist and sich der Methode des vierfachen Schriftsinnes bedient, sind die ab 1519 erscheinenden Operationes in psalmos das erste grosse exegetische Werk, in dem der Wandel der Auslegungsmethode in bereits ausgereifter Form vorliegt. Dazwischen liegt, beginnend mit der Römerbriefvorlesung, eine Periode des Übergangs" (*Lutherstudien*, vol. 1 [Tübingen: J. C. B. Mohr (Paul Siebeck), 1971], pp. 3–4).

Although for many years the tower experience was perceived to be Luther's conversion, modern scholarship has placed this belief in question and has at the very least sought to distinguish the tower experience from the beginning of Luther's reform theology. With this background, we may now turn our attention directly to the relation between Luther's description of his experience and the understanding of conversion he articulates in his early writings.

Luther's major concern in his Preface is definitely not to record step by step the route to his discovery of justification by faith. Rather, his concern is to show how he was forced by both God and the papists to take positions he had never wished to take. Left to his own choice, he would have preferred the quiet of his study to the tumult of the public forum. In his Preface Luther is at pains to demonstrate that he had in fact been an ardent papist.[15] In no way had he possessed revolutionary or even reformatory aims. In that period of his life he considered himself to be a defender of the papacy. Thus he tells his readers: "So you will find how much and what important matters I humbly conceded to the pope in my earlier writings, which I later and now hold and execrate as the worst blasphemies and abomination. You will, therefore, sincere reader, ascribe this error, or as they slander, contradiction to the time and my inexperience. At first I was all alone and certainly very inept and unskilled in conducting such great affairs. For I got into these turmoils by accident and not by will or intention. I call upon God himself as my witness."[16] Luther's description of his moment of insight

---

[15]Ernst Stracke, *Luthers grosses Selbstzeugnis 1545 über seine Entwicklung zum Reformator historisch-kritisch untersucht*, Schriften des Vereins für Reformationsgeschichte, vol. 44, no. 140 (Leipzig: M. Heinsius Nachfolger Eger & Sievers, 1926), pp. 101–105. "Luther hat in diesem Überblick die konservative Linie in seiner Entwicklung aufgezeigt; wir fanden sie in den primären Quellen, mitunter freilich etwas leichter getönt, wieder. Er hat ferner beweisen wollen, dass alles, was er tat und lehrte, aus dem Worte Gottes selbst sein Leben hatte; manche primäre Quellen, die wir kennen lernten, bestätigt das. Dazu kommt noch, dass der alte Luther keinen Gefallen daran gefunden hat, ein Bild zu entrollen von dem gewaltigen Werk der Zerstörung, dass er, von aussen durch das Andrängen der Feinde, von innen her durch den Geist Gottes getrieben, vollbracht hat, um dem Evangelium eine Gasse zu bahnen" (p. 129).

[16]*WA* 54, 179, 34–180, 4; *LW* 34, 328.

should be studied within the context of his own purpose in writing the Preface, designed for a new generation that had grown up since those difficult early days of struggle.

In his account Luther says that at the time of his discovery he had returned to interpreting the Psalter after having already lectured on Romans, Galatians, and Hebrews. He writes that he had "been captivated with an extraordinary ardor for understanding Paul in the Epistle to the Romans. But up till then it was not the cold blood about the heart, but a single word in Chapter 1[:17], 'In it the righteousness of God is revealed,' that had stood in my way. For I hated that word 'righteousness of God,' which, according to the use and custom of all the teachers, I had been taught to understand philosophically regarding the formal or active righteousness, as they called it, with which God is righteous and punishes the unrighteous sinner."[17] Although Luther had already been writing against reliance on indulgences at the expense of faith, he himself was still deeply troubled and unresolved regarding how one comes to be justified before God. To all appearances, he still considered this justification to be something that man had to achieve, even though he had come to oppose the nominalist concept that man could earn merit before God. He writes:

> Though I lived as a monk without reproach, I felt that I was a sinner before God with an extremely disturbed conscience. I could not believe that he was placated by my satisfaction. I did not love, yes, I hated the righteous God who punishes sinners, and secretly, if not blasphemously, certainly murmuring greatly, I was angry with God, and said, 'As if, indeed, it is not enough, that miserable sinners, eternally lost through original sin, are crushed by every kind of calamity by the law of the decalogue, without having God add pain to pain by the gospel and also by the gospel threatening us with his righteousness and wrath!' Thus I raged with a fierce and troubled conscience. Nevertheless, I beat importunately upon Paul at that place, most ardently desiring to know what St. Paul wanted.

[17]WA 54, 185, 14–20; LW 34, 336.

At last, by the mercy of God, meditating day and night, I gave heed to the context of the words, namely, 'In it the righteousness of God is revealed, as it is written, "He who through faith is righteous shall live"' There I began to understand that the righteousness of God is that by which the righteous lives by a gift of God, namely by faith. And this is the meaning: the righteousness of God is revealed by the gospel, namely, the passive righteousness with which merciful God justifies us by faith, as it is written, 'He who through faith is righteous shall live.' Here I felt that I was altogether born again and had entered paradise itself through open gates. There a totally other face of the entire Scripture showed itself to me. Thereupon I ran through the Scriptures from memory. I also found in other terms an analogy, as, the work of God, that is, what God does in us, the power of God, with which he makes us strong, the wisdom of God, with which he makes us wise, the strength of God, the salvation of God, the glory of God.[18]

How does this description relate to Luther's writings about conversion? First, particularly in the writings of 1518–1519, conversion is linked to the action of the Word. In Scripture the Word is at work to convert man. Christ, as the Word who has suffered humiliation and death for man, also brings about the conversion of the world. Second, Luther describes his experience in language associated with conversion and baptism. He tells his readers that he felt as though he had been born again, indeed as though he had entered paradise. Phrasing our question in another way, we may ask if Luther's developing understanding of conversion, as we have followed it through his writings, helps to illuminate the 1545 description. Why, in spite of his importunate beating upon the Pauline text, does Luther's problem persist? One answer is that Luther continued to face God in servile fear and was still convinced that although he could not earn righteousness before Him, he must make progress in faith. Although he affirmed that he had "acquired the beginning of the knowledge of Christ and faith in him,"[19] he did

[18]WA 54, 185, 21–186, 13; LW 34, 336–337. On conversion and call in Paul and Luther, see Emanuel Hirsch, Lutherstudien, (Gütersloh: C. Bertelsmann, 1954), vol. 2, pp. 68–79.
[19]WA 54, 183, 27–28; LW 34, 334.

not yet equate faith as God's gift with righteousness. Luther's attitude resembles that which was defended by Eck in the Leipzig debate. Luther, as we have seen, strongly opposed Eck's defense of the gloss from Cassiodorus: "The fear of judgment is the door to conversion."[20] Against that position, Luther proclaimed that servile fear without grace not only does not provide a door for conversion but in fact works only wrath. Such appears to have been Luther's own experience. He both raged against God and was fearful of His righteousness and wrath. With respect to Eck's argument, Luther affirmed that conversion occurs solely through the grace of God, without man's action. As an example, he cited Paul's conversion, stating that he would not have been converted if his heart had not been converted inwardly by grace. This affirmation also resembles Luther's account that his insight came "by the mercy of God."[21] In Luther's case the Word broke through his own efforts to achieve understanding. What Luther describes in his 1545 Preface is in fact the twofold action of God in conversion. Through God's alien work, the *opus alienum,* Luther was brought to the recognition that the righteousness that God required lay beyond his efforts and ability. Through God's appropriate work, *opus proprium,* he received grace mediated through the Word to know that God Himself gives man the righteousness He requires. Luther's mature understanding of conversion is reflected in this account of his experience. He offers a slightly different account of his experience in a conversation of 1532 recorded in the *Tischreden.* He tells his listeners: "The words 'righteous' and 'righteousness of God' struck my conscience like lightning. When I heard them I was exceedingly terrified. If God is righteous (I thought), he must punish."[22] In this account, as well as in his Preface, Luther appears to be describing the experience of the alien work of God, bringing him to despair and humility. In this version of the recorded conversation he says that he concluded that "if we, as

---

[20]*WA* 2, 366, 17.

[21]*WA* 54, 186, 3; *LW* 34, 337.

[22]*WA TR* 3, Nr. 3232c, 228, 24–26; *Luther's Works,* vol. 54: *Table Talk,* ed. and trans. Theodore G. Tappert (Philadelphia: Fortress Press, 1967), p. 193 (hereafter cited as *LW* 54). Copyright © 1967 by Fortress Press. Used by permission.

righteous men, ought to live from faith and if the righteousness of God should contribute to the salvation of all who believe, then salvation won't be our merit but God's mercy. My spirit was thereby cheered. For it's by the righteousness of God that we're justified and saved through Christ. These words (which had before terrified me) now became more pleasing to me. The Holy Spirit unveiled the Scriptures for me in this tower."[23] By His appropriate work, acting through the Holy Spirit, God revealed the meaning of the Scripture to Luther and brought him peace and joy.

We may now venture some general remarks about Luther's tower experience. First, for all of his preparation, the insight he received came to him apart from his own efforts. The despair he felt was itself God's *opus alienum,* which prepared the way for the *opus proprium,* in which he experienced the revelation of the true meaning of the righteousness of God. Second, Luther describes himself as changed or transformed by this experience. From a troubled, angry man he was changed into one who had experienced the resolution of his problem and had achieved a new sense of joyous conviction. In other words, Luther describes himself as one who had been converted. Third, he writes that "a

---

[23]*WA TR* 3, 228, 27–32; *LW* 54, 193–194. In one version of this conversation, 3232b, the phrase *"auff diser cloaca"* occurs (*WA TR* 3, 228, 23). The meaning of *cloaca* has been the subject of considerable debate. Erik H. Erikson, in his book *Young Man Luther: A Study in Psychoanalysis and History* (New York: W. W. Norton, 1962), made much of the word and its anal connotations but did not adequately investigate its medieval meaning and usage. See further Lewis W. Spitz, "Psychohistory and History: The Case of Young Man Luther," in *Encounter with Erikson: Historical Interpretation and Religious Biography,* ed. Donald Capps, Walter H. Capps, and M. Gerald Bradford (Missoula: Scholars Press, 1977), pp. 33–65. As Ernst Kroker pointed out many years ago in his article "Luthers Tischreden als geschichtliche Quelle," *Luther-Jahrbuch* 1 (1919), 81–131, the term *cloaca* must be understood within the monastic context of Luther's time, in which it was used to describe a state of melancholy. See also Heiko A. Oberman, "Wir sein Bettler. Hoc est verum: Bund und Gnade in der Theologie des Mittelalters und der Reformation," *Zeitschrift für Kirchengeschichte* 78 (1967), 232–252, esp. 234–242. H. G. Haile in his study *Luther* points to the limitations of the *Tischreden* as a source for information about the early Luther (pp. 239–258); see esp. p. 252, on the Gospel "discovery." See also Haile's article "The Great Martin Luther Spoof: Philological Limits to Knowledge," *Yale Review* 67 (1977), 236–246, on the tower experience and notorious psychoanalytic interpretations of Luther's own account.

totally other face of the entire Scripture showed itself to me."[24] Although, as he admits, he had already attained some understanding of the meaning of faith and righteousness, his moment of insight was a sudden occurrence in which he realized the full implications of what he had begun to recognize through his study of Scripture.

According to Luther, before the tower experience he had made some progress but had not yet attained the realization that faith is God's work in man, which gives him righteousness. He had, however, reached the point of excluding the idea that righteousness is obtained through merit. His problem was that he still perceived righteousness to depend on progress in faith— not that man thereby earned righteousness, but that God required from him this effort.[25] Thus, though he had overcome the idea that man could earn righteousness, the more subtle problem of progress in faith or, phrased differently, perseverance in conversion remained. If this is indeed an accurate representation of Luther before the tower experience, how do his writings about conversion reflect it?

Throughout his early works Luther struggles with the question of preparation for conversion. As early as the *Dictata*, he disclaims that man can earn or effect his own conversion, but the more subtle and difficult problem of whether or not a person can attain to a level of humility or passive receptiveness for conversion through his own efforts remains unresolved. Beginning with the *Lectures on Romans*, Luther more consistently proposes that God Himself works all preparation for conversion in man. In these same lectures, however, Luther remains unclear on the extent of man's responsibility for persevering in conversion through faith and humility. It is in the works of 1518 and 1519 that Luther exhibits his full and mature understanding of

---

[24]*WA* 54, 186, 9–10; *LW* 34, 337.

[25]As Saarnivaara writes: "As long as Luther was under the impression that the righteousness which God requires of man is his 'active' goodness and innocence of obedience and love, produced by the infused grace, and that He judges man according to his actual condition, it was impossible for him to have true and lasting peace in his heart" (*Luther Discovers the Gospel*, pp. 44–45).

both conversion itself and perseverance in conversion.[26] In these writings he attributes even the desire within a person to call out to God to be the work of God within him. God, through the Law, His alien work, brings man to despair and humility and to a recognition of his need, and through the Gospel, His appropriate work, He gives man faith and the knowledge of His forgiveness. The Christian is then able to persevere in conversion through faith, itself a gift and the very possession of Christ, who works through man. God both converts man to Himself and allows him to make progress in Him, to persevere in his conversion and thereby to grow in holiness. For all that he has and is man remains dependent upon God, the loving God who first converted to man in the incarnation, who both prepares man for conversion and sustains him as he perseveres in it.

In his 1545 Preface Luther displays much the same understanding of God and His action. A Christian is righteous because God gives him the righteousness He requires through faith. From our study of Luther's concept of conversion we know that he came to this understanding during 1518, as his Heidelberg disputation demonstrates, and that he articulated this perception throughout his works of 1518 and 1519. According to the chronology he offers in his Preface, during this period he also reached his insight into the meaning of the righteousness of God. His developing understanding of conversion parallels the description he gives of the route to his conversion. While this parallel does not constitute total proof of a late date for the tower experience, it does lend support to Luther's own dating

[26]F. Edward Cranz, in *An Essay on the Development of Luther's Thought on Justice, Law, and Society,* Harvard Theological Studies 19 (Cambridge: Harvard University Press, 1964), convincingly argues that with regard to these themes, "The crucial turning-point in Luther's general development occurs when he begins toward 1518–19 to recognize two 'realms' of Christian existence, two realms which are in the Christian's experience simultaneous and yet distinct. There is the Christian's existence in Christ, and there is the Christian's existence in the world; there is only one Christian individual who exists in both realms" (p. xvi). I suggest his changing ideas in this area parallel his attainment of full understanding of perseverance in conversion as both God's work in man and man's joyful responsibility through the gift of faith.

and credibility and to the opinion of those scholars who accept that date as valid.

Additional support for the acceptance of a date in 1518 comes from Luther's own writings. First, as we have already noted, in the *Operationes in Psalmos* one finds a close parallel to Luther's 1545 description. He also makes unusually frequent references in this work, written between 1519 and 1521, to Romans 1:17. Second, in his *Explanations to the Leipzig Propositions*, which Luther completed in the fall of 1519, in a strongly worded attack on scholastic theologians he writes: "I know and confess that they taught me nothing other than ignorance of sin, righteousness, baptism and the total Christian life. Nor did they teach me what constitute the power of God, the work of God, the grace of God, the righteousness of God, or about faith, hope and love. In brief, not only did they not teach me anything but what they did teach was entirely contrary to holy scripture. . . . I lost Christ then; now in Paul I have found him."[27] This passage bears important similarities to the 1545 account, and it further suggests that his "finding Christ through Paul" was a recent occurrence.

Luther's reformatory turn (*reformatorische Wende*) goes back beyond the Bernhardi von Feldkirch theses of autumn 1516, unaware as Luther was at that time that he was presenting so grave a challenge to ecclesiastical practice. This reformatory turn must be understood as a process, consisting of a series of insights and struggles. As Luther tells his readers in the Preface: "I was all alone and one of those who, as Augustine says of himself, have become proficient by writing and teaching. I was not one of those who from nothing suddenly became the topmost, though they are nothing, neither have labored, nor been tempted, nor become experienced, but have with one look at the Scriptures exhausted their entire spirit."[28] In the writings of 1518–1519 Luther speaks with a new assurance and confidence.

[27]WA 2, 414, 22–28 (*Resolutiones Lutherianae super propositionibus suis Lipsaie disputatis*).
[28]WA 54, 186, 25–29; LW 34, 338.

This new confidence may well be the result of the tower experience, the evangelical breakthrough—indeed, the conversion—which he describes in 1545 as having been decisive for his life.

Having experienced that he was "altogether born again and had entered paradise itself through open gates,"[29] Luther turned back to the task of proclaiming the true nature of righteousness. Thus in his 1520 treatise *The Freedom of a Christian,* Luther could write of righteousness through faith as not only the goal but the basis of all Christian life and work: "So also our works should be done, not that we may be justified by them, since, being justified beforehand by faith, we ought to do all things freely and joyfully for the sake of others."[30] This is the meaning of perseverance in conversion.

[29]*WA* 54, 186, 8–9; *LW* 34, 337.
[30]*WA* 7, 67, 4–6 (*Tractatus de libertate christiana*); *LW* 31, 368.

[8]

Conclusion

Throughout the preceding pages we have followed in the footsteps of the Augustinian monk and biblical theologian Martin Luther as he delivered his first lectures and preached his first sermons. In our intellectual journey we have found conversion to be a key concept in Luther's theology. We have also discovered that by concentrating our attention on his concept of conversion we have opened wide a new window on his theology and thereby gained a fresh perspective on his theological and personal development. From initial uncertainty regarding humility as preparation for grace and conversion, Luther gradually realized that God Himself works the necessary preparation in man. It was only in the works of 1518 and 1519 that he united this insight with the perception that perseverance in conversion is also God's work in man. This perseverance is not another burden laid upon man, but a joyful responsibility. Through grace and faith God gives man the strength to continue as a pilgrim until his journey's end, until that moment of conversion when he comes to see God *facie ad faciem*. Luther's understanding of conversion developed from his fundamental insight in the *Dictata* that the first and greatest conversion of all is God's conversion to man in the incarnation. Only gradually did Luther realize the implications for man of the alien and appropriate works of God in Christ, both making possible his new birth and providing the prototype for his conversion.

Through the study of Luther's concept of conversion, we brought new evidence to our analysis of his tower experience. We ascertained that it is the culminating insight—the moment of conversion—in a long process. Although Luther penned his famous description of that experience only a year before his death, we found good reason to believe that his memory was sound and his account reliable. In the writings of 1518 and 1519 Luther spoke with a full and definitive understanding of conversion. In these same writings he also described perseverance in conversion as possible only through faith, itself the result of God's grace, which alone justifies man. Thus, although we have concentrated on conversion, we have returned in the end to those concepts traditionally viewed as central to Luther's evangelical breakthrough—faith, grace, and justification. The very fact that conversion is so intimately linked to these ideas in Luther's theology demonstrates again the importance of a concept that until now has received little scholarly attention.

At many points in his writings Luther stressed the need for conversion, a theme that became even stronger after the indulgence controversy of 1517. Luther's reform efforts were aimed at effecting conversion—from works righteousness to reliance on faith; from a false dependence on ceremonies to reliance on the preached Word. For people to be converted, for them to receive faith or to renew their faith in the conversion of repentance, it is essential that the Word be preached. Luther's strongest critique of the priesthood—one that marks his great treatises of 1520, for example—was directed at the priests' failure to preach the Word and thereby to bring those who had fallen away into works righteousness and despair to true repentance and joy in the Lord. The Word is God's instrument, quite literally His sword, for slashing through and bringing to nought man's false assurance and confidence in his own works. The Word is constituted by the preaching of Christ incarnated, crucified, and resurrected, of the God who suffered and died for man's sins. Since conversion occurs through this preaching,

conversion is viewed as a work of God—of a God who in the moment of destruction wears a dark and impenetrable mask. The revelation of a new meaning of life (however this meaning is explicated in the individual case) follows on the wreckage, on the ruins of that structure. The experience of conversion lies particularly near at hand, where either an entire epoch experiences the loss of a secure world view or the individual, in the midst of an apparently well-established age, suddenly plunges into the depths and abysses of human uncertainty.[3]

From the dark days of personal uncertainty and despair Luther emerged into the brilliant light of new understanding—the insight of conversion. His conversion insight led to the end of one era and the beginning of another, the Protestant Reformation.

[3]Hans Jürgen Baden, *Literatur und Bekehrung* (Stuttgart: Ernst Klett, 1968), p. 15.

Bibliography

Works of Martin Luther

Luther, Martin. *D. Martin Luthers Werke: Kritische Gesamtausgabe.* 58 vols. Weimar: Hermann Böhlau and Hermann Böhlaus Nachfolger, 1883–

———. *D. Martin Luthers Werke: Kritische Gesamtausgabe. Briefwechsel.* 15 vols. Weimar: Hermann Böhlaus Nachfolger, 1930–1978.

———. *D. Martin Luthers Werke: Kritische Gesamtausgabe. Tischreden.* 6 vols. Weimar: Hermann Böhlaus Nachfolger, 1912–1921.

———. *Luthers Randbemerkungen zu Gabriel Biels Collectorium in quattuor libros sententiarum und zu desser Sacri canonis missae expositio Lyon 1514.* Edited by Hermann Degering. Festgabe der Kommission zur Herausgabe der Werke Martin Luthers zur Feier des 450. Geburtstages Luthers. Weimar: Hermann Böhlaus Nachfolger, 1933.

———. *Luthers Vorlesung über den Hebräerbrief nach der vatikanischen Handschrift.* Edited by Emanuel Hirsch and Hanns Rückert. Berlin and Leipzig: Walter de Gruyter, 1929.

———. *Dr. Martin Luthers Sämmtliche Werke.* 2d ed. Edited by Johann Georg Walch. 23 vols. St. Louis: Concordia, 1880–1910.

———. *Dokumente zu Luthers Entwicklung ⟨bis 1519⟩.* 2d rev. ed. Edited by Otto Scheel. Sammlung ausgewählter kirchen- und dogmengeschichtlicher Quellenschriften, n.s., vol. 2. Tübingen: J. C. B. Mohr (Paul Siebeck), 1929.

———. *Luther's Works.* 55 vols. General editors: Jaroslav Pelikan, vols.

1–30; Helmut T. Lehmann, vols. 31–55. St. Louis: Concordia; Philadelphia: Fortress Press, 1955–1976.

_____. *Lectures on Romans.* Translated and edited by Wilhelm Pauck.
Library of Christian Classics, vol. 15. Philadelphia: Westminster
Press, 1961.

Primary Sources

Augustine. *The Confessions of St. Augustine.* Translated by F. J. Sheed.
1943; New York: Sheed & Ward, 1965.

Benedict. *The Rule of St. Benedict.* Edited and translated by Justin Mc-
Cann. Westminster, Md.: Newman Press, 1952.

Bernard of Clairvaux. *Sancti Bernardi Opera.* Vol. 1: *Sermones super Can-
tica Canticorum 1–35.* Edited by J. Leclercq, C. H. Talbot, and H. M.
Rochais. Rome: Editiones Cistercienses, 1957. Vol. 2: *Sermones super
Cantica Canticorum 36–86.* Edited by J. Leclercq, C. H. Talbot, and H.
M. Rochais. Rome: Editiones Cistercienses, 1958. Vol. 4: *Sermones.*
Edited by J. Leclercq and H. Rochais. Rome: Editiones Cistercienses,
1966.

_____. *The Works of Saint Bernard of Clairvaux.* Vol. 2: *On the Song of
Songs I.* Translated by Kilian Walsh, O.C.S.O. Cistercian Fathers Series, no. 4. Spencer, Mass.: Cistercian Publications, 1971. Vol. 4: *On
the Song of Songs IV.* Translated by Irene Edmonds. Cistercian Fathers
Series, no. 40. Kalamazoo: Cistercian Publications, 1980.

Biel, Gabriel. *Canonis misse expositio.* 4 vols. Edited by Heiko A. Oberman
and William J. Courtenay. Veröffentlichungen des Instituts für europäische Geschichte, Mainz. Wiesbaden: Franz Steiner, 1963–1967.

Bonaventure. *Opera omnia.* Vol. 8. Quarrachi, 1898.

Gerson, Jean. *Jean Gerson: Selections from "A Deo exivit," "Contra curiositatem studentium," and "De mystica theologia speculativa."* Edited by
Steven E. Ozment. Textus minores, vol. 38. Leiden: E. J. Brill, 1969.

Gregorius. *S. Gregorii Magni, Moralia in Iob Libri I–X. Corpus Christianorum.* Series Latina, vol. 143. Turnholti: Brepols, 1979.

Habig, Marion, ed. *St. Francis of Assisi: Writings and Early Biographies.* 3d
rev. ed. Chicago: Franciscan Herald Press, 1973.

Hermannus Quondam Judaeus. *Opusculum de conversione sua.* Edited by
Gerlinde Niemeyer. Monumenta Germaniae historica, die deutschen
Geschichtsquellen des Mittelalters, 500–1500. Quellen zur Geistesgeschichte des Mittelalters, vol. 4. Weimar: Hermann Böhlaus Nachfolger, 1963.

Bibliography

Justin Martyr. *Dialogue with Trypho, a Jew.* In *The Ante-Nicene Fathers*, vol. 1: *The Apostolic Fathers with Justin Martyr and Irenaeus*. Edited by Alexander Roberts and James Donaldson. Revised by A. Cleveland Coxe. 1885; Grand Rapids, Mich.: W. B. Eerdmans, 1975.

McCracken, George E., ed. *Early Medieval Theology*. Library of Christian Classics, vol. 9. Philadelphia: Westminster Press, 1957.

Minge, J.-P. *Patrologia Latina*. 224 vols. in 221. Paris: Garnier Fratres, 1884–1903.

Sabatier, Paul, ed. *Le Speculum perfectionis ou Mémoires de Frère León*. Vol. 1. Manchester: Manchester University Press, 1928.

Sherley-Price, Leo, trans. *St. Francis of Assisi: His Life and Writings as Recorded by His Contemporaries*. New York: Harper, 1959.

Tauler, Johannes. *Predigten*. Edited by Georg Hofmann. Freiburg, Basel, Vienna: Herder, 1961.

————. *Die Predigten Taulers*. Edited by Ferdinand Vetter. Deutsche Texte des Mittelalters, vol. 11. Berlin: Weidmannsche Buchhandlung, 1910.

Thomas Aquinas. *Summa theologiae*. [Cambridge?], Eng.: Blackfriars, 1964–1976.

Thomas of Celano. *Leben und Wunder des heiligen Franziskus*. 2d ed. Translated by P. Engelbert Grau, O.F.M. Franziskanische Quellenschrift, vol. 5. Werl, Westfalia: Dietrich-Coelde, 1964.

————. *St. Francis of Assisi According to Brother Thomas of Celano*. Edited by H. G. Rosedale. London: J. M. Dent, 1904.

Secondary Sources

Abrahams, Israel. *Jewish Life in the Middle Ages*. New York: Macmillan, 1896.

Aland, Kurt. *Hilfsbuch zum Lutherstudium*. 3d rev. and expanded ed. Witten: Luther-Verlag, 1970.

————, ed. *Martin Luther's 95 Theses with the Pertinent Documents from the History of the Reformation*. St. Louis: Concordia, 1967.

————. *Über den Glaubenswechsel in der Geschichte des Christentums*. Berlin: Alfred Töpelmann, 1961.

————. *Der Weg zur Reformation: Zeitpunkt und Charakter des reformatorischen Erlebnisses Martin Luthers*. Theologische Existenz Heute, n.s., no. 123. Munich: Chr. Kaiser, 1965.

Allbeck, Willard Dow. *Studies in the Lutheran Confessions*. Philadelphia: Muhlenberg Press, 1952.

Altenstaig, Johannes. *Vocabularius theologie*. Hagenau, 1517.

Althaus, Paul. *Die Theologie Martin Luthers*. 3d ed. Gütersloh: Gerd Mohn, 1972.

Baden, Hans Jürgen. *Literatur und Bekehrung*. Stuttgart: Ernst Klett, 1968.

Bandt, Hellmut. *Luthers Lehre vom verborgenen Gott: Eine Untersuchung zu dem offenbarungsgeschichtlichen Ansatz seiner Theologie*. Theologische Arbeiten, vol. 8. Berlin: Evangelische Verlagsanstalt, 1958.

Bauer, Karl. *Die Wittenberger Universitätstheologie und die Anfänge der deutschen Reformation*. Tübingen: J. C. B. Mohr (Paul Siebeck), 1928.

Bayer, Oswald. *Promissio: Geschichte der reformatorischen Wende in Luthers Theologie*. Forschungen zur Kirchen- und Dogmengeschichte, vol. 24. Göttingen: Vandenhoeck & Ruprecht, 1971.

Baylor, Michael. *Action and Person: Conscience in Late Scholasticism and the Young Luther*. Studies in Medieval and Reformation Thought, vol. 20. Leiden: E. J. Brill, 1977.

Becker, Siegbert W. *The Foolishness of God: The Place of Reason in the Theology of Martin Luther*. Milwaukee: Northwestern, 1982.

Beintker, Horst. *Die Überwindung der Anfechtung bei Luther: Eine Studie zu seiner Theologie nach den Operationes in Psalmos 1519–21*. Theologische Arbeiten, vol. 1. Berlin: Evangelische Verlagsanstalt, 1954.

Benz, Ernst. *Paulus als Visionär: Eine vergleichende Untersuchung der Visionsberichte des Paulus in der Apostelgeschichte und in den paulinischen Briefen*. Abhandlungen der Geistes- und Sozialwissenschaftlichen Klasse. Jahrgang 52, no. 2. Wiesbaden: Akadamie der Wissenschaften und der Literatur in Mainz, Franz Steiner, 1952.

Bizer, Ernst. *Fides ex auditu: Eine Untersuchung über die Entdeckung der Gerechtigkeit Gottes durch Martin Luther*. 3d rev. ed. Neukirchen-Vluyn: Neukirchner Verlag, 1966.

Blank, Josef. *Paulus und Jesus: Eine theologische Grundlegung*. Studien zum Alten und Neuen Testament, vol. 18. Munich: Kösel, 1968.

Blankenheim, L. M. "Die Richtervorlesung Luthers." *Archiv für Reformationsgeschichte* 51 (1960), 1–19.

Boehmer, Heinrich. *Der junge Luther*. 6th rev. ed. Stuttgart: K. F. Koehler, 1971. Published in English as *Road to Reformation: Martin Luther to the Year 1521*. Translated by John W. Doberstein and Theodore G. Tappert. Philadelphia: Muhlenberg Press, 1946.

Bonduelle, J. "Convers." *Dictionnaire de droit canonique*, vol. 4, cols. 562–588. Paris: Librairie Letouzey et Ané, 1948.

Bornkamm, Heinrich. *Eckhart und Luther*. Stuttgart: W. Kohlhammer, 1936.

Bibliography

———. *Luther Gestalt und Wirkungen: Gesammelte Aufsätze.* Schriften des Vereins für Reformationgeschichte, no. 188. Gütersloh: Gerd Mohn, 1975.

———. "Luthers Bericht über seine Entdeckung der iustitia Dei." *Archiv für Reformationsgeschichte* 37 (1940), 117–128.

———. "Zur Frage der Iustitia Dei beim jungen Luther, Teil I." *Archiv für Reformationsgeschichte* 52 (1961), 16–29.

———. "Zur Frage der Iustitia Dei beim jungen Luther, Teil II." *Archiv für Reformationsgeschichte* 53 (1962), 1–60.

Bornkamm, Karin. *Luthers Auslegungen des Galaterbriefs von 1519 und 1531.* Arbeiten zur Kirchengeschichte, vol. 35. Berlin: Walter de Gruyter, 1963.

Bourke, Vernon. *Augustine's Quest of Wisdom: Life and Philosophy of the Bishop of Hippo.* Milwaukee: Bruce, 1945.

Brandenburg, Albert. *Gericht und Evangelium: Zur Worttheologie in Luthers erster Psalmenvorlesung.* Konfessionskundliche und kontroverstheologische Studien, vol. 4. Paderborn: Bonifacius-Druckerei, 1960.

Brecht, Martin. *Martin Luther: Sein Weg zur Reformation, 1483–1521.* Stuttgart: Calwer, 1981.

———. "Der rechtfertigende Glaube an das Evangelium von Jesus Christus als Mitte von Luthers Theologie." *Zeitschrift für Kirchengeschichte* 89 (1978), 45–77.

Brosché, Fredrik. *Luther on Predestination: The Antinomy and the Unity Between Love and Wrath in Luther's Concept of God.* Acta Universitatis Upsaliensis, Studia Doctrinae Christianae Upsaliensis, vol. 18. Uppsala, 1978.

Brundage, James A. *The Crusades: A Documentary Survey.* Milwaukee: Marquette University Press, 1962.

———. *Medieval Canon Law and the Crusader.* Madison: University of Wisconsin Press, 1969.

Buescher, Gabriel. *The Eucharistic Teaching of William of Ockham.* Franciscan Institute Publications, Theology Series, no. 1. St. Bonaventure, N.Y.: Franciscan Institute, 1950.

Chapman, John. *Saint Benedict and the Sixth Century.* London: Sheed & Ward, 1929.

Comba, Emilio. *Waldo and the Waldensians before the Reformation.* New York: Robert Carter & Brothers and Dodd, Mead, 1880.

Connolly, John L. *John Gerson: Reformer and Mystic.* Louvain: Librairie Universitaire, 1928.

198

Courcelle, Pierre. *Recherches sur les Confessions de Saint Augustin.* Paris: E. de Boccard, 1950.

Courtenay, William J. "Cranmer as a Nominalist—*Sed Contra.*" *Harvard Theological Review* 57, no. 4 (October 1964), 367–380.

Cranz, F. Edward. *An Essay on the Development of Luther's Thought on Justice, Law, and Society.* Harvard Theological Studies 19. 1959; Cambridge: Harvard University Press, 1964.

Damerau, Rudolf. *Die Abendmahlslehre des Nominalismus insbesondere die des Gabriel Biel.* Studien zu den Grundlagen der Reformation. Giessen: Wilhelm Schmitz, 1963.

———. *Die Demut in der Theologie Luthers.* Studien zu den Grundlagen der Reformation, vol. 5. Giessen: Wilhelm Schmitz, 1967.

Demmer, Dorothea. *Luther Interpres: Der theologische Neuansatz in seiner Römerbriefexegese unter besonderer Berücksichtigung Augustins.* Witten: Luther-Verlag, 1968.

Dodds, E. R. *Pagan and Christian in an Age of Anxiety: Some Aspects of Religious Experience From Marcus Aurelius to Constantine.* 1965; New York: W. W. Norton, 1970.

Dress, Walter. *Die Theologie Gersons: Eine Untersuchung zur Verbindung von Nominalismus und Mystik im Spätmittelalter.* Gütersloh: C. Bertelsmann, 1931.

Dukker, Chrysostomus. *Umkehr des Herzens: Der Bussgedanke des heiligen Franziskus von Assisi.* Bücher Franziskanischer Geistigkeit, vol. 1. Werl, Westfalia: Dietrich-Coelde, 1956.

Ebeling, Gerhard. *Evangelische Evangelienauslegung: Eine Untersuchung zu Luthers Hermeneutik.* 1942: Darmstadt: Wissenschaftliche Buchgesellschaft, 1969.

———. *Luther: An Introduction to His Thought.* Translated by R. A. Wilson. 1970; Philadelphia: Fortress Press, 1972.

———. *Lutherstudien,* vol. 1. Tübingen: J. C. B. Mohr (Paul Siebeck), 1971.

Ellwein, Eduard. *Vom neuen Leben: Eine systematische und theologiegeschichtliche Untersuchung zur Lehre vom neuen Leben.* Forschungen zur Geschichte und Lehre des Protestantismus, vol. 1. Munich: Chr. Kaiser, 1932.

Erikson, Erik H. *Young Man Luther: A Study in Psychoanalysis and History.* 1958; New York: W. W. Norton, 1962.

Ernst, Wilhelm. *Gott und Mensch am Vorabend der Reformation: Eine Untersuchung zur Moralphilosophie und -theologie bei Gabriel Biel.* Erfurter Theologische Studien, vol. 28. Leipzig: St. Benno, 1972.

Bibliography

Evans, G. R. *Anselm and a New Generation.* Oxford: Clarendon Press; New York: Oxford University Press, 1980.

Feckes, Karl. *Die Rechtfertigungslehre des Gabriel Biel und ihre Stellung innerhalb der nominalistische Schule.* Münster: Aschendorffschen Verlagsbuchhandlung, 1925.

Feld, Helmut. *Martin Luthers und Wendelin Steinbachs Vorlesungen über den Hebräerbrief: Eine Studie zur Geschichte der neutestamentlichen Exegese und Theologie.* Veröffentlichungen des Instituts für europäische Geschichte Mainz, vol. 62. Wiesbaden: Franz Steiner, 1971.

Fife, Robert Herndon. *The Revolt of Martin Luther.* New York: Columbia University Press, 1957.

Frend, W. H. C. *Martyrdom and Persecution in the Early Church: A Study of Conflict from the Maccabees to Donatists.* 1965; Garden City, N.Y.: Anchor Books, Doubleday, 1967.

Galtier, Paul. "Conversi." *Dictionnaire de Spiritualité,* vol. 2, pt. 2, cols. 2218–2224. Paris: Beauchesne, 1953.

Gilson, Etienne. *The Mystical Theology of Saint Bernard.* New York: Sheed & Ward, 1940.

Grane, Leif. "Augustins 'Expositio quarandum propositionum ex epistola ad Romanos' in Luthers Römerbriefvorlesung." *Zeitschrift für Theologie und Kirche* 69, no. 3 (September 1972), 304–330.

———. *Contra Gabrielem: Luthers Auseinandersetzung mit Gabriel Biel in der Disputatio contra Scholasticam Theologiam.* Acta Theologica Danica, vol. 4, Gyldendal, 1962.

———. "Gregor von Rimini und Luthers Leipziger Disputation." *Studia Theologica* 22 (1968), 29–49.

———. "Lutherforschung und Geistesgeschichte: Auseinandersetzung mit Heiko A. Oberman." *Archiv für Reformationsgeschichte* 68 (1977), 302–315.

———. "Luthers Auslegung von Röm. 2, 12–15 in der Römerbriefvorlesung." *Neue Zeitschrift für systematische Theologie und Religionsphilosophie* 17, no. 1 (1975), 22–32.

———. *Modus Loquendi Theologicus: Luthers Kampf um die Erneuerung der Theologie (1515–1518).* Acta Theologica Danica, vol. 12. Leiden: E. J. Brill, 1975.

———. *Peter Abelard: Philosophy and Christianity in the Middle Ages.* Translated by Frederick and Christine Crowley. New York: Harcourt, Brace & World, 1970.

Green, Lowell. "Faith, Righteousness, and Justification: New Light on Their Development under Luther and Melanchthon." *Sixteenth Century Journal* 4, no. 1 (1973), 65–86.

Bibliography

_____. *How Melanchthon Helped Luther Discover the Gospel: The Doctrine of Justification in the Reformation.* Fallbrook, Calif.: Verdict Publications, 1980.

Grimm, Harold J. "The Human Element in Luther's Sermons." *Archiv für Reformationsgeschichte* 49 (1958), 50–60.

Grundmann, Herbert. *Ketzergeschichte des Mittelalters.* Vol. 2, Leiferung G, 1. Teil of *Die Kirche in ihrer Geschichte: Ein Handbuch.* Edited by Kurt Dietrich Schmidt and Ernst Wolf. Göttingen: Vandenhoeck & Ruprecht, 1963.

_____. *Religiöse Bewegungen im Mittelalter: Untersuchungen über die geschichtliche Zusammenhänge zwischen der Ketzerei, den Bettelorden und der religiösen Frauenbewegungen im 12. und 13. Jahrhundert und über die geschichtlichen Grundlagen der deutschen Mystik.* 2d rev. ed. Hildesheim: Georg Olm, 1961.

Grundmann, Walter. *Der Römerbrief des Apostels Paulus und seine Auslegung durch Martin Luther.* Weimar: Hermann Böhlaus Nachfolger, 1964.

Grunewald, Käte. *Studien zu Johannes Taulers Frömmigkeit.* Beiträge zur Kulturgeschichte des Mittelalters und der Renaissance, vol. 44. Leipzig: B. G. Teubner, 1930.

Guardini, Romano. *The Conversion of Augustine.* Translated by Elinor Briefs. Westminster, Md.: Newman Press, 1960.

Gyllenkrok, Axel. *Rechtfertigung und Heiligung in der frühen evangelischen Theologie Luthers.* Uppsala Universitets Årsskrift 1952:2. Uppsala: A.-B. Lundquistka Bokhandeln; Wiesbaden: Otto Harrassowitz.

Hagen, Kenneth. "Changes in the Understanding of Luther: The Development of the Young Luther." *Theological Studies* 29, no. 3 (September 1968), 472–496.

_____. *A Theology of Testament in the Young Luther: The Lectures on Hebrews.* Studies in Medieval and Reformation Thought, vol. 12. Leiden: E. J. Brill, 1974.

Hägglund, Bengt. *The Background of Luther's Doctrine of Justification in Medieval Theology.* Historical Series, no. 18, Facet Books. Philadelphia: Fortress Press, 1971.

Haile, H. G. "The Great Martin Luther Spoof: Philological Limits to Knowledge." *Yale Review* 67 (1977), 236–246.

_____. *Luther: An Experiment in Biography.* Garden City, N.Y.: Doubleday, 1980.

Hamel, Adolf. *Der junge Luther und Augustin: Ihre Beziehungen in der Rechtfertigungslehre nach Luthers ersten Vorlesungen 1509–1518 untersucht.* 2 vols. Gütersloh: C. Bertelsmann, 1934–1935.

Bibliography

Hamm, Berndt. *Promissio, Pactum, Ordinatio: Freiheit und Selbstbindung Gottes in der scholastischen Gnadenlehre.* Beiträge zur historischen Theologie, vol. 54. Tübingen: J. C. B. Mohr (Paul Siebeck), 1977.

Hammerich, L. L. *The Beginning of the Strife Between Richard Fitzralph and the Mendicants.* Det Kgl. danske videnskabernes selskab. Historiskfilologiske meddelelser, 26, 3. Copenhagen: Levin & Munksgaard, Ejnar Munksgaard 1938.

Hassel, David J. "Conversion Theory and *Scientia* in the *De Trinitate.*" *Recherches Augustiniennes* 2 (1962), 383–401.

Heikennen, Jacob W. "Luther's Lectures on the Romans (1515–1516)." *Interpretation: A Journal of Bible and Theology* 7 (April 1953), 178–194.

Hendrix, Scott H. *Ecclesia in Via: Ecclesiological Developments in the Medieval Psalms Exegesis and the Dictata super Psalterium (1513–1515) of Martin Luther.* Studies in Medieval and Reformation Thought, vol. 8. Leiden: E. J. Brill, 1974.

Hennig, Gerhard. *Cajetan und Luther: Ein historischer Beitrag zur Begegnung von Thomismus und Reformation.* Arbeiten zur Theologie, 2d ser., vol. 7. Stuttgart: Calwer, 1966.

Hilpisch. S. "Conversi." *New Catholic Encyclopedia.* Vol. 4, pp. 285–286. New York: McGraw-Hill, 1967.

Hirsch, Emanuel. *Lutherstudien.* 2 vols. Gütersloh: C. Bertelsmann, 1954.

Hoffman, Bengt. *Luther and the Mystics: A Re-examination of Luther's Spiritual Experience and His Relationship to the Mystics.* Minneapolis: Augsburg, 1976.

Holl, Karl. *Gesammelte Aufsätze zur Kirchengeschichte.* Vol. 1: *Luther.* 2d and 3d rev. eds. 1921; Tübingen: J. C. B. Mohr (Paul Siebeck), 1923.

Hollenbach, M. W. "Synderesis." *New Catholic Encyclopedia.* Vol. 13, pp. 881–883. New York: McGraw-Hill, 1967.

Hübner, Hans. *Rechtfertigung und Heiligung in Luthers Römerbriefvorlesung: Ein systematischer Entwurf.* Glaube und Lehre, vol. 7. Witten: Luther-Verlag, 1965.

Iwand, Hans Joachim. *Glaubensgerechtigkeit nach Luthers Lehre.* 2d ed. Munich: Chr. Kaiser, 1951.

——. *Rechtfertigungslehre und Christusglaube: Eine Untersuchung zur Systematik in der Rechtfertigungslehre Luthers in ihren Anfängen.* Theologische Bücherei, vol. 14. Munich: Chr. Kaiser, 1961.

James, William. *The Varieties of Religious Experience: A Study in Human Nature.* 1902; New York: New American Library, 1958.

Jedin, Hubert, ed. *History of the Church.* Vol. 5: *Reformation and Counter*

Reformation. Edited by Erwin Iserloh, Joseph Glazik, and Hubert
Jedin. Translated by Anselm Biggs and Peter W. Becker. New York:
Seabury Press, 1980.

Jetter, Werner. *Die Taufe beim jungen Luther: Eine Untersuchung über das
Werden der reformatorischen Sakraments-und Taufanschauung.* Beiträge
zur historischen Theologie, vol. 18. Tübingen: J. C. B. Mohr (Paul
Siebeck), 1954.

Junghans, Helmar. *Wittenberg als Lutherstadt.* Berlin: Union, 1979.

Kantzanbach, Friedrich Wilhelm. "Christusgemeinschaft und Rechtfertigung: Luthers Gedanke vom fröhlichen Wechsel als Frage an unsere Rechtfertigungslehre." *Luther: Zeitschrift der Luther-Gesellschaft* 35
(1964), 34–45.

Keller, Ludwig. *Johann von Staupitz und die Anfänge der Reformation.*
Leipzig: S. Hirzel, 1888.

Kiessling, Elmer C. *The Early Sermons of Luther and Their Relation to the
Pre-Reformation Sermon.* Grand Rapids, Mich.: Zondervan, 1935.

Kolb, Robert. *Nikolaus von Amsdorf (1483–1565).* Bibliotheca Human-
istica & Reformatorica, vol. 24. Niewkoop: B. de Graaf, 1978.

Köster, Beate. "Bemerkungen zum zeitlichen Ansatz des reformatorischen Durchbruchs bei Martin Luther." *Zeitschrift für
Kirchengeschichte* 86 (1975), 208–214.

Kroeger, Matthias. *Rechtfertigung und Gesetz: Studien zur Entwicklung der
Rechtfertigungslehre beim jungen Luther.* Forschungen zur Kirchen- und
Dogmengeschichte, vol. 20. Göttingen: Vandenhoeck & Ruprecht,
1968.

Kroker, Ernst. "Luthers Tischreden als geschichtliche Quelle." *Luther-
Jahrbuch* 1 (1919), 81–131.

Ladner, Gerhart. *The Idea of Reform: Its Impact on Christian Thought and
Action in the Age of the Fathers.* 1959; New York: Harper & Row, 1967.

Leclercq, Jean. *Bernard of Clairvaux and the Cistercian Spirit.* Translated
by Claire Lavoie. Cistercian Studies Series, no. 16. Kalamazoo: Cistercian Publications, 1976.

_____. *The Love of Learning and the Desire for God: A Study of Monastic
Culture.* 1961; New York: Fordham University Press, 1977.

_____. *Monks and Love in Twelfth-Century France: Psycho-Historical Essays.*
Oxford: Oxford University Press, 1979.

Leff, Gordon. *Bradwardine and the Pelagians: A Study of His 'De Causa Dei'
and Its Opponents.* Cambridge Studies in Medieval Life and Thought,
n.s., vol. 5. Cambridge: Cambridge University Press, 1957.

_____. *Heresy in the Later Middle Ages: The Relation of Heterodoxy to*

Bibliography

Orthodoxy, c. 1250–c. 1450. vol. 1. Manchester: Manchester University Press, 1967.

――――. *Richard FitzRalph, Commentator of the Sentences: A Study in Theological Orthodoxy.* Manchester: Manchester University Press, 1963.

Lindhardt, Mogens. "Magna pars iustitiae, velle esse iustum: Eine augustinische Sentenz und Luthers Römerbriefvorlesung." *Studia Theologica* 27 (1973), 127–149.

Link, Wilhelm. *Das Ringen Luthers um die Freiheit der Theologie von der Philosophie.* 3d ed. Darmstadt: Wissenschaftliche Buchgesellschaft, 1969.

Loewenich, Walther von. *Luthers theologia crucis.* 5th ed. Witten: Luther-Verlag, 1967.

Lohse, Bernhard, ed. *Der Durchbruch der reformatorischen Erkenntnis bei Luther.* Wege der Forschung, vol. 123. Darmstadt: Wissenschaftliche Buchgesellschaft, 1968.

――――. *Martin Luther: Eine Einführung in sein Leben und sein Werk.* Munich: C. H. Beck, 1981.

――――. *Mönchtum und Reformation: Luthers Auseinandersetzung mit dem Mönchsideal des Mittelalters.* Forschungen zur Kirchen- und Dogmengeschichte, vol. 12. Göttingen: Vandenhoeck & Ruprecht, 1963.

Lorenz, Rüdiger. *Die unvollendete Befreiung von Nominalismus: Martin Luther und die Grenzen hermeneutischer Theologie bei Gerhard Ebeling.* Gütersloh: Gerd Mohn, 1973.

Lottin, O. "Le voeu de 'conversatio morum' dans la Règle de Saint-Benoît." *Recherches de théologie ancienne et médiévale* 26 (1959), 5–16.

McCann, Justin. *Saint Benedict.* New York: Sheed & Ward, 1937.

McSorley, Harry J., C.S.P. *Luther: Right or Wrong: An Ecumenical-Theological Study of Luther's Major Work, "The Bondage of the Will."* New York: Newman Press; Minneapolis: Augsburg, 1969.

Mauser, Ulrich. *Der junge Luther und die Häresie.* Schriften des Vereins für Reformationsgeschichte, no. 184. Gütersloh: Gerd Mohn, 1968.

Metzger, Günther. *Gelebter Glaube: Die Formierung reformatorischen Denkens in Luthers erster Psalmenvorlesung, dargestellt am Begriff des Affekts.* Forschungen zur Kirchen- und Dogmengeschichte, vol. 14. Göttingen: Vandenhoeck & Ruprecht, 1964.

Müller, Gerhard. "Die Einheit der Theologie des jungen Luthers." In *Reformatio und Confessio: Festschrift für D. Wilhelm Maurer,* edited by Friedrich Wilhelm Kantzenbach and Gerhard Müller. Berlin and Hamburg: Lutherisches Verlagshaus, 1965.

Munck, Johannes. *Paul and the Salvation of Mankind*. Richmond: John Knox Press, 1959.

Murphy, Lawrence F., S. J. "Martin Luther, the Erfurt Cloister, and Gabriel Biel: The Relation of Philosophy to Theology." *Archiv für Reformationsgeschichte* 70 (1979), 5–24.

Nembach, Ulrich. *Prediġ̣t des Evangeliums: Luther als Prediger, Pädagoge und Rhetor*. Neukirchen-Vluyn: Neukirchener Verlag, 1972.

Nilsson, Kjell Ove. *Simul: Das Miteinander von Göttlichem und Menschlichem in Luthers Theologie*. Forschungen zur Kirchen- und Dogmengeschichte, vol. 17. Göttingen: Vandenhoeck & Ruprecht, 1966.

Nock, Arthur Darby. *Conversion: The Old and New in Religion from Alexander the Great to Augustine of Hippo*. 1933; London: Oxford University Press, 1962.

Nörregard, Jens. *Augustins Bekehrung*. Translated by A. Spelmeyer. Tübingen: J. C. B. Mohr (Paul Siebeck), 1923.

Nygren, Gotthard. *Das Prädestinationsproblem in der Theologie Augustins: Eine systematisch-theologische Studie*. Translated by Christa-Maria Lyckhage. Studia Theologica Lundensia, vol. 12. Göttingen: Vandenhoeck & Ruprecht, 1956.

Oberman, Heiko A. *Archbishop Thomas Bradwardine, A Fourteenth Century Augustinian: A Study of His Theology in Its Historical Context*. Utrecht: Kemink & Zoon, 1957.

————. *Contra vanam curiositatem: Ein Kapitel der Theologie zwischen Seelenwinkel und Weltall*. Theologische Studien 113. Zurich: Theologischer Verlag, 1974.

————. "Facientibus Quod in se est Deus non Denegat gratiam: Robert Holcot O.P. and the Beginnings of Luther's Theology." *Harvard Theological Review* 55 (1962), 317–342. Also in *The Reformation in Medieval Perspective*, edited by Steven Ozment. Chicago: Quadrangle Books, 1971.

————, ed. *Forerunners of the Reformation: The Shape of Late Medieval Thought Illustrated by Key Documents*. Translations by Paul L. Nyhus. New York: Holt, Rinehart & Winston, 1966.

————. *The Harvest of Medieval Theology: Gabriel Biel and Late Medieval Nominalism*. 2d rev. ed. Grand Rapids, Mich.: W. B. Eerdmans, 1967.

————. "'Iustitia Christi' and 'Iustitia Dei': Luther and the Scholastic Doctrines of Justification." *Harvard Theological Review* 59 (1966), 1–26.

————, ed. *Luther and the Dawn of the Modern Era: Papers for the Fourth*

International Congress for Luther Research. Studies in the History of Christian Thought, vol. 8. Leiden: E. J. Brill, 1974.

———. "Reformation: Epoche oder Episode." *Archiv für Reformationsgeschichte* 68 (1977), 302–315.

———. "The Shape of Late Medieval Theology: The Birthpangs of the Modern Era." *Archiv für Reformationsgeschichte* 64 (1973), 13–33.

———. "Simul Gemitus et Raptus: Luther und die Mystik." In *The Church, Mysticism, Sanctification, and the Natural in Luther's Thought: Lectures Presented to the Third International Congress on Luther Research,* edited by Ivar Asheim. Philadelphia: Fortress Press, 1967. Published in English in *The Reformation in Medieval Perspective,* edited by Steven Ozment, pp. 219–251. Chicago: Quadrangle Books, 1971.

———. " 'Tuus sum, salvum me fac': Augustinréveil zwischen Renaissance und Reformation." In *Scientia Augustiniana: Festschrift für Adolar Zumkeller, OSA,* edited by Cornelius Petrus Mayer and Willigis Eckerman. Würzburg: Augustinus, 1975, pp. 349–394.

———. *Werden und Wertung der Reformation: Von Wegestreit zum Glaubenskampf.* Tübingen: J. C. B. Mohr (Paul Siebeck), 1977. Revised and abridged as *Masters of the Reformation: The Emergence of a New Intellectual Climate in Europe.* Translated by Dennis Martin. Cambridge: Cambridge University Press, 1981.

———. "Wir sein Bettler. Hoc est verum: Bund und Gnade in der Theologie des Mittelalters und der Reformation." *Zeitschrift für Kirchengeschichte* 78 (1967), 232–252.

———. "Wittenbergs Zweifrontenkrieg gegen Prierias und Eck: Hintergrund und Entscheidungen des Jahres 1518." *Zeitschrift für Kirchengeschichte* 80 (1969), 331–358.

O'Connell, Robert J. *St. Augustine's Confessions: The Odyssey of a Soul.* Cambridge: Belknap Press of Harvard University Press, 1969.

O'Meara, John J. *The Young Augustine: The Growth of St. Augustine's Mind up to his Conversion.* London: Longmans, Green, 1954.

Ozment, Steven E. "An Aid to Luther's Marginal Comments on Johannes Tauler's Sermons." *Harvard Theological Review* 63 (1970), 305–311.

———. *Homo Spiritualis: A Comparative Study of the Anthropology of Johannes Tauler, Jean Gerson, and Martin Luther (1509–16) in the Context of Their Theological Thought.* Studies in Medieval and Reformation Thought, vol. 6. Leiden: E. J. Brill, 1969.

———. "Luther and the Late Middle Ages: The Formation of Reformation Thought." In *Transition and Revolution: Problems and Issues of*

European Renaissance and Reformation History, edited by Robert M. Kingdon, pp. 109–152. Minneapolis: Burgess, 1974.

———, ed. *The Reformation in Medieval Perspective.* Chicago: Quadrangle Books, 1971.

Pannenberg, Wolfhart. *Die Prädestinationslehre des Duns Skotus im Zusammenhang der scholastischen Lehrentwicklung.* Forschungen zur Kirchen- und Dogmengeschichte, vol. 4. Göttingen: Vandenhoeck & Ruprecht, 1954.

Pantin, W. A. *The English Church in the Fourteenth Century.* Cambridge: Cambridge University Press, 1955.

Pascoe, Louis B. *Jean Gerson: Principles of Church Reform.* Studies in Medieval and Reformation Thought, vol. 7. Leiden: E. J. Brill, 1973.

Pesch, Otto Hermann. *Theologie der Rechtfertigung bei Martin Luther und Thomas von Aquin.* Walberger Studien der Albertus-Magnus-Akadamie, Theologische Reihe, vol. 4. Mainz: Matthias Grünewald, 1967.

Peters, Albrecht. *Glaube und Werk: Luthers Rechtfertigungslehre im Lichte der heiligen Schrift.* 2d ed. Arbeiten zur Geschichte und Theologie des Luthertums, vol. 8. Berlin and Hamburg: Lutherisches Verlagshaus, 1967.

Pinomaa, Lennart. *Der existenzielle Character der Theologie Luthers: Das Hervorbrechen der Theologie der Anfechtung und ihre Bedeutung für das Lutherverständnis.* Helsinki, 1940.

———. *Der Zorn Gottes in der Theologie Luthers: Ein Beitrag zur Frage nach der Einheit des Gottesbildes bei Luther.* Helsinki, 1938.

Poschmann, Bernhard. *Penance and the Anointing of the Sick.* Translated and revised by Francis Courtney. Freiburg: Herder; London: Burns & Oates, 1964.

Prenter, Regin. *Der barmherzige Richter: Iustitia dei passiva in Luthers Dictata super Psalterium 1513–1515.* Acta Jutlandica, Aarsskrift for Aarhus Universitet, 33, 2, Teologisk Serie 8. Aarhus: Universitetsforlaget I; Copenhagen: Ejnar Munksgaard, 1961.

———. *Spiritus Creator.* Translated by John M. Jensen. Philadelphia: Muhlenberg Press, 1953.

Raeder, Siegfried. *Das Benutzung des masoretischen Textes bei Luther in der Zeit zwischen der ersten und zweiten Psalmenvorlesung 1515–1518.* Beiträge zur historischen Theologie, vol. 38. Tübingen: J. C. B. Mohr (Paul Siebeck), 1967.

Raitt, Jill, ed. *Shapers of Religious Traditions in Germany, Switzerland, and Poland, 1560–1600.* New Haven: Yale University Press, 1981.

Bibliography

Ritschl, Otto. *Dogmengeschichte des Protestantismus.* Vol. 2: *Orthodoxie und Synkretismus in der altprotestantischen Theologie.* Pt. 1: *Die Theologie der deutschen Reformation und die Entwicklung der lutherischen Orthodoxie in der philippistischen Streitigkeiten.* Leipzig: J. C. Hinrichs, 1912.

Rosin, Wilbert, and Preus, Robert D., eds. *A Contemporary Look at the Formula of Concord.* St. Louis: Concordia, 1978.

Rost, Gerhard. *Der Prädestinationsgedanke in der Theologie Martin Luthers.* Berlin: Evangelische Verlagsanstalt, 1966.

Rühl, Artur. "Der Einfluss der Mystik auf Denken und Entwicklung des jungen Luther." Dissertation, Philipps-Universität Marburg, 1960.

Ruhland, Friedrich. *Luther und die Brautmystik nach Luthers Schriftum bis 1521.* Giessen: Otto Kindt, 1938.

Runciman, Steven. *A History of the Crusades.* 3 vols. Cambridge: Cambridge University Press, 1951–1954.

Rupp, Gordon. *Luther's Progress to the Diet of Worms.* 1951; New York: Harper & Row, 1964.

————. *The Righteousness of God: Luther Studies.* London: Hodder & Stoughton, 1953.

Saarnivaara, Uuras. *Luther Discovers the Gospel: New Light upon Luther's Way from Medieval Catholicism to Evangelical Faith.* St. Louis: Concordia, 1951.

Schinzer, Reinhard. *Die doppelte Verdienstlehre des Spätmittelalters und Luthers reformatorische Entdeckung.* Theologische Existenz Heute, no. 168. Munich: Chr. Kaiser, 1971.

Schmiel, David. *Via Propria and Via Mystica in the Theology of Jean le Charlier de Gerson.* St. Louis: Oliver Slave, 1969.

Schmitz, Philibert. "Conversatio (conversio) morum." *Dictionnaire de Spiritualité,* Vol. 2, pt. 2, cols. 2206–2212. Paris: Beauchesne, 1953.

Schoeps, Hans Joachim. *Paul: The Theology of the Apostle in the Light of Jewish Religious History.* Philadelphia: Westminster Press, 1961.

Schwarz, Reinhard. *Fides, Spes und Caritas beim jungen Luther.* Arbeiten zur Kirchengeschichte, vol. 34. Berlin: Walter de Gruyter, 1962.

————. *Vorgeschichte der reformatorischen Busstheologie.* Arbeiten zur Kirchengeschichte, vol. 41. Berlin: Walter de Gruyter, 1968.

Schwiebert, E. G. *Luther and His Times: The Reformation from a New Perspective.* St. Louis: Concordia, 1950.

Seeberg, Reinhold. *Lehrbuch der Dogmengeschichte.* Vol. 3: *Die Dogmenbildung des Mittelalters.* 6th ed. Basel: Benno Schwabe, 1960. Vol. 4, pt. 1: *Die Lehre Luthers.* 2d and 3d rev. ed. Leipzig: A. Deichertsche Verlagsbuchhandlung, Werner Scholl, 1917.

Bibliography

Seils, Martin. *Der Gedanke vom Zusammenwirken Gottes und des Menschen in Luthers Theologie.* Beiträge zur Förderung christlicher Theologie, vol. 50. Gütersloh: Gerd Mohn, 1962.

Selge, Kurt-Victor. *Die ersten Waldenser.* Vol. 1: *Untersuchung und Darstellung.* Arbeiten zur Kirchengeschichte, vol. 37/1. Berlin: Walter de Gruyter, 1967.

Smalley, Beryl. *The Study of the Bible in the Middle Ages.* 1952; Notre Dame, Ind.: University of Notre Dame Press, 1964.

Söderlund, Rune. "Der meritum-Begriff der 'Heidelberger Disputation' im Verhältnis zum mittelalterlichen und zur späteren reformatorischen Theologie." *Lutherjahrbuch* 48 (1981), 44–53.

Spitz, Lewis W. "Psychohistory and History: The Case of Young Man Luther." In *Encounter with Erikson: Historical Interpretation and Religious Biography,* edited by M. Gerald Bradford, Donald Capps, and Walter Capps. Missoula, Mont.: Scholars Press, 1977.

———. *The Reformation: Basic Interpretations.* 2d ed. Lexington, Mass.: D. C. Heath, 1972.

———. *The Religious Renaissance of the German Humanists.* Cambridge: Harvard University Press, 1963.

Stange, Carl. *Die Anfänge der Theologie Luthers.* Studien der Luther-Akademie, n.s., vol. 5. Berlin: Alfred Töpelmann, 1957.

Steidle, Basilius, ed. *Regula Magistri: Regula St. Benedicti.* Rome: Herder, 1959.

Steinmetz, David C. "Luther and the Late Medieval Augustinians: Another Look." *Concordia Theological Monthly* 44 (1973), 245–260.

———. *Luther and Staupitz: An Essay in the Intellectual Origins of the Protestant Reformation.* Duke Monographs in Medieval and Renaissance Studies, no. 4. Durham, N.C.: Duke University Press, 1980.

———. *Misericordia Dei: The Theology of Johannes von Staupitz in Its Late Medieval Setting.* Studies in Medieval and Reformation Thought, vol. 4. Leiden: E. J. Brill, 1968.

———. "Religious Ecstasy in Staupitz and the Young Luther." *Sixteenth-Century Journal* 11, no. 1 (Spring 1980), 23–37.

Stelzenberger, Johann. *Die Mystik des Johannes Gerson.* Breslauer Studien zur historischen Theologie, vol. 10. Breslau: Müller & Seiffert, 1928.

Stendahl, Krister. *Paul among Jews and Gentiles and Other Essays.* Philadelphia: Fortress Press, 1976.

Stock, Ursula. *Die Bedeutung der Sakramenten in Luthers Sermonen von 1519.* Studies in the History of Christian Thought, vol. 27. Leiden: E. J. Brill, 1982.

Stracke, Ernst. *Luthers grosses Selbstzeugnis 1545 über seine Entwicklung zum Reformator historisch-kritisch untersucht.* Schriften des Vereins für Reformationsgeschichte, vol. 44, no. 140. Leipzig: M. Heinsius Nachfolger Eger & Sievers, 1926.

Tentler, Thomas. *Sin and Confession on the Eve of the Reformation.* Princeton: Princeton University Press, 1977.

Thaidigsmann, Edgar. "Kreuz und Wirklichkeit: Zur Aneignung der 'Heidelberger Disputation' Luthers." *Lutherjahrbuch* 48 (1981), 80–96.

Thomas, Hedwig. *Zur Würdigung des Psalmenvorlesung Luthers von 1513–1515.* Weimar: Hermann Böhlaus Nachfolger, 1920.

Trinkaus, Charles, ed. *The Pursuit of Holiness in Late Medieval and Renaissance Religion.* Studies in Medieval and Reformation Thought, vol. 10. Leiden: E. J. Brill, 1974.

Troeltsch, Ernst. *Gesammelte Aufsätze.* Vol. 4. Tübingen: J. C. B. Mohr (Paul Siebeck), 1925.

Vercruysse, Joseph. *Fidelis Populis.* Veröffentlichungen des Instituts fur europäische Geschichte Mainz, Abteilung für abendländische Religionsgeschichte, vol. 48. Wiesbaden: Franz Steiner, 1968.

———. "Gesetz und Liebe: Die Struktur der 'Heidelberger Disputation' Luthers (1518)." *Lutherjahrbuch* 48 (1981), 7–43.

Vogelsang, Erich. *Die Anfänge von Luthers Christologie nach der ersten Psalmenvorlesung.* Berlin and Leipzig: Walter de Gruyter, 1929.

———. *Die Bedeutung der neuveröffentlichen Hebräer-Brief Vorlesung Luthers von 1517/1518.* Tübingen: J. C. B. Mohr (Paul Siebeck), 1930.

Vorster, Hans. *Der Freiheitsverständnis bei Thomas von Aquin und Martin Luther.* Kirche und Konfession, vol. 8. Göttingen: Vandenhoeck & Ruprecht, 1965,

Walch, Johann Georg. *Historische und Theologische Einleitung in die Religions-Streitigkeiten der Evangelisch-Lutherischen Kirche, von der Reformation an bis auf ietzige Zeiten, Vierdter und funfter Theil.* Jena, 1739.

Watson, Philip. *Let God Be God!: An Interpretation of the Theology of Martin Luther.* Philadelphia: Muhlenberg Press, 1949.

Weier, Reinhold. *Das Theologieverständnis Martin Luthers.* Konfessionskundliche und kontroverstheologische Studien, vol. 26. Paderborn: Bonifacius Druckerei, 1976.

Weilner, Ignaz. *Johannes Taulers Bekehrungsweg: Die Erfahrungsgrundlagen seiner Mystik.* Studien zur Geschichte der katholische Moraltheologie, vol. 10. Regensburg: Friedrich Pustet, 1961.

Wernle, Hans. *Allegorie und Erlebnis bei Luther.* Basler Studien zur deutschen Sprache und Literatur, vol. 24. Bern: Francke, 1960.

Wicks, Jared. *Man Yearning for Grace: Luther's Early Spiritual Teaching.* Washington and Cleveland: Corpus Books, 1968.

Williams, Watkin. *Saint Bernard of Clairvaux.* Historical Series of the University of Manchester, no. 237; Historical Series no. 69. Manchester: Manchester University Press, 1935.

Wolf, Ernst. *Luthers Prädestinationsanfechtungen.* Rostock: Richard Beckmann, 1925.

_____. *Staupitz und Luther: Ein Beitrag zur Theologie des Johannes von Staupitz und deren Bedeutung für Luthers theologischen Werdegang.* Quellen und Forschungen zur Reformationsgeschichte, vol. 9. Leipzig: M. Heinsius Nachfolger Eger & Sievers, 1927.

Wolf, Herbert. *Martin Luther: Eine Einführung in germanistische Luther-Studien.* Stuttgart: J. B. Metzler, 1980.

Workman, Herbert. *The Evolution of the Monastic Ideal: From the Earliest Times Down to the Coming of the Friars.* 1913; Boston: Beacon Press, 1962.

Zur Mühlen, Karl-Heinz. "Luthers Kritik am scholastischen Aristotelismus in der 25. These der 'Heidelberger Disputation' von 1518." *Lutherjahrbuch* 48 (1981), 54–79.

_____. *Nos extra nos: Luthers Theologie zwischen Mystik und Scholastik.* Beiträge zur historischen Theologie, vol. 46. Tübingen: J. C. B. Mohr (Paul Siebeck), 1972.

Index

Abelard, Peter, 38n, 39n
Absolution, 119, 166–167
Achievement, 62n, 78, 108, 112, 155
Adam, 51, 79, 87, 104–105, 106n, 144, 154, 169–170, 172
Adhesion, 31
Albrecht of Mainz, Archbishop, 125, 161
Alien work (*opus alienum*), 121, 154–155, 162–163, 171–173, 183–186, 189–190. *See also* Works.
Alypius, 30
Ambrose, 30
Amor dei, 47–48. *See also* Love.
Amor sui, 47–48, 59, 85n, 156, 171. *See also* Love.
Amsdorf, Nikolaus von, 192
Antony, 30
Appropriate work (*opus proprium*), 121, 154–155, 162n, 183–184, 189–190. *See also* Works.
Aquinas, Thomas. *See* Thomas Aquinas.
Aristotle, 110–111
Attrition, 166
Augustine, 19n, 22, 26–30, 36, 42, 52, 57n, 59n, 65n, 86, 101, 105–106, 141, 144, 161, 175n, 179, 187
Augustinianism, 19n, 157n
Aversion (*aversio*), 26–27, 48, 61, 65n, 66, 101, 105, 155

Baptism, 20, 22, 31, 34–35, 44–45, 53, 63n, 72n, 73–74, 81n, 87–90, 96, 100–101, 105–106, 110, 119, 154, 168, 172, 182, 187
Barth, Karl, 86
Baylor, Michael, 18
Bernard of Clairvaux, 35–39, 43, 57n, 116n, 140
Bernhardi, Bartholomäus, 134, 140, 146–151, 187
Biel, Gabriel, 44, 47, 60n, 71, 72n, 89, 96n, 134, 140, 156. *See also* Nominalism.
Birth, 81, 101, 110–111, 143, 153, 172, 190
Bizer, Ernst, 17
Boehmer, Heinrich, 15
Bonaventura, 41, 42n, 60n
Bornkamm, Heinrich, 15, 17
Bradwardine, Thomas, 175n

Caesarius of Arles, 32
Calvinism, 192n
Canon law, 50, 167n
Carthusians, 37
Cassian, 32
Cassiodorus, 59n, 171, 183
Celano, Thomas of. *See* Thomas of Celano.
Charity (*caritas*), 18, 29, 46, 47n, 145. *See also* Love.
Christ, 20–21, 29, 44, 64, 65n,

Index

Index

Index

Library of Congress Cataloging in Publication Data

Harran, Marilyn J., 1948–
  Luther on conversion.

  Bibliography: p.
  Includes index.
    1. Conversion—History of doctrines—16th century.   2. Luther, Martin,
  1483–1546.   I. Title.
  BT780.H27   1983   248.2′4   83-7194
  ISBN 0-8014-1566-7